Islands In A Circle Sea

BY THE SAME AUTHOR

Dolphins Under My Bed
The first stage of a journey that became the adventure of a lifetime.

Turtles In Our Wake
Exploring some of the Mediterranean's loveliest islands.

A Thousand Miles From Anywhere
Crossing the Atlantic to winter in the Caribbean.

Osprey Summer – A Very American Experience
From Florida's salt marshes to the rocky shores of New England.

---oOo---

There is in many of us the desire for a little adventure before it gets too late. David and Sandra Clayton decided to give up the security of home and jobs and turn a daydream into a reality. In this final book about their trans-Atlantic voyages they take the reader through the great diversity of climates, cultures and scenic beauty of the North Atlantic islands. Although they cannot know it, their idyllic few years of freedom are also the beginning of the end of an era, as the tragic events of 9/11 and the wars and atrocities that follow begin to change the world.

Reviews for earlier books in this series:

'Sandra writes with wit and charm … This is travel writing at its best.'
Cruising Magazine (UK)

'… her ability to see the humor even in everyday situations will keep you laughing, while her sensitive, evocative descriptions of people, places, and nature will captivate you …' Cruising World (US)

'I loved it. I've read all of Sandra's books and for me this is the best. Roll on the follow-up. Ian Mackelden

'I have all four of the books so far and can't wait for the next to come out.'
R M Daley

Sandra Clayton

Islands In A Circle Sea

Malvern Partnership

Published by Malvern Partnership
PO Box No 162, Heber City, Utah, 84032, USA

Copyright © Sandra Clayton 2016
First edition published 2016

ISBN: 978-0-9915904-2 -1 (Paperback)
         978-0-9915904-3 -8 (ePub)

Maps: Copyright © David Clayton

Cover photographs: Copyright © Sandra Clayton
        Front: Sunset
        Back: Author with Toby at Nassau

Disclaimer:
This book is an account of journeys undertaken at a particular time and not in any way intended as a guide or an aid to navigation. Nor should it be considered as a recommendation of any particular place or destination. The names and identifying details of individuals and vessels have mostly been changed to protect people's privacy.

Website: https://sites.google.com/site/sandraclaytonauthor/

CONTENTS

The Bahamas

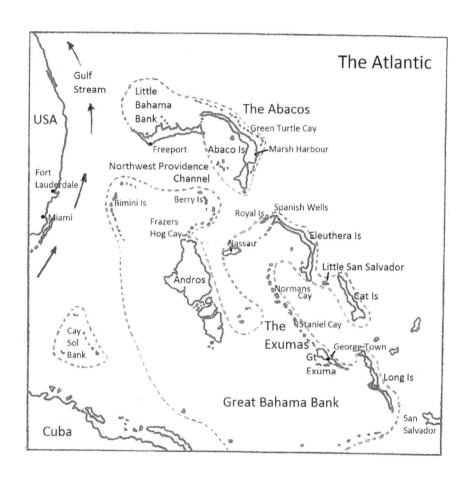

The dotted line shows the outer edges of the sandbanks.

Florida to Virginia

Virginia to New Jersey

New Jersey to Massachusetts

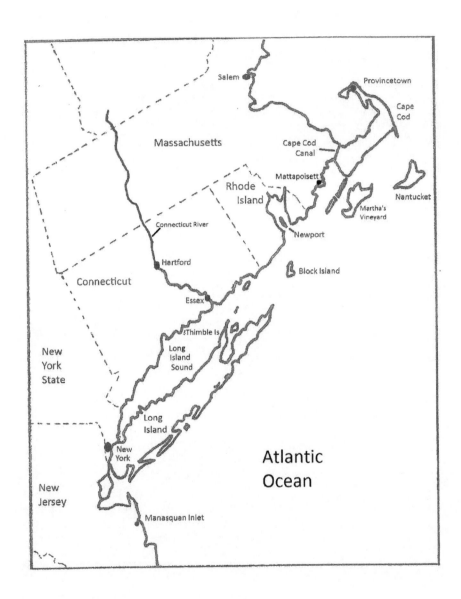

Maine to New Brunswick

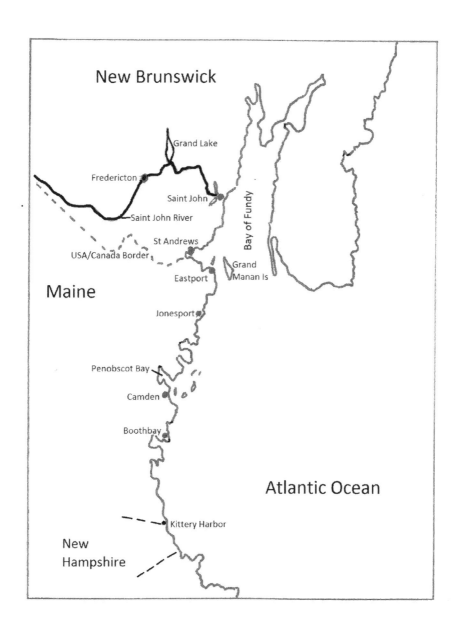

Atlantic Winds and Currents

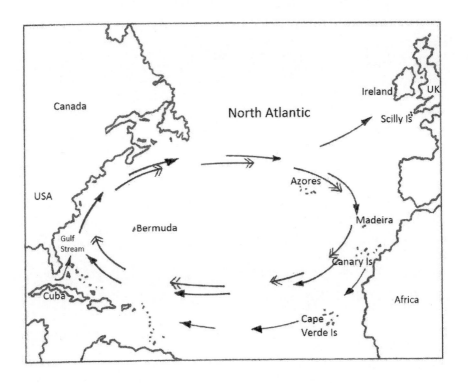

Feathered arrows show winds and solid ones the currents.

The Circling Sea

Ask for word association regarding the North Atlantic Ocean and the response is likely to be, 'grey, bleak, violent.' Archive film clips of WWII winter Atlantic convoys will come to mind, or scenes from *The Perfect Storm*. And I have to admit that, in the early days, when David brought home a book about cruising the North Atlantic islands my heart sank. At the time I was yearning for the warmth of the Mediterranean and the Caribbean.

But far from a uniform state of wintry greyness, the North Atlantic has many latitudes and climates ranging from the temperate to the tropical. It also contains an enormous variety of islands – from the palm-fringed coral sands of The Bahamas and the sun-kissed beaches of Bermuda, to the volcanic Azores brimming with summer flowers.

There is also the vast array of North America's Atlantic islands ranging from the sub-tropical Florida Keys up to New England's Nantucket and Martha's Vineyard; not to mention all those gracing the coasts of Maine and Canada. This book charts our voyages among quite a few of them.

From time immemorial mariners, including Columbus, have been aided in these trans-Atlantic journeys by a vast clockwise circle of currents and trade winds that have traditionally carried their ships south and west from Europe to the Americas; and then north and east back to Europe.

Within this great circling sea lie the North Atlantic Islands - which, of course, include Great Britain, where our voyages first began.

Acknowledgements

Voyager's Crew would like to express their gratitude for and to the following:

Atlantic Coast, Second Edition, published by MAPTECH, Inc.
Atlantic Islands, published by Imray Laurie Norie & Wilson Ltd.
Canadian Hydrographic Service Charts.
Guide to Cruising Chesapeake Bay, 2000 Edition, Chesapeake Com. Inc.
Herb Hilgenberg for his weather forecasting and ship routing skills.
Imray Charts, published by Imray Laurie Norie & Wilson Ltd.
Jack, Skipper of the sailing yacht *Dutch Concrete.*
Janet and Les Kierstead for their good company and all their kindness.
Maptech Chartkits.
Maptech Embassy Guides - *The Bahamas.*
Pantaenius Yacht Insurance.
Reeds Nautical Almanac: North American East Coast.
Stars and Planets: A Companion Guide for Amateur Astronomers,
+2nd Edition, published by Barron's.
Skipper Bob Publications.
The Atlantic Crossing Guide published by Adlard Coles Nautical, 4th edition.
The Intracoastal Waterway Chartbook, Third Edition, published by International Marine, a Division of the McGraw-Hill Companies.
United States Army Corps of Engineers for maintaining the ICW.
World Cruising Routes, by Jimmy Cornell, published by Adlard Coles.

And especially to David's brother, Tony, for all his onshore support throughout our travels.

About Voyager

Voyager is a heavy cruising catamaran that was built by Solaris Yachts at Southampton. They built strong, comfortable boats but ceased trading after a disastrous fire spread from a neighbouring yard. *Voyager* is their Sunstream model, 40ft long x 16ft wide with twin 27hp diesel engines.

She is a typical British catamaran in that she has a small mainsail and a large genoa which is her main source of power. She is cutter rigged and therefore has a small staysail as well as the other two sails.

Her two hulls are connected by a bridge deck with a cabin on it which provides the main living area, or saloon. It contains a large sofa, a coffee table, a dining table and a chart table. Opposite the chart table, and overlooking the galley, the starboard dining seating quickly converts to a breakfast bar which also makes an ideal dining area for any meal on a bouncy sea as there is less potential for loose objects to move about.

From the saloon, you enter the starboard or right-hand hull down three steps. Immediately in front of you is the galley. Turn right and there is an additional food preparation area, storage for cutlery and crockery and a large chest refrigerator. In the stern is a double bunk, a wardrobe, dressing table and clothing cupboards. Underneath the bunk is one of *Voyager*'s engines. At the bow end of this hull there is a head containing a toilet, wash basin and a bath.

The port hull contains in its stern an identical suite to the one in the starboard hull plus a shower, toilet and vanity. There is a further cabin in the bow of this hull but for the voyage we converted it into a storage space with a small workbench and vice.

Out on deck *Voyager* has a deep, well protected cockpit and all her sails can be handled from within it.

Prelude

One northern winter evening David had one of those moments I had come to recognize. They usually turned out to be life-enhancing in the long run, if a bit disruptive during the transition period. This one would be rather more disruptive than most.

What if, he said, *we sold the house and sailed away to somewhere warm*? It took a while, thanks to an economic recession and the collapse of the housing market, but eventually home became a 40-foot catamaran called *Voyager*.

Like many before us we had headed for the Mediterranean, and then on to the Caribbean. But, with the Hurricane Season approaching, we had to make a choice. We could leave the North Atlantic Hurricane Zone by sailing south, which would get quite hot, or go north to the USA.

We had decided on the latter and spent the summer exploring America's Atlantic Intracoastal Waterway, or ICW for short. It is a system of rivers, lagoons, lakes and ocean inlets connected by man-made canals that meanders for twelve hundred miles through the towns, marshes, cedar forests and peat bogs of five states - Florida, Georgia, the two Carolinas and Virginia. From there we had just kept on going, sailing into Washington, Chesapeake Bay, New York Harbour and as far north as New England before heading south again.

Now, however, with our US visas about to expire, we have set off from the Florida coast for a winter in the islands. More than seven hundred of them. Mostly uninhabited. And known collectively as The Bahamas.

THE BAHAMAS

1
The Berry Islands

During the day we spot our first flying fish since leaving the Caribbean last spring. And a large sting ray leaps from the water close beside us, curving its wings over its back like a bird before swooping underwater again. After weeks of largely motor-sailing in the narrow, sheltered waters of America's Intracoastal Waterway, we are back out on the Atlantic Ocean. Wide spaces all around, a big sky and all sails up.

The plan is to head across the Straits of Florida for Alice Town in the Bimini Islands. It is an official port-of-entry for clearing into The Bahamas and the closest one from Fort Lauderdale, with an approximate travelling time of nine and a half hours.

Our route crosses the Gulf Stream, a warm ocean current flowing up from the Gulf of Mexico and which might best be described as a powerful river flowing through the Atlantic Ocean. In the Straits of Florida it is up to 45 miles wide and travels north at around two-and-a-half knots. Although some reports say it can reach as high as five - one knot equalling a nautical mile covered in one hour, and roughly equivalent to 1.15mph.

What this means in practical terms is that if the wind is in an opposing direction to this current, the sea becomes violent. Even when the adverse wind has dropped, or changed to the same direction as the current, the sea remains turbulent for days afterwards. So finding a suitable weather window for a passage across it is important and can take a little time.

The present one is expected to last only a couple of days. After that, cold fronts will travel down from the north bringing more high winds from the opposing direction and making the sea state untenable again.

Unfortunately, everything seems to conspire against us today, not least some confusion about what had yesterday seemed a straightforward weather forecast. The result is that, despite getting up at dawn for an early start, we are late setting off. Then we encounter head winds that aren't supposed to be here, but gusting to 21 knots and making the Gulf Stream *very* bouncy.

We are also picking up sargassum. This floating weed keeps settling against our keels, rudders and propellers, slowing the boat down to almost nothing and leaving us with no choice but to spend time shunting back and forth in an effort to float it off.

Then the fan belt on the port engine snaps.

We carry six spare fan belts of varying sizes, because even *Voyager*'s port and starboard engines use different ones. Unfortunately, when David goes to get one, due to some oversight in the provisioning department he finds that while we have two spare belts for the starboard engine, there isn't one for the port.

Down to one engine, and reducing our speed even further, there is now no chance of us reaching Alice Town before sunset. And because the entrance to its harbour is surrounded by shoals, it is not a place to approach in the dark unless you know it very well.

Instead we alter course for the Northwest Providence Channel and an unplanned night passage. It is no great hardship in this warm December night. And so, with Great Isaac Lighthouse flashing reassuringly in the gathering darkness, we head for the Berry Islands instead.

One of the islands there - Great Harbour Cay - is also a port-of-entry and a place to officially clear into the country. That's the thing about The Bahamas. With over 700 islands, cays and islets, like the Corporation buses of my youth, if you miss one there's bound to be another one along quite soon. And this way we shall arrive in daylight.

The Berry group of islands curve around a northern corner of an enormous semicircle of shallow water created by a vast bank called, appropriately, Great Bahama Bank. In places the water covering it is less than a foot deep.

Shallow water is a feature of The Bahamas. It may even have given the archipelago its name, since one theory is that it comes from the early Spanish explorers who called it *baja mar* as in *shallow sea*. But, as with so many places we've been to, there are alternative theories as to how this island country got its name.

We sail through a balmy night ablaze with stars. At 2.30am an enormous, blood-red moon sinks in the west, its lower rim looking as if it is dripping into the sea. We drift on, under glittering starlight until cloud gradually moves across the sky producing a very dark night after all the earlier brightness.

We see only two other vessels. One I had initially assumed to be a fixed red light on one of the islands, and something I am aware of for some time before it proves it isn't stationary at all. The other - a tug pulling a barge – is only identifiable by the navigation lights it is showing.

It turns out that the red glow I had assumed to be a shore light belongs to a small yacht on a collision course with our starboard bow. And rather than a large red light a long way off, it is in fact a relatively small one quite close. Ultimately too close.

Instead of the mandatory red, white and green tricolour on its masthead, this yacht has a red lamp tied in its rigging. The whole point of the tricolour is that it tells you which direction an otherwise invisible vessel on a pitch-black sea is travelling.

I get my first clue that this is not a red light on a distant island when the tug towing the barge changes course to go around it. So I begin to think it must be some sort of buoy, although none is shown on the chart. But I decide to alter course anyway and am just doing so when a small yacht under sail looms out of the darkness and passes very close to *Voyager*'s starboard quarter. So close, in fact, that even in the blackness I can see it clearly for a moment. There is nobody on deck and its skipper, if indeed it has one, is fortunate that the tug driver and I have avoided it.

At dawn we turn to starboard, round Little Stirrup Cay, and make our way down a narrow channel to a navigational marker our cruising guide says is three miles ahead. It is quite difficult to identify because it is a mere shadow of its former self.

Something about The Bahamas that you quickly get used to is that, thanks to the annual season of hurricanes and tropical storms, bits fall off things — navigational markers especially but sometimes bigger things like boundary walls and even roofs — and are not necessarily replaced quickly or even at all.

This present marker is a case in point. It began life as a tripod of three sturdy pilings with a radar reflector on the top. The reflector has gone now, along with one of the piles, leaving the remaining two so weakened that they also are likely to disappear in the next storm. An additional aid to navigation here is supposed to be a wrecked fishing boat but, if it is still around, it is no longer visible above the surface.

After completing the three miles to the two ailing piles, to reach Great Harbour Cay you then turn to port on a bearing of 111° for a further four miles, much of it under the impression that you are heading directly for a cliff face. It is only when you are very close, and convinced there is nowhere to go, that you make a 90° turn and enter a narrow cut - just one more of the many reasons for not approaching these islands at night.

We pass through the cliff face and enter a lagoon. As we do, a large manatee surfaces beside us. The water is shallow, green and so clear you can see individual blades of grass growing in the sand below you.

Great Harbour Cay measures somewhere around seven miles by two. A cay (pronounced *key*) is defined as a small, low island composed of a coral reef with sand on top. That sounds rather barren, yet cays can be surprisingly fertile, sustaining human populations and even agriculture. This one, our first landfall in The Bahamas, is heavily wooded. Its combination of low green hills, pale blue translucent water and spectacular beaches – not to mention the entire lack of any other human presence - is the quintessence of Paradise for many. Including us.

2
The Columbian Exchange

There had been a number of early African and European contacts with what came to be called The New World but the most significant - in terms of impact on the Americas and the course of European history - was that of Christopher Columbus. And it happened here, in The Bahamas.

His first landfall was at an island he named San Salvador - as in *Holy Saviour* - as one of his stated intentions was to bring Christianity to the peoples he found during his travels. Like the rest of the archipelago, the island had no natural resources worth exploiting apart from its people. Those he found on San Salvador, the Lucayans, (who had, incidentally, named their island Guanahani long before) Columbus described as 'sweet and gentle' and decided they would make excellent slaves.

Sailing under the auspices of the Spanish court, Columbus made this first of his four Atlantic voyages in 1492. Exactly where in The Bahamas he landed is in dispute as it is not known which of a number of Bahamian islands is Columbus's San Salvador. It may or may not be the one given that name in 1925; it was simply thought by historians to most likely fit the bill.

But then most facts about Columbus are in dispute, apart from his treatment of islanders. Contemporary observers cite evidence of a brutal tyrant who, along with his two brothers, not only enslaved indigenous populations for the purpose of working them to death, but used torture and dismemberment to discourage resistance.

The man himself proves elusive. DNA has failed to establish exactly whose bones lie in the impressive tomb dedicated to Christopher Columbus inside the entrance to Seville cathedral in southern Spain. Human remains moved between countries many times over the centuries as territories changed hands, and those in the Seville tomb may belong to his brother.

The Dominican Republic, in the Caribbean, claims to house the authentic bones in its own tomb at Santo Domingo Este, although as yet no DNA testing has been done on them.

Even Columbus's likeness was painted posthumously as no authentic portrait is known to exist. And although described as an Italian from the Republic of Genoa, modern historians have pointed out that, surprisingly for an Italian – even when writing to Italy - he never wrote in Italian but in a Spanish rich in the idioms of Catalonia, a region of northeast Spain.

In the end, like most things, it comes down to the bragging rights. Whichever place can claim the goods – be it bones, a battle site or the birthplace of a famous son – that will be the place which attracts people who want to be photographed standing in front of a piece of history. And tourism is how many places and people survive.

One of the things *not* in dispute is that Columbus never set foot in North America, despite so many places there being named after him. Another undisputed fact is that his voyages - and the colonizers who followed his route - would eventually change whole continents through the movement of peoples and cultures, animals and plants.

In what is termed 'the Columbian Exchange', wheat and horses from Europe changed the diet and agriculture of the New World. While the latter's maize, tomatoes and potatoes became staples of the Old World and helped increase its populations.

Europe in its turn wiped out entire New World populations and cultures through warfare and slavery, especially in the mines in the relentless pursuit of gold and silver. Also by introducing its extensive range of contagious diseases including bubonic plague, yellow fever, measles, influenza and - most devastating of all – smallpox, because indigenous populations simply had no resistance to them.

Meanwhile the riches plundered from the New World, and shipped back to the Old, transformed the balance of power in 16th century Europe.

3
Great Harbour Cay

There is a small marina in the lagoon but our intention is to spend the winter at anchor in these islands. So we decide to drop our hook in the lagoon temporarily while we go and complete the entry formalities, buy a new fan belt from the marina store and then set off for an anchorage. Ah. Ignorance, as they say, is bliss.

Trying to find a suitable place to anchor, and with supposedly six feet (1.8m) of clear water beneath us (we need only half that), we go aground on a sand bar. The tide is falling rapidly and with only one engine we are unable to drag ourselves off it again. So we launch the dinghy and David rows to the marina.

When he gets there it is not only low tide but the pontoon is designed to accommodate people stepping off large, high-sided American power boats. So he holds a conversation with the feet of the marina manager, who says he doesn't have a fan belt, but David can probably get one from around the corner at the blue shed in the direction he's just come from.

He also tells him that Customs & Immigration insist on boarding yachts that are clearing-in, but will not do so while they are at anchor. We have no option but to enter the marina. We don't mind. We are a little tired after a day and a night at sea and means we shan't have to move again today. It will also give us a chance to find a fan belt, as David doesn't manage to spot the blue shed on his way back in the dinghy. By 2pm the tide has risen sufficiently to allow us to float *Voyager* off the sand bar and motor into the marina.

As soon as we are tied up, and with our quarantine flag raised, we go and pay for our berth; then return to *Voyager* and wait for Customs and Immigration to arrive. The Bahamas is the only country we've ever visited where an official comes to you, instead of you hiking miles to find him. Although, given the forms the marina manager has given us to complete in advance of his visit, we suspect it might have more to do with wanting a look at your boat than extreme courtesy.

The first question on the Immigration form to catch our attention is the one asking if, during the previous six weeks, any members of the crew have succumbed to plague, cholera, yellow fever or smallpox. (The very things, in fact, that Columbus and his crews brought here with them.)

Next, have we found any rats or mice on board carrying plague during the same period? In more than two-and-half-years at sea we have never had any kind of rodent on board. But even if we had, the form does not explain how you would know if it had plague or not. We can only assume you'd have to check its armpits and groin for the characteristic lumps, or buboes, that human victims presented during the Black Death. That's supposing you could safely catch a rodent and hold it on its back while you have a look.

We are not sure if these questions are a reflection on the usual quality of vessels visiting these islands, or whether the immigration form hasn't been updated since Fletcher Christian was a lad. But I buff up the galley sink and draining board to a high shine anyway, while David tidies up on deck, so that *Voyager* will look wholesome for the Immigration Officer.

He makes a slightly incongruous visitor to a yacht, with his business shirt and tie, grey trousers, and his leather-soled shoes skating across *Voyager's* gelcoat. After a polite greeting he takes a seat in the cockpit and after inspecting our documents and the completed forms opens a small leather attaché case containing a book of cruising permits and a rubber stamp.

Removing both he smiles and says he is pleased to agree our request and issues us with a permit. Then with his attaché case closed on his lap, and his hands folded on top of it, he talks with nostalgia of Cornwall and English literature. As British subjects, until independence in 1973, it seems Bahamian school children sat British GCE examinations and quite a few visited the British Isles.

Late afternoon a sports fishing boat berths nearby and two holiday-makers disembark with their catch of lobsters. Someone hangs up a set of scales on the dock and the crustaceans weigh in at around eleven pounds apiece. The holiday divers are ecstatic and pose with them for the camera.

Next morning, in conversation with our neighbour, an American, David asks if he has a spare fan belt we could buy from him. He doesn't have one the right size, but says that when his local mechanic arrives he may be able to help us. When the mechanic arrives he takes our damaged fan belt away saying he will be about half an hour.

Three hours later, and not sure if we are required to have left the marina by now, the man on the neighbouring boat tells David where to find the mechanic. On the way, the driver of a pick-up truck offers him a lift and David rides island-style in the back. After quite some time he is dropped off at the blue shed he had been told was just around the corner yesterday. However, no-one there knows anything about our fan belt, or recognizes David's description of the mechanic. Nor do they sell fan belts.

We need the old one back to make sure we get a new one of the right size when we finally find somewhere to buy one. Frustrated, David begins the long walk back, but is spotted by another man in a truck who, without even asking, appears to know all about his situation. He drops David off at the marina saying, 'I find him.'

Our American neighbour is mystified. After another hour, the original man – formerly known as 'the mechanic' and whose description nobody had recognized - arrives with *two* fan belts. One is a new one, the other second-hand. The latter is a perfect fit. Money changes hands. And with two engines now functioning, and often in very shallow water, we motor cautiously away.

4
Getting Our Bearings

Our first sortie out among the islands brings us up against a conundrum. David has a particular island in mind. It contains a sheltered cove as well as being a recommended anchorage, although as always he has identified a few bolt holes along the way just in case.

By the time the GPS tells us we are approaching the island we want, the light has become hazy. Even so, there should be enough visibility to see the entrance the chart is telling us is on the coastline alongside us. It is only after climbing up onto the doghouse roof that I can see into something looking vaguely like the cove we are seeking, only instead of being alongside, it is about half a mile behind us.

We decide not to risk the one beside us, as many of these little coves are full of rocks. Instead we continue on to one of David's boltholes but that doesn't tally with the GPS co-ordinates either, and worryingly we arrive at it far more quickly than we should have.

We end up in an area called Great Harbour, a large shallow bay, and anchor in the shelter of the eastern end of Great Stirrup Cay. After all the dark and sometimes peaty waters of America's inland waterways it is lovely to watch your anchor sliding into white coral sand and its chain snaking away from it along a pristine seabed.

The evening is delightful too, and I prepare a meal out in the cockpit while David, sitting at the chart table in the saloon, begins to work out our position on the chart from the GPS co-ordinates. He discovers that, according to the chart, we are sitting on top of a little scrap of land called Goat Cay which is in reality - and also visible to us - over half a mile away.

Turning over the chart he finds a line of small print at the bottom and the mystery of why nothing appears to be where it is supposed to be is solved. The note tells him that this chart has been taken, 'From British Surveys in 1836 and 1885.'

This would also account for why we keep touching bottom. There is always a lot of movement with sandy sea beds and even modern charts have problems keeping up to date. With charts whose information is more than 150 years old (despite having been purchased only weeks ago) your only chance of staying afloat would appear to be constant vigilance.

Nevertheless, being presented with such an historic document is an opportunity to observe those things of importance to 19th century mariners. For instance, the maker of this chart has written on a neighbouring island, 'wood, water and vegetables' which, of course, tells anyone using it that on this particular island he will find timber for repairing ship damage as well as fuel for cooking, along with fresh water.

'Vegetables', plus fruit and berries where they could find them, supplemented a crew's monotonous diet of pork in brine, fish and hardtack on a long sea voyage. Even more importantly they contained the Vitamin C necessary to prevent scurvy. And, providing an additional bit of historical colour, all the depths on this old chart are given in fathoms, not metres or feet. Traditionally used for measuring water depth, a fathom equals six feet or 1.82 metres and was originally based on the distance between a man's outstretched arms.

As for the discrepancy in distance, it *is* only around half a mile. And once you know about it you can at least see that far and get your bearings. Unlike parts of the South Pacific, apparently. David read a report recently which said that some of the islands there are as much as nine miles from where the charts say they are.

Something we have forgotten about since leaving the harbours and sheltered inland waterways of the United States is the size of the sea swell you get around a small island. It had not been apparent in the protected waters of the lagoon on our first night in The Bahamas. But this anchorage is quite exposed and when a great expanse of tidal water comes into contact with a small piece of land the swell is enormous. So when you drop your hook for your first night off an exposed, uninhabited little island, with the wind rising and the Atlantic crashing against its windward side – or, as in this case, foaming over the top of it - you can feel a little vulnerable.

However, directly opposite us, on a neighbouring island, there is a tiny lighthouse. As dusk settles, its light comes on and it is good to know that, isolated as we are, its beam will flash throughout what promises to be a dark, overcast night. As well as a comforting light, it will also provide a stationary point by which to judge if *Voyager* is dragging her anchor in this heavy swell.

We stand on our foredeck in the gathering gloom and count – two flashes with a 20-second pause between. We continue counting, silently, as it flashes through several more sequences. Grateful for its reassuring presence through the coming night, we turn toward each other and smile contentedly. Then the light goes out and doesn't come on again.

After a very rolly night we decide to head south down the Berry Island chain in search of quieter anchorages. The sea during this journey is so turbulent that as you move around the boat you don't dare let go with one hand before ensuring that the other has a grip on something solid. And, with every step you take, you pause to look down at what your foot is wavering towards, because as you rise and fall with the boat it would be so easy to fall and injure yourself, or simply go overboard. And with no-one within sight or hearing, and rescue services a very long way away, keeping yourself intact is your most important survival technique.

We arrive off the southern tip of Little Harbour Cay (not to be confused with *Great* Harbour Cay) just before mid-day, after nearly five hours on a bouncing sea. On the way David had spent some time adjusting latitude and longitude on the present chart to take into account the half-mile variation he found yesterday - only to then discover that this one has already been altered to modern standards.

The approach to the anchorage is through a wide channel between two islands - Little Harbour Cay and Cabbage Cay - but the chart shows a group of rocks in between them. Unnervingly, the cruising guide puts the rocks much closer to the channel than the chart does. And if anything the sea is even more turbulent as we enter the channel than it was in open water. So we enter with me surging up and down on the bow trying to get an early sighting of the rocks we need to avoid.

They are described as 'awash' which means just below the surface but I never catch a glimpse of any rocks at all on my downward plunges, even in this clear water, which is worrying. Because I'm convinced I'm looking in the wrong place and terrified we're suddenly going to hit them.

Once inside the first part of the anchorage the water becomes calmer, but quickly gets very shallow. As we feel our way in, I anxiously aim the binoculars at a white board with black lettering on it. It takes some time, straining to focus in the blistering sunlight, before I can make out what it says. A warning, presumably. More rocks, maybe. Or some other terrible danger to which we are inexorably heading. I am beginning to get one of my headaches from staring into the sun when I am finally able to read it.

'Welcome to Little Harbour Cay,' it says. 'Home of Flo's Conch Bar and Restaurant. Call on Channel 68'.

The cruising guide says it gets rolly here, and for a quiet night to pass through and anchor on the south side of Guano Cay. Which is what we do, lowering the anchor into white sand and water that is an extraordinary, glistening, turquoise.

Before we left Florida, AT&T said that we would be able to use our cell phone without problems in The Bahamas and relieved us of an $800 deposit. David had tried to make a call from Great Harbour Cay, where we cleared in, to his brother Tony to let him know that we had arrived safely. It was very sheltered there and we had not been able to get a signal. No matter, we would call him as soon as we left the next day.

We had tried again and again. But whenever our cell phone's will-o'-the-wisp signals finally produced a line, all an increasingly-enraged David could get on dialling was a recorded voice telling him to ring the operator. But when he dialled the number for the operator in our AT&T phone book, all he got was a recorded voice telling him to ring his local operator, only there wasn't a Bahamian number for him to dial.

So, we set off in the dinghy for the small settlement at Little Harbour Cay to find a telephone. Flo's Conch Bar, the first place we try, doesn't have one. And nor does anybody else. The nearest one, it turns out, is at Great Harbour Cay —where we had cleared in.

On the way back to *Voyager* we stop off to say Hi to the couple aboard an American yacht which has just anchored not far from us. They are from Puerto Rico and in the process of making their way home. They are feeling the cold, they say, and keen to get back south. They do not have a phone either but offer to use their SSB radio transmitter to ask a friend of theirs to send an email to a friend of ours in England asking her to telephone David's brother and tell him we are alive but unable to contact him direct.

The forecast now is for three days of high winds. We decide to stay put. Our American neighbours come over in their dinghy next day to tell us that our email has gone off. They have also decided to head off home despite the forecast. We thank them for their kindness in sending the email for us and wish them a safe journey.

Far from feeling the cold we are finding the temperature here delightful and given our sheltered anchorage begin to explore our surroundings. We dinghy ashore to beaches strewn with coral and conch shells and fringed with palm trees. We swim, amble along the sands, and on one of the days follow a path to an abandoned house. There is something deeply romantic about the idea of living in serene isolation on your very own sub-tropical island. And a fascination with old abandoned houses and the ghostly echoes of the lives once lived in them.

Another morning we walk across the island to a beach on its Atlantic side and find it strewn with debris washed here by storms. Old footwear, wooden planks and broken pallets. Sadly there is also a vast amount of plastic. All the usual suspects, from individual drinks bottles and polystyrene beakers to laundry liquid containers and bleach bottles, toys, nappy liners and the ever-present nylon fishing nets. It is a material that never breaks down completely, even in the sea. But here, a wind-blown tide has driven this collection above the water line, so it will grace these otherwise pristine sands indefinitely.

Within a couple of days the wind rises even higher than forecast, and we are glad we stayed where we are. Our wind generator howls through the night and even our sheltered anchorage becomes quite turbulent.

Come morning we can see spume rising out in the channel through which we arrived at this anchorage. It is the water churning violently over the rocks that we failed to spot when we entered a few days ago. At least now we shall know where they are when we leave. The weather forecast says two cold fronts are arriving, tonight and tomorrow, and could mean we shall need to remain a little longer.

It is no hardship, and even in Paradise the basics need attending to. I do laundry and David services the engines using for the first time the new, manual, oil extractor pump he bought before leaving America. When we first set off he'd bought an electric one. Expensive and not something to be discarded lightly, it had proved to be fiddly, ineffective and made oil changes a chore. This little manual one is simple and effective.

Finally, with forecast winds of 10 -15 knots, we set off for the Bahamian capital, Nassau. It turns out to be 17-23 knots but the passage is less violent than it might have been.

5

Nassau

You have to radio up Nassau Harbour Control and ask for permission to enter. Once given, you then make your way in between two foaming breakwaters and two sets of buoys.

As we set off the Harbour Control Officer wishes us a good day as if he meant it. Then it's up the three-mile long harbour and past the cruise ships, including the Disney ones with the Mickey Mouse smoke stacks. The graffiti on the cruise ship dock, in wobbly white paint – presumably the result of having to stand in a bobbing dinghy to write it – says, 'God Loves You'.

Over to our left is the most extraordinary edifice, a multi-storied fantasy building comprising two towers joined by a bridge near roof level. It is utterly at odds with the '700 largely uninhabited islands and generally undeveloped nature of The Bahamas,' we had been lead to expect. In truth, it is an astonishing hotel to find perched on a small island.

Nevertheless, it is hard to find anything negative to say about a harbour whose control officer wishes you a good day as if he meant it; where you are assured, even in the midst of Mammon, that God loves you; and you are about to anchor in a nation's capital whose water is so surprisingly clean.

The harbour is a long stretch of water bordered by the shoreline of New Providence Island - on which the nation's capital Nassau stands – and Paradise Island on which the astonishing hotel is situated.

The anchorage is very crowded and we make four attempts to set our anchor in a seabed that turns out to have very poor holding. As we make our second attempt a man in a dinghy arrives alongside to convey verbatim a message he does not understand but hopes we will. It is from the couple from Puerto Rico at our last anchorage saying that our friend in England has sent an email to their friend, who has called them on their SSB radio to say that David's brother has been informed of our safe arrival – thereby making the yachtie grapevine in The Bahamas more effective than AT&T.

A man on a neighbouring catamaran also calls a greeting to us. It is Martin, a man we met when we first set out to find a boat, and long before we set off cruising. We arrange to meet up later.

This is a busy harbour with a lot of competition for space. A sea plane on take-off works hard to get up enough speed to clear the mastheads of the anchored yachts and for a time we appear to be on a collision course with it as we try to find enough room somewhere our anchor will hold.

We end up out on the edge of the anchorage, near a collection of pilings in which we take no particular interest. We are just grateful to have finally come to rest. As soon as he is satisfied that we are securely attached to the seabed David takes the dinghy ashore in search of a supermarket. After many days at sea, and at anchor, we are low on food.

Soon after he leaves, another man in a dinghy arrives offering to sell me computerized charts. We don't have the means to use them and they are probably pirated anyway. But he also mentions in passing that we should expect a container ship to drop its anchor very close to our starboard bow. There is not a lot I can do about it for the moment. Given the trouble we have had with this seabed so far I am not about to try re-anchoring single-handed and so return to my chores.

Not long afterwards I am down in the galley and suddenly the day turns very dark. When I go outside there is *Seaboard Spirit*, her bottle green hull towering over *Voyager*'s starboard quarter. Its captain glares down at me from a great height.

'Well placed!' he shouts.

'We'll move,' I call back up to him.

This huge container ship then slides alongside, drops an anchor off our starboard bow, reverses, moves forward to another spot, drops a second anchor, and then reverses slowly into her dock – the collection of pilings we had ignored when we were anchoring ourselves.

The helmsmen of its two pilot boats have been grinning broadly at me throughout. They were probably expecting me to have hysterics. I might have, had I not been forewarned.

When David returns he says, 'How close did it get?' I hold my hands over our starboard side, palms a couple of feet apart.

'*That* close?' he says.

Shortly after dusk we crawl into bed exhausted, from the turbulent seven-hour sea passage getting here plus repeated attempts at anchoring on a very hot afternoon. Not to mention a hot and tiring trip into town for David and a small but contained nervous breakdown for me.

We are just drifting into sleep when the sound of fusillades and mortar attacks echo around us. It is a spectacular firework display. I go up on deck and watch from the cockpit. David, less taken with fireworks than I and far more tired, can be heard moaning softly from below, 'Why won't they let me sleep?' as the boat reverberates to each multi-coloured thunder-clap.

Well into December now, the further south we have travelled into temperatures in the 90s/30s the more aware I am of the incongruousness of the English robin perched on a snowy shovel handle on our calendar. David and his brother exchange them at Christmas - sun-soaked exotic for British traditional.

High winds will keep us at Nassau through Christmas and New Year. It is no hardship, being warm, sunny and very friendly, with plenty of places to go and so complete an absence of insects that you can dine on deck in lamp light of an evening without attracting a single one.

Our first outing, however, is to sort out our phone. We leave our dinghy at the dock provided by BASRA, the Bahamas Air & Sea Rescue Association, and set off on foot for Bah Tel Com.

Downtown

Near the harbour the streets have no pavements so you walk against the traffic which drives on the left, British style, but in American left-hand-drive cars. The roads are very narrow - making the journey even more precarious – as do the storm drains, some of them without grilles. There is a quiet air of neglect. Paint peels off wooden houses. Torpid dogs lie among crumbling concrete and tumbling bougainvillea. Yet in the commercial district when you reach it, the buildings would not be out of place in many an affluent European city and there are a *lot* of banks.

On reaching Bah Tel Com we find we have arrived at its Accounts Payable office. The security guard (everybody here seems to have one) re-directs us to the Enquiry office and tells us where to get a bus to it.

As people board the bus they call out, *Good mornin', good mornin', good mornin'*. And those already on the bus respond. The driver, a lovely man, asks us where we are from and then, for our 75 cents fare, provides us with what is effectively a guided tour of the town. After having pointed out the major landmarks, and wishing us a happy stay, he deposits us at the doors of Bah Tel Com.

The Enquiry office is very crowded with customers sitting, standing and leaning in every available space and we expect a long wait. So we are amazed to be sent almost immediately to see someone who can help us.

Someone at AT&T, it seems, was negligent with the facts. AT&T does *not* have an agreement with anyone in the Bahamas and our phone is useless. Disappointed, angry and frustrated at the amount of time and money wasted, we catch a bus to the shopping area to find FedEx and send a Christmas package home. Despite charging only the basic rate, Fed-ex gives us a 20% seasonal discount as well.

We also find a shop selling discount phone cards to use on the public phones - 42 minutes for $10 - and a very helpful lady who gives us instructions on how to use it.

David calls AT&T.

Back in the anchorage there has been constant activity on and around the container ship, which has been unloaded and is currently being reloaded. With its departure to be expected in the near future, David decides to move *Voyager* well away from the spot where its first anchor is lying to avoid another close encounter when it is hauled up.

I keep trying to tell him that the new spot he has chosen will put us directly over the ship's *second* anchor, but he's having trouble getting our own to bite, it is a hot afternoon, and in the end he gets uncharacteristically irritable and tells me to just *stop going on about it*. We *are perfectly all right where we are*, he says. He can see the bottom and there is *no sign of an anchor down there.*

Martin and Queenie come over for a few cold beers late afternoon and share a meal with us early evening. Queenie is a six-year-old Husky with charming manners and an affectionate nature. She has also had her Christmas bath and her fur, of a texture and density designed for the Arctic tundra, exudes the pleasant scent of aloe vera shampoo whenever she stirs in the warm Bahamian sunshine. The four of us are sitting companionably in the cockpit when the sky goes dark. Three yachtsmen and a dog turn as one and crane their necks up at the towering bottle green bows of *Seaboard Spirit*.

'See,' I mutter resentfully. 'I told you we were over his second anchor.'

Martin is leaving Nassau tomorrow to visit friends on another island and suggests we move into his spot, which is not only in the anchorage proper but in a nice solid bit of sand. Next day, securely anchored and no longer in the way of commercial shipping, we begin the first of many trips into town.

Whether you shop, or simply wander, Nassau is a pleasure not least because it has so many civil, cheerful, friendly, helpful people. Politeness is endemic. Workmen, seeing you going astray, will stop what they are doing and say, 'It's a long way round, that way. Quicker to go the other.' And as you prepare to pass one of the public areas being tidied, anyone working near the pavement will automatically switch off his mower or strimmer until you are safely past any flying grass or chippings.

The focus of Nassau is Bay Street. It runs parallel to the shoreline and down it you will find the tourist shops, Parliament Square and the public buildings. It is also the centre of island life.

Nassau's public buildings mostly date from the nineteenth century. A few of them are even older. Which isn't bad going for the capital of a country inside the Atlantic Hurricane Zone. They are solidly built, as one would expect survivors to be, but painted pink and white, which gives an unexpected light-heartedness to them – even the gaol and courthouse.

The gaol, an octagonal building dating from 1797, is now the public library. Its cells are lined with shelves of books, old documents and records, Bahamian newspapers from colonial times to the present and artefacts belonging to people who walked this land before Europeans ever set foot on it.

When you pass down one short stretch of Bay Street you wonder who on earth buys all these precious stones and Rolex watches, but then you remember the cruise ships and Paradise Island's massive hotel and the lure of luxury goods Duty Free. Through open doors there are glimpses of black interiors, subtle lighting, plate-glass counters and shining chrome. One specializes in emeralds, another in diamonds, or the jaw-droppingly-priced Rolex watches. Meanwhile, across the street, is a local institution.

The Straw Market is a ramshackle place of haphazard wooden stalls piled high with hand-woven bags and hats. The stalls' proprietors rearrange their stock for best effect, chide the occasional loose child in the narrow aisles or sit on a stool, tranquilly embroidering daisies in white wool on the crown of a straw hat.

Down the street, the policeman directing traffic is a joy. In a spotless, belted white jacket and gloves, black trousers with a red stripe down the seam and a peaked cap to match, he doesn't so much direct the traffic as conduct it. From his podium. A small, wooden box he brings with him, painted black and placed precariously in the middle of the busy intersection. The 'orchestra' around him, tensed behind the dusty windscreens of trucks, cars and buses, awaits his cue. Until, with an exaggerated sweep of an arm, a small flourish or simply the flick of a wrist he sets the various sections in motion. The only thing missing is a baton.

Another day we continue beyond the town centre and along the waterfront to Fort Charlotte. On the way, the conch vendors stand inside their sentry-box type stalls, serving customers over narrow counters formed by a ledge on the closed, lower half of the door. Some young men pull a large silver fish from the sea. In a clump of trees a local population of stray dogs bark at one another.

We pass Haynes Oval cricket ground. Then climb up to Fort Charlotte, wander round it and through it and down into its dungeons; then up on to its barracks, converted into a stand for the football pitch below. And from there onto the beach, overlooking the west entrance to the harbour with its creamy sand and transparent water. The ocean is the most stunning blue and today's brightness makes the small, white Paradise Island lighthouse shimmer against the hazy blue of the sky.

On the return to town, and on the premise that as travellers we should try the local speciality at least once (unless it is still moving or involves eyeballs) we stop off at a restaurant for our first taste of conch. We have always assumed it would be tough, so we choose the grilled-in-foil option, hoping that would have a softening effect; the alternative being deep fried in breadcrumbs which has never seemed a good thing to do to shellfish.

From the first bite it is apparent that the best thing about the conch is its shell. By the time the maître d' comes round to ask if we are enjoying ours we can only nod, with a grim smile, as our jaws are locked in a life and death struggle with something that has the taste and texture of boiled bicycle inner tube. And by slicing it in its tinfoil – in a doomed attempt to stop its liquor from making your fries soggy – you inevitably end up getting bits of tinfoil between your teeth.

Given the great quantities of conch devoured here daily, we wonder if perhaps our taste buds are at fault. So we ask some fellow-travellers their opinion, discreetly, as we leave the restaurant together. They say eating tennis shoes would be preferable and we all head for a nearby ice cream parlour to take away the lingering taste of tinfoil.

Neighbour from Hell

Along with Martin's spot in the anchorage we inherit his neighbour. His name is Doug and his wife has just flown home in response to some unspecified emergency on her side of the family. Doug has remained with their boat. He comes over to introduce himself.

In truth, he is up the back steps before his dinghy touches our stern, and tying it up as his feet hit our afterdeck. His opening gambit is to tell us, at length, about the superior holding capabilities of his own Danforth anchor compared to ours and from now on our quality of life will go rapidly downhill.

For Doug, we quickly discover, is a Bite-Your-Tongue Person. He asks what you are doing, have done, or are going to do, and then tells you stridently and at great length how in fact you ought to do it, or should have done it or could have done it better. To put in a word of self-justification about any aspect merely prolongs the ordeal. To even begin to explain the very sensible reasons behind your decision to do something in a particular way is merely to extend his monologue, so you bite your tongue and will him to go away.

In an attempt to try and reduce the opportunities for him to harangue us, when we hear his outboard approaching we meet him at whichever quarter he is about to land on, thereby blocking his route into the cockpit, and especially the saloon, so that he can't settle himself down in comfort for hours. Then we stand nodding passively, in blazing sun, wind or occasionally drizzling rain - as he instructs us on the finer points of re-charging batteries, repairing water makers, applying varnish, getting more out of an engine or keeping eggs fresh without a refrigerator - and willing him to go away.

As the days pass, and with still no sign of his wife's return, an air of doom settles over *Voyager*. We begin staring into the abyss. Thinking the unthinkable. Having him with us for Christmas.

The forecast is promising very bad weather and the prospect of days shut in with Doug forces us to consider our options. There are only two. We can leave the anchorage and risk getting blown to pieces off an exposed island somewhere. Or we can remain here in a protected harbour anchored to a solid patch of sand until life with Doug becomes so unbearable we clasp hands and throw ourselves over the side.

We are slipping inexorably into a state of melancholia when Doug's wife returns, bringing several guests with her. And with new opportunities open to him, Doug forgets all about us. Once confident that he will not be back, and with joy in our hearts, we start putting up the Christmas decorations.

Paradise Island

A long, modern road bridge connects Paradise Island with Nassau. We walk across it one morning, partly to have a closer look at the astonishing hotel, but mostly because someone has told us that it has large pools of marine life around it.

As we get closer I am reminded of Joni Mitchell's protest song, *Big Yellow Taxi* with its line, 'paved Paradise and put up a parking lot.' They undoubtedly found Paradise here, but thought it would be even better if they put in air conditioning, a casino and around twenty floors of luxury suites and hotel rooms.

So now Paradise Island is indistinguishable from Las Vegas, and the local pleasure boats take cruise ship passengers – the ones who want to experience an idyllic uninhabited island with a beach of pink coral sand and transparent water - to nearby Rose Island instead.

The enclosed 'bridge' near roof level that connects the hotel's two massive tower blocks is apparently a sumptuous suite with a nightly rate that would feed and house a local family for a twelvemonth. The building itself is the initial phase of what is destined to become a massive hotel complex, themed resort and water park. And, like the one in the Joni Mitchell song, this hotel is pink.

With its roof overhangs, and motifs vaguely reminiscent of Mayan temple buildings, it was originally called Trump Towers but renamed Atlantis. One can't help wondering if this is an appropriate allusion since, according to the myth, the ancient city-state of Atlantis sank into the sea along with the island it stood on.

We enter its wide front entrance and pass through the casino, with its banks of slot machines, roulette wheels, blackjack, craps tables, and games of Twenty One. But we are not here to gamble so we slide quickly past the croupiers, hopeful-faced but bereft of customers at this time of day, and dart out through the back door.

Outside an employee is explaining to a visiting couple how the people of the Lost Island of Atlantis would have experienced some part of daily life - the sort of thing you see done quite a lot in historic American towns by people in colonial dress - so we move swiftly on.

When we finally arrive at a pool, a young Bahamian woman is standing calf-deep in its water feeding sting rays. They are so graceful and very beautiful, some black with white spots and a prominent forehead shadowing their eyes that gives them an almost amiable expression. Sting rays can, of course, give a painful, very occasionally fatal sting. One of these swims effortlessly alongside the woman's bare leg and, as she lowers her hand to stroke it, its closest wing curls around her fingers in a gentle caress.

We wander to another pool with a list of feeding times but no sign of life, then over a jungle bridge beside an artificial waterfall, to the beach where local entrepreneurs appear to have retained their rights to sell souvenirs and hire out jet skis behind a hotel notice disclaiming any responsibility for these goods and services.

It is here that we discover the island's great treat - by accident. Well, more through typical local courtesy, really. As we are leaving the beach I notice a stone bollard with a list of attractions on it. It also has a young man leaning on it, although he does not obscure the list at all. His back is mostly towards us, but becoming suddenly aware of us reading the list he moves quickly aside, apologising. He wasn't in our way, I tell him, I was simply curious about the 'predator pool' listed on the notice beside him.

There will be nothing in it until feeding time, he says. 'But there is something you should see first. You walk under the fish.' And he gives us directions.

It is unlike anything we have seen before. The open pools at ground level are joined to underground caverns of perspex so that you walk through them with marine life above and on both sides of you.

You may have a dead-eyed shark at your shoulder one minute, and a doe-eyed, navy-blue frilly creature wafting above your head the next. It is wonderful to see up close all the things you never wanted to meet while wearing a wetsuit and snorkel - like sharks, sword fish and barracuda. And then suddenly you are surrounded by shoals of delicate little reef fish shimmering in their carnival colours.

There is also more than a touch of whimsy here. The children's water chute goes through the centre of the predator pool via a clear plastic tube; while the predators go via a clear plastic tube through the restaurant where they get to see human feeding time.

We tear ourselves away and follow the predators back aboveground, to watch them being fed in the pool outside. Added to the sword fish, barracuda and rather muscular sharks is a tiny hammerhead and a nurse shark, and some much larger stingrays than we saw earlier. These are grey and flat, with their eyes on top of their heads, and not something you would consider stroking at all.

Christmas

The weather now confirms the forecasts. It becomes cold, wet and very windy. During a lull in the rain we go ashore to do the last of our Christmas shopping. On the way we are hailed from a sloop and invited to the French Canadians' Christmas Eve Pot Luck, tonight, ashore.

'9pm to 3am,' she says. 'Bring a dish and whatever you want to drink.'

Pot Luck is a Canadian institution and an easy way to have a party for lots of people without investing a large amount of time, effort and money. The host arranges the venue and everybody chips in.

'The anchorage,' someone had told us earlier, 'is 60 per cent French Canadian. They're all on the run from their winter.'

In town there are carol-singers outside Barclays Bank. Like most of the other pedestrians we stop in the street to listen. As the applause and the singers melt away, the woman beside me says softly, 'How lovely, to sing greetings to God.'

She has such an air of tranquillity and kindliness that – though not normally a toucher of strangers - I squeeze her elbow and wish her the season's greetings. I am rewarded with the kind of smile that says it truly is Christmas.

With a large chocolate cake balanced on the top of our shopping - our 'dish' for the party tonight - we dinghy back to *Voyager* just before it starts to rain again. This is not the sort of weather we had been expecting from a Bahamian Christmas.

By Christmas morning the weather has turned really bad but, if nothing else, the blustery winds and lashing rain outside add an extra cosiness to the saloon. We have the tree up and decorated as usual, Christmas cards from family and friends strung across a bulkhead, candles lit and the aroma of a roast dinner wafting up from the galley.

Blustery it may be, but it is still quieter than the Christmas we spent last year, rising and troughing on Atlantic rollers en route to the Caribbean through the fallout from Hurricane Lenny.

During lunch, Bahamas Radio entertains us with Christmas songs, including a reggae *Rudolph the Red Nosed Reindeer* and a soul *White Christmas*. By afternoon the wind is gusting up to Gale Force 8, which means that our wind generator is producing more than enough electricity to power our small television. So, instead of an audio tape of the Nine Lessons and Carols from Kings College, Cambridge of last year, we have a full colour video. Plus those good old Christmas standards, *Miracle on 34th Street* and *It's A Wonderful Life*.

In between time we need to keep an eye on our position. A number of boats drag during the course of the day and have to re-anchor. There is also rumoured to be a partial eclipse of the sun today, and there may well be. But the only thing visible is total cloud cover.

By bedtime it is gusting up to Gale Force 9 and we take turns keeping a night watch. We have also laid out a second anchor. At around 4am David notices through the darkness that the car ferries moored beside the bridge appear to be getting closer to *Voyager*'s stern.

Unfortunately it is not the ferries that are on the move, but us. We are also dragging two entangled anchors and while I keep *Voyager* hovering, David hauls them up and separates them. By the time we re-anchor, the wind is lessening and it has stopped raining.

I take over the watch, sitting in the cockpit in a murky pre-dawn light, the harbour choppy from the wind. Suddenly, my eyes are drawn to the waves under the bridge, which appear to be lifting into the air. It takes a moment to realize that they are not waves at all but flocks of young seagulls sweeping just above the surface of the water. Indistinguishable from the chop at first, once clear of the bridge they begin rising as if the waves themselves are growing wings and taking flight. Flock after flock of them. Waves transforming into wings. Silent, rhythmic, they rise and pass beside us before disappearing into a glowering western sky.

Another cold front is forecast, with more strong winds.

Then & Now

Nassau was named after a Dutchman from the House of Orange-Nassau who married his Stuart first cousin and, as King William III and Queen Mary, they later reigned Britain and its dominions.

As for dominions, and the vexed question of colonization, and all the appalling destruction of indigenous populations, languages and cultures, there is something to celebrate here. And it has to do with slavery.

Depopulated by Columbus and those coming after him in pursuit of riches, in the years 1714-18 Nassau became a pirate haven for the likes of Edward Teach, aka Blackbeard, and Anne Bonny. There were Spanish and French incursions as Europe's major states fought each other for hegemony in the Caribbean and surrounding areas, but The Bahamas was ultimately colonized by Britain.

The population increased considerably with the Revolutionary War (1775–1783) or War of Independence if you are American, when some of those loyal to the British Crown fled here from the American colonies and brought their slaves with them. Several years before that war began, however, a trial had taken place in London which would have an even more dramatic effect on the future of The Bahamas.

Slavery in England and Wales was not authorized by Statute and its existence in the British Empire – including the American colonies - was ambiguous. But clarification came in 1772 in a case which established that slavery was not supported by Common Law either.

James Somerset, a young man of African descent, had been purchased in Boston, Massachusetts by a man called Stewart. But on reaching England Somerset escaped. He was recaptured and imprisoned on a ship while Stewart made plans to transport him to Jamaica for sale to a plantation owner. However, during his period of freedom, James Somerset had been baptized and his English godparents claimed that no Christian should be transported from England or Wales against his will.

The judge in the ensuing court case, Lord Mansfield, found for the claimants and the judgement he handed down from London's Kings Bench is considered a milestone in the movement to abolish slavery worldwide.

In England that fight was taken up by William Wilberforce (1759-1833) who, for 26 years headed the parliamentary campaign against the British slave trade. His efforts, and those of others like him, resulted in the Slave Trade Act of 1807 which made trading in slaves throughout Britain's dominions illegal. Sadly this only banned *trading* in slaves, not owning them, and the usual vested interests held up the abolition of slave-owning for nearly three more decades, until legislation finally became a reality in 1833 a few days before Wilberforce died.

In the meantime, the abolition of trading at least enabled the Royal Navy to intercept slave ships on the high seas from 1807 onwards and thousands of Africans being transported to a life of misery in America and the Caribbean were freed and resettled here.

The Bahamas became a haven, with the British government freeing American slaves aboard domestic US ships driven ashore by bad weather, and providing a sanctuary for American slaves and Black Seminoles escaping from Florida.

Today, Bahamians are still predominantly African in origin, but though independent since 1973 they retain some links with British culture. One of them is celebrating Boxing Day on December 26, although the way they do it, with Junkanoo, is unlike anything the British have ever done.

The weather on Boxing Day, however, is foul. But we are saved from any feelings of guilt about not struggling ashore in driving rain to watch it by the fact that there will be a repeat performance on New Year's Day.

On one of the days the America's Cup yacht, *New Zealand*, takes out a party for a blustery early morning sail. Under mainsail only, it sets off with gusto towards the harbour entrance but is soon back, decanting its saturated passengers into its tender. The best place to be at present is tucked up at anchor or in your hotel.

As the Old Year draws to a close, however, the wind and rain fall away and as if to celebrate the fact, as well as a new beginning, Paradise Island provides us all with a stupendous New Year's Eve firework display. As it ends, others begin across the harbour on New Providence Island.

A glance at our log tells us that during the year just ended we have travelled 5,245 miles.

Junkanoo

With daylight approaching, on New Year's morning we go ashore to watch Junkanoo. The parade takes place between 1am and 11am but a sign on the BASRA dock warns yachtsmen not to leave their dinghies there during the hours of darkness as they may be stolen; so we leave *Voyager* at dawn and tie up the dinghy as it gets light.

You walk the length of Bay Street - cool, silent and deserted at this time of the morning - until you become aware of a continuous sound in the distance that gets louder and louder until finally you reach the barriers blocking motor traffic from entering Bay and Elizabeth Streets. But by then the colour and movement has exploded upon your senses and the sound has taken your breath away.

The parade's route is a large rectangle: down Bay Street, turn right into Elizabeth, right again into Shirley, right at Frederick and back into Bay Street. We slide into a front row space at the barrier on the corner of Elizabeth and Bay, opposite two smiling senior policemen in full dress uniforms, and Junkanoo unfolds before us.

Hundreds of people undulate down the street, watched by hundreds more from the pavements and buildings. It is vibrant, good humoured and above all it is *happy*. What captivates is the vitality. This parade has already been going since 1am, but after six hours they are still dancing. And smiling. And they still have another four hours to go.

The work that has gone into the costumes is awe-inspiring - especially given the size of some of them. One we estimate as easily 12ft wide by 12ft high, but is still carried by a single person.

A theme is agreed each year. For this one it is constellations, such as those in the southern sky known collectively to astronomers as the Southern Birds — Pavo the Peacock, the Phoenix, and Apus the Bird of Paradise. And northern constellations such as Cygnus the Swan.

The use of colour is spectacular. I mean, they use everything and each costume should be a hash of colour, but it isn't. So much planning goes into them that because, rather than despite, so many colours, they create a dazzling effect. But even more, because each costume uses all the colours, there is the most stunning harmoniousness to the procession and the most tremendous sense of community spirit.

But what really blows your mind is the sound. There are a lot of wind instruments: trombones, clarinets, tubas, French horns and trumpets. There are cowbells, cymbals and whistles and basically anything you can carry and play a tune on. But what gets you, finally, are the drums. Home-made, many of them. Some basic. Some as beautifully decorated as the people playing them. And big. Their sound is deep and resonant. Their rhythm bounces off the buildings and rises up from the street.

First it hits you in the diaphragm, and then your brain and suddenly you're vibrating along with everybody and everything else, including the street itself, and you can't keep still. And you give yourself up to the colour and movement but most of all to the sound, along with all the other people lining your section of street. Young, middle-aged and well-matured, tiny children and teens, they all smile and vibrate on the same wavelength as you. And the narrow street, with its tall buildings, contains the energy of the sound and bounces it back at you, again and again.

As for stamina, as if the heavy costumes weren't enough to support for ten hours – and with the morning warming up nicely, too - some of the musicians are encircled by the tubing of wind instruments so big that there is no other way to carry them.

In a lull between the departure of one group of musicians and the arrival of the next, the man beside me explains that a group of friends or family members will choose a subject and then start making the costumes in March for the two parades, the one on Boxing Day and the other on New Year's Day. But if anybody should wonder why it would take from March to December, one glance at the individual costumes tells you why. I ask the man where the tradition came from. 'The British,' he says. 'We just kept it going.'

It's a kind thought, but we British are too phlegmatically northern European to have anything this vibrant in our genes. And, as I will discover later, although the Junkanoo's development remains subject to debate, it is pretty much agreed that its origins lie in West Africa.

Whatever its journey I am grateful, on this first morning of a New Year, to the people of Providence Island for their spontaneity, good humour and community spirit. Including the self-deprecating figure gliding along the edge of the parade, in jeans, black hoodie and small rucksack with his quiet smile, determined walk and a large coil of wire in one hand.

If he carried a logo on his back it would say something like Junkanoo Emergency Services. But he doesn't need a logo. Everybody on the street knows who he is. He's the repairman. The guy with the spare parts who comes to your aid if a wire support snaps or the foam rubber taking the weight on your shoulders or hips comes adrift and the heavy costume begins to chafe.

According to the local paper, Atlantis puts on its own Junkanoo in-house. But nothing could ever recreate this feeling of the street pulsating under your feet or the sense of something coming to fruition that has been planned and sewn and glued in so many homes, over so many months, by so many people and performed with such spontaneity. Not for any commercial reason, but for themselves alone.

A massive hotel complex, such as the one on Paradise Island is due to become, will bring enormous changes to Nassau at all levels. A rise in the standard of living for the local community is likely to be one of them, but changes in other ways, too. Things that have always been taken for granted, or not even noticed until much later.

Rose Island

Leaving Nassau Harbour, you pass the tiny ruined Fort Montague which once guarded its eastern entrance, sail past The Narrows and the wrecks off Athol Island and from there it is only a short distance to Rose Island. It is probably the longest, thinnest island we have ever seen. Its recommended anchorage, Bottom Harbour on the south side of the island, is really just a bay with another tiny island and a reef protecting it. From there we take the dinghy ashore, to a low stone jetty.

The shoreline is rocky, but a narrow path between the trees takes you to a very lovely beach on the north side of the island. The water is crystal clear and the sand the palest pink. It is quite deserted and utterly tranquil.

There is a little holiday place here, abandoned now, but still with springy lawns between the cabins, a system of rainwater collection and solar panels for power. It would be a blissful place for holidays, which is probably what its owners thought. But for many a Bahamian project the environment proves that bit too difficult for it to survive. So now the island is uninhabited. Just the local tour boats bringing people from the cruise ships for an hour or two, and yachtsmen like us.

On another day we dinghy to one of the little islets forming the reef around our anchorage. The water surrounding it is so shallow we have to get out of the dinghy some way off and float it behind us as we wade ashore. There are crabs living in holes in the sand, which is creamy white here with an almost liquid texture that oozes silkily between the toes. The sand is so pale, and the water so clear and shallow, that the sea is almost colourless, just a tiny hint of blue.

Early evening, a setting sun of polished copper sinks into the sea, back-lighting a frieze of small clouds in the western sky and hanging a golden halo around each one. An airliner flies below them, a very long way away. It is undoubtedly travelling very fast although distance makes it appear to be hardly moving at all. It has no meaning here, speed and hectic movement. Not among this tranquillity.

As evening progresses, the western sky becomes a translucent red, like wine in a glass with a candle flame beneath it. When I look again later it has become opaque, and burnt orange.

It had been warm below deck when we'd gone to bed but with two hulls you can have an identical bunk each on sticky nights. At around 1am

I feel the boat shift and go up on deck to check our anchor, but David is already there. When we had gone below for the night the wind had been coming from the south and *Voyager* was being sheltered by the small island. Now the wind is coming from the west. The anchorage is open to the west and the wind is sweeping into it from the open sea with nothing to obstruct it.

Voyager's anchor hasn't shifted, but David will stay on deck a while anyway. I go below and make tea. We sit in the cockpit and drink it slowly, watching an enormous moon sink behind Rose Island. If the setting sun had been polished copper, this setting moon is burnished brass.

6
The Exumas

There are two particularly desirable cruising areas in The Bahamas. Each is an archipelago which takes its name from its largest island: the Exumas in the south, and the Abacos in the north. We decide to explore the southern one first, and then meander north as the weather gets hotter.

The distance from Rose Island to the Exumas is only thirty miles, and the water so clear you can see individual blades of sea grass and the trails of small marine creatures in the sand 20 feet/6m below. It is the clearest water we have ever sailed in and every now and then a sting ray leaps out of it, taps its fluting wings together over its back, and sinks below again.

Allans Cay
Our first stop is Allans Cay. We find the anchorage fairly crowded and finish up at the north end of it, in what appears to be our own tidal stream, always facing the opposite direction to everyone else. Because of the strength of the current we make our first attempt at Bahamian mooring.

To do this, you lay out your first anchor in the conventional way, but let out far more chain than would be normal, and drop back to its fullest extent. Then you drop your second anchor, also from the bow, and once it is set you haul in the chain from the first anchor until you are lying half way between the two in your planned position.

The theory is that when the tide changes, the chain from the first anchor will go slack, the boat will turn through 180° and fall back on the second anchor keeping you within a limited area.

It is a convention in these islands as it enables a large number of boats to fit into relatively small anchorages. And it works well for monohulls. In fact, people go off and leave their boats anchored this way for days, even in bad weather. Unfortunately, a catamaran's two hulls turn it into something of a cat's-cradle, with every tide change requiring the mess to be sorted out with boat hooks and various ropes that takes about half an hour before we are comfortably settled again. With four tide changes in twenty-four hours, including during the night, something has to be done.

The problem is that we don't carry two lots of chain, so our second anchor uses rope. And, when this rope goes slack, it doesn't sink as quickly as the chain on our main anchor and it gets caught between the hulls and around the rudders as the boat turns. Fortunately, enlightenment comes with breakfast. David lowers a chum — a lump of lead loosely hooked around the second anchor's rope — so that the minute the rope goes slack it is quickly pulled to a depth that allows *Voyager*'s twin keels to pass over it, tangle free. From now on Bahamian mooring will not be a problem.

Allans Cay is famous for its iguanas, a very large lizard whose species can be traced back millions of years. They are endangered, protected, and according to our cruising guide very partial to lettuce which they will take from your hand. We only have cabbage on board but they seem to find that an acceptable alternative — the main criteria being green and crunchy. Even the birds here are tame. As we stand talking to a couple from Michigan, a mockingbird walks around our feet before wandering off to rootle about in our dinghy for something edible.

At another beach, at the far end of the anchorage, as we walk the dinghy ashore through the shallow water, a number of much larger iguanas come elbowing out of the scrub and down the beach demanding food. As it is not forthcoming they become resentful. It's not our fault. We exhausted our stock of greens with the other lot. These hiss at us in displeasure. At around three and a half feet/1m long, and with worryingly large claws, we beat a retreat. Fortunately, they don't like water so we wade through the shallows towing the dinghy behind us until we are far enough away to enjoy the rest of the beach without them.

Highbourne Cay

According to the forecast the wind is set to rise considerably tomorrow so we head off to Highbourne Cay, for shelter as well as a change of scene.

The wind, when it arrives at our new anchorage, is from the east and since we are on the west side of the island it is sheltered and comfortable. A Bahamian sunset cuts a brief but glorious swathe of gold across the tops of the waves before disappearing in cloud. During a restful night David, his mind still exercised by the disturbances of the previous ones, sits bolt upright in bed and stares out across the anchorage.

'We're dragging,' he says. Then he spots the only other boat here and adds, 'But if we are, we're into synchronized dragging,' falls back onto his pillow and is asleep again.

Next morning we dinghy into the marina. It is spotless, newish, with only one yacht and four large motorboats tied up in its incredibly clean, blue water. There is a nice little shady office, and a porch with chairs, and in one corner of it some coconut halves and water bowls for the colourful wild birds feeding there. As we walk to the counter to ask directions to the shops the birds, now fully breakfasted, begin to walk out – not in a random fashion as one might expect, but very orderly, in neat little columns of their own species.

The store is only a few minutes' walk away. When we get there it is closed. We ask a man working in his garden if it opens today. Oh, yes, he says. She is making a delivery. She will be back in about a quarter of an hour. We find a shady tree and sit under it.

When the store owner returns we, and the skipper of the other anchored boat, browse through her refrigerated storeroom, then get into her aging van to go to her house to collect loaves of freshly-baked bread. The roof of the van has rusted into small holes in places which have been filled with chewing gum to keep the rain out.

Nowhere is tranquillity all the time, of course. Late afternoon we are enjoying a glass of wine and a game of Scrabble at the saloon table. I hear an engine, and get up in time to see a helicopter go over very low and very fast but some distance away. A few minutes later we hear a strange swishing noise outside and both of us get up to look. Coming towards us, at enormous speed, is a powerful wave and we just have time to act before it reaches our starboard beam.

We've never been hit with quite such force before, not even crossing the Atlantic; the speed and violence of it being accentuated by the shallowness of the water. David grabs the glasses to avoid wine and broken glass everywhere while using his left hip and shoulder to keep the computer and TV from hurtling off the chart table. I run down the galley steps and wedging one foot against the cupboard behind me for balance, wrap my arms around the pots and pans beside the sink and the crockery on the draining board.

Everything else: books, videos, cameras, spectacles and Scrabble board hit the floor. By the time *Voyager* has stopped thrashing from side to side and we have staggered outside, there is not a thing to be seen apart from a flat expanse of shining blue water.

Normans Cay

Looking out from the cockpit at the route to Normans Cay is quite intimidating. You zigzag through narrow channels, in swirling currents and back eddies, between tiny islets, coral heads and half-submerged rocks. Once clear of these you turn right and sail placidly for half an hour or so and then make your way between two rocks and over a very shallow sandbar to enter the inner pool of Normans Cay.

It is called Normans Pond and the entrance is only four feet/1.3m deep which is too shallow for most yachts and the reason we currently have it to ourselves.

The cay itself forms an elongated horse shoe, providing a wonderfully protected anchorage. It is also extraordinarily beautiful with its different shades of blue water and the land green with coconut palms, low shrubs and palmetto. Add a bright, shining sky and it really is Paradise.

As we motor forward to choose a place to drop our anchor, a large sting ray, probably five feet/1.5m across, leaps from the water. It is one of the black ones with white spots, and the raised forehead. And so beautiful. In what looks like sheer exuberance, it rises several feet from the water and claps the rippling edges of its great wings over its back before sinking again.

Later that evening, the sting ray swims around us, close to *Voyager*'s hulls. Its motion is wonderful, just below the surface of the water, with only its wing tips slowly breaking the surface. I am standing at the rail, watching it when, with a huge but effortless leap, it is level with my face. Like a dolphin or a whale, a sting ray appears to be as keen to get a look at you as you are to observe it.

Next morning we dinghy ashore to the nearest beach for a swim, with our masks and snorkels. No effort is required on our part as the current gently carries you along parallel to the beach. And as you travel you are accompanied by thousands of tiny fish. Like swimming in a fish tank only without the glass walls. Just you, and the brightly coloured little fish, and the sun streaming through the crystal clear water onto the sandy bottom. A sand so pale it is almost white, and so soft your feet sink into it.

These are perfect days. We swim and laze and read and eat and go to bed when it gets dark and rise with the dawn. We have the anchorage to ourselves, and the temperature is ideal. At night we go to bed under skies so clear that the Milky Way near blows your mind, and fall asleep trying to name the Fixed Stars.

Every morning we listen to World Service international news at 6am Local Time; to the British news half an hour after that; and then the Waterway Radio & Cruising Club weather forecasts. The latter is run by Americans using single side band (SSB) also known as ham radios.

Before every transmission there is a call for any priority, emergency or medical issues to 'come now'. In the Caribbean there was only one medical emergency that we heard of but there were depressingly regular reports of people having nocturnal intruders on their boats, of dinghies being stolen from their sterns - and once, even a whole yacht went missing. There was also the occasional mugging ashore. Here, the closest thing to a crisis so far has been a jelly fish getting sucked up into a yachtsman's water maker.

There are so many beaches around the anchorage you can swim off a different one each day. Although some of them are so delightful they get a second visit from us. At one of them the beach falls away at a certain point so you can snorkel with your body floating in shallow water, which is deliciously warm, while looking down onto shoals of colourful reef fish below you in deep water.

After these swimming trips we return to *Voyager* for coffee and what has now become the traditional game of backgammon. Today, as usual, while the coffee brews in the galley, on deck we pour fresh water warmed in the sun over ourselves to remove the salt from our bodies. With the sun sparkling on the blue water and a light breeze in the palm trees, David looks around us and says, 'Not a bad place to be in the middle of January.' We are still the only boat here. It is utterly tranquil.

Warderick Wells

We find Warderick Wells Cay another tranquil place to be – once you get settled there. The nearest anchorage is buoyed and all of them are taken. There is another, idyllic place according to the cruising guide, where you can use your own anchor, but to reach it means a four-mile detour around a sandbar. But it is well worth the trip. For not only is it very beautiful, we also have it all to ourselves.

Weather-wise, these remain glorious days of light breezes and cloudless skies, while the nights continue to blaze with stars and the planet Venus is so bright it lights up the sea like moonlight.

This island is also home to the HQ and principal visitor centre of the Exuma Land and Sea Park, the first marine conservation of its kind in the world. Set up in 1958, it covers 176 square miles and is managed by The Bahamas National Trust.

With one exception – where the buoys are - you may drop an anchor where you like as long as it is not on coral. And while you are welcome to enjoy the area's attractions to the full you are also required to leave everything where you found it.

In 1986 it became a No-Take Zone. Take anything away from the Park's waters and the Park Wardens will fine you $500 per incident per person aboard your boat. A single fish, lobster, shell or other souvenir, counts as one incident. And your boat may be confiscated. Which is probably why – for a popular watering hole - this entire area is still so unspoilt more than four decades after the first Park Wardens set about protecting it.

Warderick Wells is a cruiser's dream. Your surroundings are stunning. And with its undersea caves, coral reefs teeming with reef fish and the haunt of sea turtles, the swimming and snorkelling are superb.

Staniel Cay

After completing the long route back around its sandbank, we set out through the north-east entrance into a lively sea and a six-hour sail. Our course is to the south end of Compass Cay and along the tortuous route through rock-strewn Pipe Creek to Staniel Cay. There we anchor in water so shallow that we touch bottom during the night. However, it is very soft sand and such a gentle bottoming that we hardly notice.

Staniel Cay is where scenes for the James Bond movie *Thunderball* and Disney's *Splash* were filmed, among others, although the experience doesn't seem to have affected this little settlement much. We clamber ashore onto the yacht club's very tall dinghy dock and a resident gives us directions to the shops.

The pink one, she says, sells bread, fruit and veg; the blue one sells canned goods; while the general store up the creek has 'the best presented meat' – which I never do understand - and a small chandlery.

To reach it you pass the settlement's tiny cemetery which has a commemorative seawall opposite. On it a local artist has painted portraits of the deceased, not in formal poses but in the roles they carried out in life – as nurse, barber, boat skipper.

The coast road, which has been eroded in places, shows the only signs of damage from last year's hurricane. The airport, alongside the creek, is a concrete square, and although we don't want to risk giving offence by asking him, we think the man in uniform sitting on a plastic chair under a small garden pagoda in one corner of it is air traffic control.

The grotto which featured in the 007 and Disney movies is a large cavern inside the island. Access is from the sea and to get into it you swim through one of the various tunnels, depending on the state of the tide, and whether you are a diver or a snorkeler. At low tide even a mask and snorkel are optional.

Once through one of these tunnels you emerge into a large cavern filled with sunlight, through a hole in the roof, lighting up the water and the brightly coloured reef fish. You need to choose the right time, however, as a swimmer can be swept out to sea by the ebbing tide.

The reef at Staniel Cay is another spectacular place to snorkel, with its fascinating coral and so many different types of fish - one minute iridescent blue; the next, shimmering white with long fins curving from head to tail. We also find ourselves being followed at times by shoals of small, semi-transparent ones with large black eyes. You don't know they're there unless you turn around suddenly and – just like the children's game - they all stop dead and wait for you to move on again before they do. Sometimes, depending on the light, their bodies are virtually invisible, so all you see when you turn around are hundreds of black eyes staring back at you.

And then the weather changes.

Winter weather in The Bahamas is notoriously changeable but also largely predictable. From around mid-November to early March the islands are prey to winds called Northers sweeping down from Florida and Georgia. The first indication is a sudden wind shift locally. After that a strong wind arrives dragging a cold front behind it, as cold air from the north collides with Bahamian warmth. This is followed by darkening skies, gusting heavy rain, a thunderstorm or a squall.

Fortunately the forecasters give very good predictions of their arrival. The only thing they can't tell you is how long a particular Norther will last. It may be 24 hours, or days. And sometimes one will show every sign of going away, only to flare up again. The important thing for yachtsmen is to attend to the forecasts, be anchored somewhere appropriate when one is expected, and have bolt holes in reserve on lengthy passages.

The latest Norther announces its arrival with a dramatic wind change, sending our stern whipping round towards the little reef in front of the beach opposite. More importantly our bow is now facing an inlet through which the new wind direction is coming, and its increased strength is producing a swell fit to lift our anchor.

Happily the answer is just around the corner in the main anchorage and we motor into a protected, *Voyager*-size, space. There we settle down under a thunderstorm and high winds - although not as high as those occurring north of The Bahamas today, where it apparently reached over 50mph. And, after the recent balmy days, as well as turbulent it also turns cold.

Mind you, when I say *cold*, there's a tendency nowadays to go looking for your woolly slippers when the thermometer sinks to 70°F/21°C. And, though we experience a drop in temperature, it is nowhere near Miami's which reached a rare low of 44°F/6.7°C this month, requiring conservationists to rescue not only manatees but even turtles.

I have to say that it had never occurred to me that cold water would be a problem for the cold-blooded turtle. But it seems the shallow water of Florida's lagoons cools faster than the ocean, and a prolonged drop in temperature in a shallow lagoon sends them into shock.

Meanwhile a fellow-cruiser we meet says he has just heard from his son back home in Niceville, on the Florida Panhandle, that the temperature there has sunk to a nippy 28°F/-2°C.

On the way north to The Abacos we stop off at Nassau to collect our mail and stock up, there being so few shops even on those islands which are inhabited. We also have a lot of marine life cluttering up our hulls and reducing our speed by easily a knot and a half. So, with the weather conducive, David finds a shallow, deserted spot, dons his wetsuit, goggles and snorkel and begins scraping Voyager's hulls free of barnacles.

Meanwhile I clean the decks and back steps while keeping an eye open for him. I never leave him underwater unobserved. People in power boats – and, as we have recently seen, in helicopters - can cause huge water surges, while blood from even minor cuts can attract sharks. You can also turn thoughtlessly underwater, get caught up on something and drown in minutes.

A large sting ray swims only yards away from the boat all the time that David is below. It throws itself upwards a number of times, but mostly just drifts about. Its bluish-black hue under water is indistinguishable from David's wetsuit and I suggest to him, on one of his returns to the surface for air, that the ray might have designs on him.

'If the worst happens,' I tell him, 'I want you to know I'll stand by you.'

7
Eleuthera

Between The Exumas chain and The Abacos is a very long, narrow island called Eleuthera. To avoid an overnight passage we decide to break our journey at Royal Island, a small dot on its north-west tip.

We set sail for it after the weather forecast. There will be northerly winds tomorrow which will mean wind on the nose if we leave our departure until then. But if we go now, we are promised a broad reach in a 10- to 14-knot wind all the way. Sadly, it dies away around lunchtime so we take in the genoa and motor instead. Half an hour later it begins to rain. Then the wind rises suddenly, starting from the south-east and working its way round to the north so that by the time we arrive at Royal Island it is bang on the nose. This is the result of the cold front arriving which was not due until tonight.

Royal Island

The cruising guide suggests you look for the wreck of a freighter to the south of Royal Island to use as a waypoint. We have difficulty identifying the freighter but eventually decide that an obscure conical shape is now all that is left of it above water. Using this as our starting point we set a course to take us through the reefs to the eastern entrance of the harbour recommended by the cruising guide.

On trying to enter, however, we are rapidly down to less than three feet/1m over coral heads, which can tear a hull to shreds. On trying to reverse out, we run solidly aground. Fortunately we are on a rising tide, and are soon able to get off and reverse our way out of the entrance.

We then head west to the other entrance and radio for confirmation from any boats already anchored inside. *Southern Comfort*, an American ketch, gives us very clear instruction and, as we slowly approach the entrance between rocks, a yacht called *Icon* radios us up to confirm that we have plenty of depth ahead of us.

Of course, as we approach the entrance, the wind speed increases until it is gusting 24 knots. Fortunately the bottom is sand and weed and the anchor bites solidly first time and no sooner are we settled than the wind drops, the rain stops and the sun comes out. We radio and wave our thanks to *Southern Comfort* and *Icon*. As we sit with a mug of tea in the cockpit, a large turtle paddles past in the sunshine.

One of your initial thoughts on arriving in the Bahamas is: how have these islands escaped development? Then you begin to find expensive holiday projects begun and abandoned because they couldn't survive economically. There are plenty of reasons: in a lot of areas the water is too shallow for cruise ships; it can be an awkward journey to anywhere other than Nassau or Freeport because guests must travel to the islands from these major airports by small boats, or small planes if there is a runway locally; resources such as drinking water and power can be a problem, as is obtaining supplies; it is also a hurricane zone.

Ultimately the undergrowth, including a giant form of tradescantia – previously only known to me as a pretty green-and-white striped pot plant - reclaims it all. One such venture is here at Royal Island and in the afternoon we go ashore and climb a steep hill to investigate Royal Island Harbour's abandoned and decaying yacht club and hotel.

It is in an idyllic spot and must have cost a small fortune to build. After wandering through its once impressive interiors we follow its paved and walled walks and the encroaching undergrowth to the other side of the island. There you find yourself looking down on a natural pool, perfect for swimming in, on the edge of a translucent blue sea.

Back on board, during the afternoon, a dinghy comes alongside. The Canadians are here in force and we are invited to a Pot Luck Supper to be held in the ruins of the yacht club. I should love to, and even have a plate and bottle ready but, as dusk and the local insect population descend, decide against it.

We recently re-read Charles Dickens' *Hard Times*. In it there is a wonderful description - by Mr Sleary, riding master with a small, travelling circus - about how a performing dog, taken away by its owner some years earlier, has managed to find the circus again following its owner's death. In short, Mr Sleary says, he probably asked other dogs.

This evening, as David watches me secure the insect screens against the invisible horde, he suggests that something of the sort could explain how mosquitoes find me while missing so many other people. And he could be right because I have had mosquitoes find me in a way that has made me wonder if they may have gone to www.victims@mosquitos.com or some equivalent website thinking, 'I'm looking to produce the biggest, reddest, itchiest weals in the history of mosquito bites, with peripheral swelling of at least an inch in diameter and itchiness lasting a minimum of three days. So who is there available in my area allergic enough to my bite to produce this kind of result?'

And she (only female mosquitoes bite people) logs on, enters her location and requirements, and is presented with my listing, provided by *hundreds* of other satisfied customers. It says to look for a catamaran named *Voyager*, and that although maximum precautions are taken on board, such as insect screens, and no apertures after lights-on, the companionway door keyhole is occasionally neglected and offers easy access. The victim also has the useful habit of poking her feet and lower legs out of her bedding, and if the would-be record-holder only has the patience to wait silently behind the curtains until she is asleep ...

And in no time I'm sitting up in bed scratching, and groping around for the tube of itch cream, while David and all the people in all the other boats around us, express doubts that there is even a mosquito about.

Spanish Wells

From Royal Island it is a long sail to Marsh Harbour, the sea is quite rough and we shall have to beat, so it will be an uncomfortable day. In these conditions we could also arrive late and have no desire to navigate the reefs after dark. So we decide to break our journey at Spanish Wells. It has no recognized anchorage but a trawler yacht has anchored to the left of the harbour's eastern entrance and we tuck into the small bay behind it.

The town looks very prosperous. The houses are large and well-maintained and the harbour is lined with new and very expensive sports fishing boats. It is, in fact, the most salubrious settlement we shall ever encounter in The Bahamas. It is unique in another way, too. It is the most uniformly uncivil place we shall ever encounter in The Bahamas and could not have made us less welcome had we been a leper ship.

Late afternoon four young men on jet skis roar around *Voyager* until we have to sit down and hold on, or risk falling over. Then they go and do the same thing to the trawler yacht anchored in front of us.

We set off early next morning.

As we reach the harbour entrance a small freighter comes out with two men on the bridge and three others leaning over the bow. I wave. They glare back at me. The vessel, which is coming out quite quickly, makes no attempt to slacken speed to allow us to cross its bows although we have right of way, so we have to increase to full revs to avoid it; which is something we hadn't wanted to do because the water is so shallow in this direction.

Once past the harbour's entrance there is a series of wooden piles. Most of them are going across the bay, where we don't want to go, but a shorter line of them points towards the open sea. Unfortunately there is no connection between the two lines of piles to help you reach the one you want.

A pilot boat pulls alongside. I ask its skipper which of the piles we should be heading for. He says we need a pilot to take us through. He stares meaningfully at me. I do not respond. He roars away. I decide Spanish Wells will freeze over before it gets a cent out of us.

When you finally reach the piles you want, there is no indication which side of them you should pass. We take a punt. It gets very shallow and we go aground. A number of small boats roar past, but none of them acknowledges us so asking directions is not an option. We finally haul ourselves off and get to the line of piles we need and decide we should be OK. Some of them run in pairs, some of them don't.

We reach one pair and assume we should go between them, but one has been knocked askew and the space between seems limited, so we go around them and run ground. David puts *Voyager* into reverse but has to stop abruptly because the pilot boat roars across our stern ahead of the large leisure craft it is piloting – ignoring the piles – and out to sea. The pilot looks at us sourly.

'Watch where he goes!' yells David over the howl of their engines as he struggles to stop Voyager hitting one of the piles in their wash. When it has subsided and we stop crashing up and down, David reverses out from the piles and we copy their route out through the heads. The piles, it seems, being entirely irrelevant to your reaching the heads safely.

There is a vintage motor yacht anchored out here, of the old traditional style, looking like a miniature 1930s ocean-going liner. As we get level, half a dozen elderly people rise to their feet and, along with the chef serving them breakfast, stare at us. 'Good morning,' I say, as we slide past. Not expecting a response, I am not disappointed.

As we finally leave Spanish Wells behind, the man in the pilot boat roars past, having left his latest client. I wave. He looks sourer than ever.

Our cruising guide says the local patois here is laced with a West Country burr from the original settlers. I can't say that the voices I've heard over the VHF bear anything I recognize from Devon or Cornwall although the sweet nature of the few we've encountered has put me in mind of that region's infamous wreckers immortalised in Daphne du Maurier's novel, *Jamaica Inn*. And, oddly enough, I will subsequently come across the following description of this area's past:

'At this time, "wrecking", or the salvaging of shipwrecked boats, became a mainstay of the economy. In fact, various tricks were used to lure the ships to the reefs, in the northern part of the island. In fact, at a large reef off Spanish Wells, a reef called Devil's Backbone, there are many wrecks today attesting to the success of the following ruse; lanterns were put on donkeys at night, and moved to strategic areas, to fool the captains into thinking they were the lights of lighthouses, and cause the ships to go off course onto the rocks. This was especially popular in Spanish Wells, and Harbor Island. The local population even resisted the construction of lighthouses, in the time of 1845-1870, although more than 300 vessels had shipwrecked over the years, since "wrecking" provided a boost to the local economy.'

More recently, in the late 1970s and early '80s, the local economy benefited from becoming a relay station between Columbia and Florida in the cocaine trade, until the Bahamian authorities put a stop to it.

Once free of Spanish Wells, you work your way around two starboard headlands when, the cruising guide says, you should look for jeep tracks. Then, with your back to them, steer 350 degrees magnetic, putting a reef with crashing surf on your starboard side. Get it wrong and you meet up with a reef on your port side. We assume 'jeep tracks' mean the two narrow, parallel concrete slabs running down into the water. And we obviously don't get our turn entirely right as we end up in very shallow water at one stage. But out at sea we bowl along at over 6 knots.

A check of the GPS tells us that we will arrive at Little Harbour at about 5pm which is later than we should have liked because our exit from Spanish Wells took longer than expected. It is a rolling sea but nevertheless a pleasant passage and one providing a special treat.

It is an odd thing but while I'm the one who seems to know intuitively when dolphins are about, David is always the one to spot a whale. He gives a shout and points, and I'm just in time to see a Humpback breach. We now know why so many of the pictures you see of humpbacks show only their tail flukes. They move so fast that by the time you grab your camera the tail is the only part still visible. We keep a lookout for ages afterwards but never see it surface again.

8
The Abacos

At 4.45pm we reach our waypoint, about half a mile off Little Harbour - the southernmost anchorage on the island of Great Abaco - which means we shall be settled before dark. Although even in daylight it turns out to be one of our more memorable approaches. A minor nightmare, really.

From the waypoint you get into the anchorage through a narrow channel between two reefs, only one of which you can see. It is called The Boilers, and that's just what it looks like - boiling water.

The notes on the chart say that to enter this channel safely you should aim for the disused lighthouse keeper's house until you get 150 yards off-shore and then turn to starboard. That keeps you in safe water between the end of the starboard reef and the off-shore rocks. Since the lighthouse itself has gone, it isn't obvious which of the deserted dwellings scattered over the headland once housed the lighthouse keeper. And none of them is in the spot shown on the chart anyway.

I go out onto the foredeck; most immediately to try and identify the house but also because, once *Voyager* is between the reefs, from the cockpit it is impossible to see where the reefs begin. It does not help that it is low tide and, as a result, all our safety margins are reduced. By going up to the bow I hope to give David maximum warning if we are getting too close.

In the end we choose one of the ruined houses and aim for it. The next problem immediately becomes apparent. On our new course the Atlantic rollers, which had provided such an enjoyable passage all day, are now pushing us from behind and driving us forward at alarming speed. To make matters even worse, the rollers are not *directly* on the stern but a little towards the port quarter, and thereby pushing us to starboard.

The reef to port, which is boiling and foaming, provides some sort of guide. But there is nothing on the chart, or in the cruising guide, to tell us how wide the channel is and thus how much leeway we have before Voyager collides with the edge of the starboard reef. David puts on full power to keep control which means we are going even faster, and much faster than he would have wished. But there is no option but for him to keep going and for me to continue clinging on while staring over the bow in the hope that if we are about to hit something I will see it in time.

An additional hazard is that the rollers are now hitting shallow water, creating breaking waves and *Voyager* is surfing. A roller will lift her stern and she accelerates down the wave. Then, as it passes under her, the bow comes up just as another roller passes under her stern and starts the process going all over again.

All of this is adding to our unwanted speed. Meanwhile the wind, which had been a gentle 8 knots when we entered the channel, has been rising steadily. I can't bear to think what it will be like if it gets much stronger, and understand at a very fundamental level why there are so many wrecks around The Bahamas.

As we approach the shore we also find the words '150 yards off' something of a problem, especially with so much at stake, and at such times you really do crave a more accurate use of language: such as, is that 150 yards off our chosen building; off the cliff face; or off the rocky shore running out from the cliff? And what does 150 yards look like exactly? In the end, you say, 'Oh, sod it!' hang a right, and vow *never* to do this again.

And suddenly we are in a millrace travelling parallel to a horribly rocky shore, being dragged about at speed while thrashing from side to side; because after making our turn, the Atlantic rollers previously on our stern are now hitting us on the beam again. Things up on the foredeck are violent. But David is wrestling with the steering wheel and all I can think is, *the last thing he needs right now is a man-overboard drill*, throw my arms around the furled genoa and hang on for dear life.

I continue to stare into the foaming water in the forlorn hope of seeing any obstruction in time, until a roar to my right makes me look up at a huge breaking wave hanging over our starboard beam. It is well that I am clinging to the genoa because, David tells me later, when it hit us my feet left the deck completely.

The whole episode must take only minutes but it seems to go on forever. Then quite suddenly we pass between two further reefs and enter the anchorage. The difference is positively surreal. From what felt like roaring, imminent destruction, all is now utterly tranquil. People are swimming, lazing in their cockpits and one couple is placidly paddling a canoe back from a local bar. We quickly drop anchor behind Lynyard Cay, pour ourselves very large drinks and give ourselves up to a stunning sunset. We are now officially in the Abacos.

Marsh Harbour

Marsh Harbour, on the large island of Abaco, is the major town in the Abacos archipelago, the one with the majority of services available and hence very popular with cruisers. We had expected its anchorage to be crowded but despite lots of boats there is still plenty of room for us.

Ashore, the first person we meet is one of the announcers on the Channel 68 Cruisers Net which broadcasts every morning and to which we have been gratefully listening since arriving in The Bahamas. She imparts all the useful information a cruiser needs, including where to find the shops, the supermarket, the chandlers and where to dispose of refuse.

The Abacos are more developed and populated than the Exumas, although not all that much. And despite holiday developments and a well-established residential area Marsh Harbour does not seem to have succumbed much to commercial or personal pressures. One shop owner tells us that sometime soon she is intending to get someone in to repair her roof in case they get any serious rain this year. When she names the hurricane that did the damage, we realize it is the one that went through two years ago. It obviously doesn't pay to do things in too big a rush here.

As well as a very good supermarket there is a wet fish shop which is a real treat. It has a six-toed cat on the threshold which is so sleepy you can do almost anything with it. When it stretches, it puts one large, six-toed paw over its face as if it were yawning politely.

At the post office we discover that there is no franking system on the island as a girl with a huge pile of letters in front of her sticks three stamps on each envelope.

Marsh Harbour is a dusty, sprawling town with very neat gardens and smartly painted houses. It is also very polite. I get chatting to an American about Dostoyevsky – the way you do - while our smalls rotate in neighbouring machines at The Pond Wash Launderette. We are sitting outside, on either side of the doorway, so anyone entering walks between us, although not close. Yet every person who passes, male or female, says, 'Excuse me' because they are crossing our conversation. When I mention this politeness to the American she says she thinks it is the British influence. How kind, I think. Especially since in US supermarkets Americans do something similar all the time.

Nor is concern for others confined to adults. Two adolescents, leaving a shop and finding people making the tiniest of detours around their laid-down bicycles, hurry to pick them up out of the way, full of apologies. Although we do choose the wrong person to ask about the Wanted posters around town concerning a recent murder, and are regaled in gory detail. The perpetrator, it seems, is still at large – hence the posters - although nobody appears unduly worried.

With our provisioning done, David checks the charts to find out the best route for us to leave here, as we do not want to repeat our Little Harbour entry experience. Tilloo passage seems favourite but a new cold front is due so we decide to wait for it to go through.

At its height, around 5 o'clock in the morning, it spins us through 180° and then clears off leaving behind dripping-wet days and 25-knot winds. So we stay where we are a bit longer.

With time to pass I dig out a remaindered book I found in a bookshop somewhere. When you live on a boat, often without access to radio or television, you buy books by the yard. At $7 plus tax, for 1200 pages, this one had been a bargain. Not a history offering analysis and synthesis, but a chronology, a list of world events in date order. And just the thing for wet, blustery days. We dip into the centuries. Fascinated.

Things like: London's origins go as far back as at least 400BC when a Celtic king called Belin had an earth wall built around a group of huts beside the Thames, along with a wooden quay. Belin's Gate, the water gate cut into the earth wall to give access from the quay to the little settlement, is the site of London's Billingsgate fish market.

And though we'd heard of the Emperors Charles the Good, the Bald and the Bad, we take a delight in the discovery of Louis the Stammerer and Louis the Pious (both 9th century Kings of France), Michael the Drunkard (a Byzantine Emperor), Michael the Lame, the Quarrelsome, the Penniless and, perhaps reflecting on his namesakes, Michael of the Wry Smile.

To divert us further during this inclement weather we dig out a bottle from our dwindling wine store and, by now in advanced reading mode, address ourselves to the description on the back.

'This incomparable wine displays the soft, round character and velvety texture typical of the Merlot grape. Its taste is characterized by radiating plum and berry fruit flavours accented with a hint of oak. Like the simple grace of a Monarch butterfly, the vanilla-spice aroma of our famous Merlot will captivate your interest immediately!'

Try as we might, our palates fail to detect any radiating plums or berries, the vanilla-spice doesn't reveal itself either and I find myself wondering where the equally elusive hint of oak might have come from in a wine which undoubtedly spent the whole of its brief life prior to bottling in a stainless-steel tank.

Do wine people really detect such flavours, or just get blind drunk on the stuff and make it all up while rolling hysterically about on the office carpet? Although you have to give them credit for the Monarch butterfly.

We have not visited a fraction of the places in The Bahamas we should have liked to, but if we want to explore Maine this year we need to make a start. However, we have enjoyed our time here so much that we intend to return next winter.

Leaving The Bahamas

Our departure turns out to be something of a farce. Or alternatively an object lesson in trying to navigate unmarked rocks. For having decided on Tilloo Cut for our exit from the Sea of Abaco, and David studying the chart thoroughly, we can't find it; or if we have, it simply doesn't look right. We seek another exit, run aground, struggle afloat again and finally flag down a dinghy with three Americans in it who very kindly return to their yacht and fetch their pilot book for us.

We opt for the exit south of Man-O-War Cay instead, but with afternoon approaching decide to anchor for the night and have another go tomorrow when there will be more hours of daylight by which to get into clear water before dark.

Next morning - despite having, as we thought, carefully written down the waypoints given in the Americans' pilot book - instead of motoring safely out to sea between two reefs we find ourselves heading back to last night's anchorage. In the end we ask directions from a man in a small day fishing boat who very kindly offers to lead us.

Once back out in the Atlantic, we head south on a broad reach all the way down the long coastline of Abaco Island to Hole in the Wall on its southern tip. We are then able to set a course, along the Northwest Providence Channel, to just north of Great Isaac.

Off Great Isaac, the last island we pass before leaving the Bahamas for Florida, we acquire a passenger. Around the size of a young sparrow with blue and yellow plumage, our bird book describes it as an immature Northern Parula Warbler whose preferred habitat is humid woodland. So not a seabird.

After flying aboard, it clings to the starboard shroud panting for a bit, then embarks on an inspection of us and the boat. It stands around on our shoulders, hands and laps, and the chopping board I am using to prepare vegetables for dinner, tours the saloon and investigates every open hatch. It is also quite taken its own image reflected back from the glass in a picture frame.

By its beak we judge it to be a fruit eater, so we give it a piece of apple to hydrate it, which it attacks vigorously, and then, in the glow of a rather lovely sunset, goes looking for a berth for the night. It is seriously into comfort. It tests the cushions, folded towels, a sweatshirt, and finally settles into a protected corner of the sofa.

It could not know, of course, that once we began our night passage its sleeping quarters would be subject to lamplight, and movement at the chart table with hourly log entries and three-hourly watch-changeovers and, sometime during the night, it disappears. We are sorry we have driven it out to sea and a sixty-mile flight to land and wonder, not for the first time, at the extraordinary stamina of tiny birds.

It is a very dark night with no moon but lots of stars, a relatively calm sea and an enjoyable night passage. We arrive at Fort Lauderdale comfortably at dawn.

When you enter this port, the Intracoastal Waterway is directly ahead of you and very quickly you are in Millionaires Row. As we enter this salubrious residential area there is a streak of colour from the saloon into the cockpit. It seems our stowaway did not leave during the night after all, but simply found a quieter berth.

And while we droop blearily in the dawn light, the little bird stands on a davit for a moment, looking refreshed and invigorated, observes the choice of luxuriant gardens on offer, and zooms off into one of them without a backward glance.

UNITED STATES OF AMERICA

9
The East Coast

We have several things in mind for this voyage up America's east coast and one of them is to visit places we had to leave out last year, either because of bad weather or time constraints.

By far the longest part of last year's journey up the east coast had been the Intracoastal Waterway, or ICW – over a thousand miles of inland waters from southern Florida to Norfolk, Virginia. It had been a joy but, because of its many bridges and speed restrictions, we decide that a sea passage – aided by the Gulf Stream – will enable us to get north much faster. This will leave us more time to explore New England than we had had last year, and also achieve our ultimate goal, the coast of Maine.

Accordingly at the beginning of March we leave southern Florida and go out to sea. It has become very hot and, according to the forecasters, is ten degrees hotter than usual for this time of year. The increased heat combined with a long-standing drought has resulted in wildfires in central Florida and, though twenty miles offshore, we sail up the coast with the smell of burning in our nostrils.

We bowl along the Gulf Stream at 9 knots accompanied by flying fish. This strong, wide current was used to great effect from the 16th to early 19th centuries by Spanish ships carrying vast wealth, from Central and South America, home to the King of Spain. These enormous riches - gold, silver, spices, gems, hides and hardwoods - were first of all transported to the coast by llama and mule train, then loaded onto the ships. Where we are currently sailing is part of the sea area once called The Spanish Main, as in 'mainland Spanish America', and a term now used only in stories of the pirates who preyed on Spain's treasure ships.

Unfortunately for us, during the night the wind changes direction and the motion of the Gulf Stream becomes uncomfortable. Then downright intolerable. In fact, it gets so violent at one stage that the glass falls off the barometer and rolls across the saloon.

It is too awful to continue so we bump and bang and lurch our way back into the ICW at the Cape Canaveral Inlet, back among the manatees and pelicans, and anchor in Titusville with burnt embers still on our decks from the distant wild fires. And surprisingly, after what at Fort Lauderdale had been overpowering heat, we are now back in body warmers. As we make an early start for Daytona next morning, the temperature is only 45°F/7°C and it is noticeable that the flying bridges of passing trawler yachts are deserted, the helmsmen snug at their inside steering positions.

We see our first osprey nest of the season, very tall and built right up to the navigation light, with a small anxious face peering over the top. At the north end of the Indian River, almost at the Haulover Canal, six white pelicans doze on a sand bank with one brown one in the middle.

There are stalking herons, darting kingfisher, and small flocks of busy sandpipers on the river banks. On the sandbars, mixed flocks share space without rancour - pelicans, gulls, terns and cormorants with more busy little sandpipers running in between. And there are lots of dolphins.

The wind is so cold that for once we are glad it is on the nose and we can get some protection from the windscreen. We reach Daytona before dark and anchor south of the Seabreeze Bridge.

The town throbs to the sound of motor bikes. It is Bike Week, an annual event which began in 1937 and includes the Daytona 200 and other races. A newly passed ordinance allows people to ride the streets without crash helmets because it seems the bikers favour black top hats to go with their black waistcoats.

Our elderly supermarket packer provides a litany of fatalities that he has either heard about or witnessed personally – 'fifteen last year alone,' he says. Hundreds of thousands flock to this motor cycle rally every year which, as well as races, offers concerts and street parties. The distant roar of motor cycles can be heard until the approach of dawn.

And while top hats, greying ponytails and mid-life crises fly about on Harley-Davidsons at Daytona, down the road at Cape Canaveral the space shuttle *Discovery* is launched, taking supplies and astronauts up to the International Space Station.

Haul-Out at St Augustine

We have difficulty finding somewhere with a travel-lift wide enough to lift *Voyager* out for her annual hull-scrape and anti-fouling until we reach St Augustine. Founded by the Spanish in 1565 as Spain's northernmost settlement, it is America's oldest town and along with a big enough travel-lift has an excellent chandlery with a very helpful owner.

When a boat is out of the water, everything takes twice as long. You have to carry all your stuff down a ladder and the minute you reach the bottom you inevitably find you've forgotten something.

I set myself up in the shade under the stern with a chair, improvised workbench, propellers, paint, brushes, white spirit and clean rag. Determined to have a positive day working on the boat, despite the no-see-ums being rife, I have dressed appropriately including long sleeves, socks and elasticised trainer bottoms.

I have also sprayed my hair, hands, face and all my clothing liberally with an excellent personal insect repellent. But when I put down the canister I find it is the similarly packaged aerosol which claims to kill even cockroaches on contact and warns you not to get the contents anywhere near your skin. I climb back up the ladder and wash it all off; and change my shirt as well since I don't think I should be inhaling this stuff either.

David had set off on his bicycle earlier for the chandlers and the supermarket. The paint he has left me for the propellers is in a can which has been used before and which resists all my attempts to remove its lid. After ten minutes struggle the only thing that has loosened is the two halves of my wrist joint. Another climb up the ladder for a heavy duty screw driver and a hammer finally gets a result but when opened, there is a skin on the paint like a quarter inch of aluminium.

The only way in is with a Stanley knife, but since it begins to fragment once cut, the only way to get the skin out without spoiling the paint is with my fingers, which I hate doing, and only after I've done it do I read the can's label which says under no circumstances should you get it on your skin.

I had painted the props during the last haul-out and don't remember anything like this. I try to get the stuff off with white spirit, but that doesn't work, and nor does hot water and soap, all of which takes quite a time. But at least I'm not sticky and leaving metallic finger prints behind me anymore. The next delay is that I can barely stir the wretched stuff, the sludge in the bottom being so thick that it all but finishes off my wrist.

I've almost completed the second propeller when David returns and says sorry, that's the wrong paint, and fetches the right one.

Despite prolonged scrubbing with soap and nailbrush, and doing all the washing-up without gloves, my hands are a shade of grey reminiscent of the decaying bodies of the un-dead in horror films, although my finger nails are a sleek and very attractive silver. But I do wonder, a little anxiously, if they will glow in the dark.

Next day it rains. And the next and the next. Given that when we'd arrived everybody was complaining about the four-year drought, it is ironic that with *Voyager* out on the hard it now rains so steadily we have trouble finding a couple of dry hours in which to slap on the anti-fouling paint. It costs us days more than it should have in hardstanding fees and the yard doesn't even offer a rain-making discount. But finally we are back in the water and on our way again.

Back on the Water

All along the US east coast, bulky or heavy cargo that is unsuitable for road or rail (such as coal, stone or hard core) is transported by tug and barge. The barges can be over 300 feet/92m long. At sea, the tug pulls the barge on a very long steel hawser. At night the barge has only one tiny light, located on its stern. From some angles it is not visible. Even when it is, it is not difficult to mistake this tiny light, which is nearly 1000 feet/300m behind the tug's own lights, as belonging to a different vessel entirely. And on dark nights at sea we have sometimes wondered how often unwary yachtsmen try to pass between the two.

By contrast, in tight places, like rivers and canals, the tug *pushes* the barge and it can be unnerving to turn a bend in a narrow river and see one approaching you. In wider inland waterways, such as the naval dockyards at Norfolk, Virginia, one tug will routinely push six barges (and sometimes even nine) but so slowly you can barely see them moving.

Because we are trying to maximize our travelling time, and setting out as soon as it is light, we experience some early-morning river fog. Sometimes it is a particular locality that produces it, sometimes it's the result of the sun warming water that still has the night's chill on it. But it means that although we may set off in a clear morning, after an hour or so we can be in fog. We are glad of our radar.

One particular morning we approach the pretty little hamlet of Tilghman on the Knapps Narrows in Chesapeake Bay in gathering mist - startling the life out of the bridge operator who isn't expecting anybody to be about - and emerge the other side into dense fog.

There is no sound, just enveloping greyness; our only contact with the outside world the radar screen which begins showing large obstacles all around us. It is only when we creep towards the first one that we can see it is a barge at anchor, and full of rocks. It is surreal, plotting our way through dozens of them by radar, watching them loom up out of the fog like ghost ships only to disappear in seconds.

The last dot on the radar screen turns out to be the Coast Guard. Like the bridge operator, they aren't expecting anybody either. Absorbed in a training exercise, they jump like startled rabbits as we glide past.

10
Maryland

Our May stop-over at Maryland's capital, Annapolis, coincides with two major annual events in a busy week at the Naval Academy which is just across the bay from our pontoon. Wednesday is Commissioning Day for the year's new intake, while Friday is Graduation Day.

Shortly after 2pm on Commissioning Day the US Navy demonstration squadron, the Blue Angels - six blue F/A-18 Hornets with yellow trim - arrive. They are preceded by a 4-engined navy transport plane which does two low level passes getting below the Academy's roof level on its second one. Then come the Blue Angels – America's version of Britain's Red Arrows.

Four Hornets stay together making passes in tight wing-tip to wing-tip formation at roof top level. The other two make passes flying head-to-head at one another, avoiding collision by a hair's breadth. One gets so low the pilot is able to heel and let the starboard wing pass between two of the spotlight towers round the football ground - all boats with tall masts having been cleared from the nearby anchorage as a precaution.

Sometimes the jets are the right way up, other times upside down and later flipping just at the point of passing. Towards the end all six fly wing-tip to wing-tip, looping the loop. Everywhere you look there are spectators, on the docks, on the roof of the Charthouse restaurant, on boats and, of course, in the Academy grounds. The regular Wednesday night yacht race is a bit of an anti-climax after that. Particularly as there is only a breath of wind for them to come in on.

On Friday, President George W Bush arrives by twin-engine helicopter to give the Graduation speech to the 902 midshipmen who've successfully completed their four-year course. The ceremony traditionally ends with them all hurling their hats into the air.

In between the two events, rather than give up our prized spot opposite the Naval Academy, instead of sailing to Baltimore we take the bus. There are several three-masted sailing vessels tied to its busy quay. One of them is the *USS Constellation*, launched in 1854 and the last sail-only warship to be built by the US Navy.

Baltimore is very different from Annapolis, which despite being the State's capital is small, old and cosy. This is a big city of wide streets, tall modern buildings and noisy. We haven't done noise for a while. And it's a bit of a shock. So we take a water taxi to Fells Point for a leisurely walking tour of the city's 18th century past.

Baltimore's historic area is quite small, thanks to the Battle of Baltimore, fought as part of the War of 1812; the Civil War Riot of 1861; the Great Railroad Strike of 1877 (strikers versus federal troops); the Great Baltimore Fire of 1904 (which destroyed 1,500 buildings in 30 hours); and the 1968 Riots following the assassination of Dr Martin Luther King, Jr.

Nevertheless, we enjoy our tour of the old waterfront and surviving streets of houses, culminating in a wood-panelled pub called Bertha's Mussel Bar for lunch. Then back to the city centre and the Aquarium. It is beautifully done but crowded even on a weekday, and let down by the acoustics which magnify sound in some places until it roars.

I have to make a confession here. I was already well-stricken in years before I discovered that seahorses were not a fairy story, like elves and pixies, when I spotted a tiny, brown, mummified one among the clutter on a bring-and-buy stall some years ago, bought it, and took the little thing home. As still the only one I had ever seen, the aquarium's seahorse exhibition is a revelation. They are glorious. The colours take you by surprise, black, bright yellow, and some are striped, with the water dragons anything up to 10in/25cm long. One species has appurtenances like sprigs of leaves which help them float and act as camouflage.

I don't think seahorses have a very exciting life in the wild. They hold the record as the slowest swimmers in the world (five feet/1.5m an hour) and clinging to a strand of sea grass and floating seems to be as good as it gets, apart from the courting season. But I do feel sad to see these little creatures in such small glass tanks under artificial light in all this noise.

11
New York

By the end of June we are on our way into New York. The impression you're always given (especially by Americans themselves) is that it is violent, rude, crude, drug-riddled, crime-ridden, anti-people and over-priced. Even some American yachtsmen we've met who lived in New York

State shuddered at the thought, saying, 'We don't go to the city.' Yet still it draws you.

As to cost there is a place, the secret passed from cruiser to cruiser, where - if you are fortunate - you can find a vacant mooring buoy in a small basin in the Hudson River off the end of 79th Street. There are only ten of these buoys, but when we reach the basin there is one free. It is also the one closest to the dinghy dock. This is an advantage because we have been warned that at times there is a very strong current which, combined with blustery conditions, can make a dinghy ride ashore quite challenging.

The mooring buoy has no pick-up line attached to it, which may account for why it is still available, because when I hook onto it I find it is far too heavy to raise. David rushes forward to help and holds on to my feet while I hang headfirst over the starboard bow threading a line through its ridiculously small eyehole. While this is going on we have 20 knots of wind and 2 knots of current to add a little interest.

We had planned on staying only three days, assuming that if the muggers hadn't got us by then, the July heat would. The wilting mooring superintendent says summer is unbearable and this isn't a good time to be here. But that afternoon a cold front from Canada begins moving south, bringing with it fresh, Spring-like days in the low 70s, which is ideal for sightseeing. Our first day ashore is delightful and we book for a week. Housed for a mere $15 a night (buy six and you get one free) - and just four blocks from Central Park – we set out to do the Big Apple.

We do the galleries and museums, Grand Central Station and the famous districts - The Bowery, Little Italy, Chinatown. We have to do the districts. You never forget the songs of your youth and in among Elvis, The Rolling Stones and The Beatles we had Ella Fitzgerald singing *Manhattan*.

The old docks area of Seaport has one of the few remaining cast iron sailing ships (built, like *Voyager,* at Southampton). We also wander into the foyer of the World Trade Centre, which is rather modern, hum and haw a bit and decide that - given all the attractions on offer - one panoramic view of the city will do and opt for the Empire State Building.

We should never have believed that a city with so intimidating a reputation could exhibit such courtesy and kindness. Ask for directions and people go to no end of trouble, and if you hesitate anywhere for more than half a minute somebody asks if you need assistance.

There are also some big-city absences that you can't help noticing: no litter (except Chinatown, which is a shock as everywhere else is so tidy);

no gangs of youths; no drunkenness (there are laws banning alcohol from being consumed away from licensed premises); no graffiti and no aggressive beggars.

Getting around isn't expensive either. We buy a cheap, go-anywhere, combined subway and bus ticket for the week and find the underground sociable, clean and air-conditioned. Our only previous knowledge of it had been a scene in a Woody Allen movie where two muggers assault the elderly passenger beside him. Someone even offers me their seat. And of course we are within easy walking distance of Central Park.

Central Park is as it is always portrayed, peopled by the hyper-active, the eccentric and the borderline mad. Cyclists, roller bladers, power walkers, joggers, and dog-owners holding conversations with resigned pets who look as if they've heard it all before. There are also the sleepers, including a young woman in pink satin top and trousers with her gold bag looped through the bars of the back of the bench and her matching gold sandals hooked on by their heels. And hot, tired horses pulling carriages filled with tourists past notices asking people not to hire them, saying that they are overworked and kept in poor conditions.

We go into St Patrick's Cathedral. A service is in progress but it does not dim the noise of the cash registers in the shop whose doors open onto the main body of the church.

Museums

Inside the entrance to the American Museum of Natural History a very nice, elderly man patiently explains the complex and confusing multiplicity of options - and their various costs – that are available to visitors. After that, organisationally speaking, everything goes downhill.

First of all is the counter which may or may not sell tickets (the sign behind it is obscure) and 'manned', in the loosest sense of the word, by three women: one of whom appears to be arranging the odds and ends necessary to sell tickets, and two who appear to be doing office work behind the glass shields.

The one we - and all the other people backing up across the foyer - think *may* be about to sell tickets finally gathers up the odds and ends in front of her that we had all wrongly assumed had something to do with selling tickets, and says she doesn't actually work there. But as she walks away, the second woman along the counter finally lifts her head from her paperwork, blinks in surprise at the long line of hopeful-looking customers staring at her and asks if we want something. Once we have her attention, there is only the complex pricing structure to get through.

The lure in coming here has been the new Planetarium in the Rose Centre for Earth & Space. Locating it is a feat of orienteering since the only signs during the quarter mile walk to get to it from the ticket counter say either 'Exit' or 'Garage' and the security and cleaning staff look haggard from the amount of times they have had to direct people, including us.

Just as we fall up the steps to it, a woman who is clearly management asks sweetly, 'Do you need help?'

'Just some proper signs,' I reply churlishly.

The actual Space Show, however, is superb. You lean back in your seat in the darkness and watch the cosmos - in all its breath-taking enormity - unveil itself across the theatre's 67-foot-wide hemispheric dome. It illustrates, as nothing else can, the way in which our own vast galaxy is merely a pinprick of light in the totality of Space.

And this is only as much as astronomers can see for now, not what could be out there. It alters your view of existence, putting your own little life into perspective. Perhaps we should all have a glimpse of this every morning before we begin our day.

The Planetarium is housed in a new annexe, but much of the original museum is surprisingly old-fashioned, whole rooms lined with floor-to-ceiling, glass-fronted displays of stuffed animals arranged in appropriate landscapes and the donors' names prominently shown. It is redolent of rich people in safari suits shooting anything that moved then sending the little corpses home with a label to ensure their own immortality. It even smells musty. But the dinosaur exhibition is tremendous.

Trying to leave the building proves as difficult as getting in, and that sense of the triviality of one's own little life compared to the enormity of Space, gets reversed. Finding your way out becomes the only thing on your mind.

There are Exit signs everywhere, but having followed some for a time they disappear. After a while you pick up another set, and another, but they all fail. One of these false trails deposits us in an exhibition of Asian and African cultures. Another finds us watching a film about black holes.

And then, inexplicably, we are in a deep circular metal pit. By now we have become disorientated; and alone, everyone else having disappeared. For two people who have navigated themselves unerringly from one side of the North Atlantic to the other – and to all the various landfalls in between - it is woeful.

Then my claustrophobia begins to kick in. I crave the sight of a window. It's been so long since I last saw one and I want reassurance that the world is still out there. I wonder if visitors spend days in here until recovered by staff; incoherent, with rumpled clothing and poor personal hygiene.

Looking up, we can see that the floor level above us is sporting another Exit sign. Not knowing how we got into this apparently sealed space, and half-mad by now anyway, we begin to discuss the best way of scaling the sheer metal sides of our pit.

Afterwards, neither of us can remember how we finally got out: of the pit or the building. But by the time we get back to *Voyager* her mooring rope is almost worn through and, with the universe now entirely forgotten, we set about replacing it before the current carries her away.

In the afternoon we visit the Guggenheim, just a walk away through Central Park. This museum building was designed by Frank Lloyd Wright. It spirals from ground to skylight, is impossible to get lost in and full of light.

Another jaunt another day is a bus ride down Broadway to The Morgan Library at 29 East 36th Street which has an exhibition of 120 Master Drawings from the Cleveland Museum of Art. It is simply but superbly done and in a lovely setting.

J Pierpont Morgan was a 19th century financier who, on one infamous occasion invited the presidents of the other major banks to his library and then locked them in for the night so that they couldn't foreclose on a bankrupt New York City. By morning, thanks to Morgan, the crisis was over and the city survived.

His library is a little piece of the Italian Renaissance relocated in the centre of Manhattan and you can visit the east and west rooms with their tiered bookshelves, magnificent ceilings, red damask wallpaper, marble fireplaces and his desk.

Each item in the exhibition has a small white card beside it saying why the drawing in front of you is worthy of inclusion in this collection of master drawings. There is none of the usual hyperbole, just why it is worth a candle in simple terms and it gives a whole new perspective on artists you knew only as oil painters. Most riveting of all is a Tiepolo, a back view of revellers from the Venetian *Carnivale* returning home in the rain, done in brown ink and wash.

Have you ever wanted to lift a picture from a gallery wall and run with it, so you could take it home and love it and look at it for as long as you lived? For me, this is it. Wiser counsel prevails, however. What he actually says is that he refuses to be an accessory and will be forced to turn me in.

So we take the subway to Greenwich Village instead, for lunch at a sidewalk trattoria in Bleecker Street and a walking tour through some of the leafier residential areas. And Washington Square Park, where film students appear to be doing a remake of *The Good, The Bad and The Ugly* only people keep strolling through their 'set'.

Fourth of July

We spend the evening of the Fourth of July with thousands of other pedestrians on the long, elevated FDR Drive which runs parallel with the East River and overlooks the fireworks barges provided annually by Macy's department store.

The massive crowd (vehicles have been banned for the duration) is policed by benign armed cops and dotted here and there with Guardian Angels - an organisation of mainly African American young men in red and white uniforms dedicated to protecting and assisting victims of crime.

As dark descends, twenty tons of explosives ascend, reflected in a million Manhattan windows. It isn't the best firework show the city has ever had. The sky is cloudy and there is no wind to blow away the smoke so, after the first few bursts, much of the effect is lost.

The crowd takes it philosophically. As it begins to drift away, mostly in family groups, chatting and laughing, somebody turns on a radio.

A female reporter gushes, 'I can't *begin* to describe what effect this *incredible* show is having on the people here watching!'

'Where *is* this woman?' asks a man cheerfully.

'L.A.' offers another.

And in the swarm off FDR Drive I notice the policemen, head and shoulders taller than almost everybody, patient despite the great mass of us swirling round them, ignoring their directions and ducking under barriers we aren't supposed to. But most of all smiling amiably. They look so good-natured about it all. Later, I will remember that especially.

To get from the East River, to our boat on the Hudson, we walk across Manhattan; initially as part of a wall-to-wall pedestrian force flowing around surprisingly tolerant motorists gridlocked by thousands of people. But gradually the crowd thins.

It is lovely to walk through the city at night. The top of the Empire State Building is red, white and blue, while the lights of Times Square reflect their flickering colours onto the faces of the dwindling revellers. Finally we are into deserted streets. It should feel threatening, but it doesn't. And for two people who normally err on the side of caution going ashore in foreign ports after dark, tonight is an exception for us.

At around midnight, after 22 blocks, we hail a cab, but only because it has begun to rain and we still have another 20 blocks to go. And, like Cinderella and her coach, time is of the essence. We need to return to *Voyager* during slack water after high tide - but *before* they release the nightly water surplus from somewhere further up the Hudson that sends a turbulent current through our Basin. Otherwise our dinghy's little two-stroke engine won't cope and we'll be swept away.

I am overwhelmed at how considerate people in this city have been. Not least the taxi driver tonight who had questioned us gently as to our safety, given the deserted place we'd asked him to leave us. When we'd explained about our boat on the river, he'd taken a route which dropped us right over the Basin so we didn't have to walk through the underpass we normally use, at this time of night. Our last sight of him is when we turn and wave to him, still sitting in his stationary vehicle watching anxiously as we scramble over a low wall and disappear down a dark river bank to retrieve our dinghy.

With the tide just right, but in pouring rain now, we shed much of our clothing in the cockpit to keep the saloon dry. Wet and tired, and nothing like as captivating as Tiepolo's home-going revellers from the Venice *Carnivale*, we have nevertheless had a super day.

Strong currents in the night cause wind against tide for a time. It is a noisy, disturbed night and in the early hours of the morning David is out on the foredeck adjusting our mooring rope.

The Districts

Next day we walk from Battery Park, where the ferries set off for Liberty and Ellis Islands, round to South Street Seaport with its old sailing ships. Then up through the Financial District past City Hall and the Supreme Court to the places made famous by Ella Fitzgerald in that memorable song.

Delancey Street is like an old Hollywood gangster movie set, with fire escapes up the front of the tenement buildings. Both Delancey and Mott

Streets, and much else that used to be Little Italy are now part of Chinatown, where very small, elderly women sit on tiny stools in the street playing cards for money, while their menfolk play dominoes.

Manhattan was not simply a lyrical love song, beautifully sung. It was also a paean to a city, albeit a wittily satirical one. To begin with, the lovers in it are short of funds. If they weren't, like the people in the opening lines they would be vacationing at Niagara Falls, where the better-off could afford to escape the worst of the city's summer heat. Hence the ironic:

And tell me what street
Compares with Mott Street
In July?
Sweet pushcarts gently gliding by.

Mott Street in the 1920s, when this song was written, was a big food market and it takes little to imagine the stench rising from fish, meat and other produce being shoved about on 'sweet' handcarts in the July heat.

It's very fancy
On old Delancey
Street, you know.

Delancey Street, on the Lower East Side - a major arterial road incorporating The Bowery - with its rattling streetcars and the train station where:

The subway charms us so
When balmy breezes blow
To and fro.

The only breezes down there would have been the underground trains hurtling through!

At around 2.30am there is a loud bang against our hull. We both rear up together and rush on deck. Opening the companionway doors we see a complete marina pontoon drifting down river. It had obviously struck our port bow on the way, as there is a gash in the gelcoat. Fortunately it had been only a glancing blow, and could have been far worse.

Much later and a long way away, on a fuel dock in a sheltered little backwater where people tend not to venture far and only in fine weather, a rather snooty berth holder will wander over and ask how it happened.

'We were hit by a pontoon,' I will reply without thinking.

'Don't you mean that *you* hit a *pontoon*?' he asks with that special contempt reserved by certain types for catamaran sailors and women.

I turn off the water hose reflectively. 'Not *really*,' I tell him. 'We were tied to a mooring buoy off Manhattan at the time. The pontoon was doing three knots.'

Before we leave the city we do the laundry and visit Barnes and Noble. You can while away the day in an American book shop, with comfy chairs and broad window ledges covered in magazines. They even provide coffee. But we can't afford to loiter today. We have to leave our buoy on the optimal tide for Hell Gate and, before we do, we need to stock up our food cupboards.

Fairway, on Broadway, is a supermarket with a difference - there's a buzz, a busyness, a don't-get-in-the-way-and-waste-time air about it. Stack it high, keep it moving. Mountains of apples, melons, tomatoes. A vast wet fish counter. A Cheese Cave of quite extraordinary dimensions. Ecuadorian chocolate. And outside, a huge flower stall. *Please Pay Inside*, a sign above it says. And people do.

We have enjoyed New York so unbelievably much and are sorry to leave, apart from the fact that we've used up all our energy. We need to put our feet up for a bit but plan to stop off here again on the way back. We take on fuel at the Imperial Yacht Club, which doesn't answer the VHF and has a *Closed* sign on its shed, but is nevertheless open for business.

Then it's down the Hudson, round the corner of Manhattan and up the East River, past Brooklyn, U Thant Island, Roosevelt Island, through Hell Gate at slack water, past Rikers and La Guardia airport and into Long Island Sound. In the Sound we anchor off City Island, between the little yachts on buoys, and bounce mightily until the last of the boy racers goes home. And then it is just peace and a quiet night. Most of the boats on the buoys have no-one aboard. Nobody bothers you. It is restful here.

12
Small Settlements

The Thimble Islands

One of the places that we failed to visit last year, because of bad weather, was Connecticut's Thimble Islands. If you continue up from New York to the top of Long Island Sound you come to them.

They are mostly little more than large, smooth boulders sloping gently down to the water, with trees and shrubs on top, although before the last Ice Age they were the tops of hills. Among their more interesting names are Mother-in-Law Island and East Stooping Bush. Some have quite large houses on them. It is an area of very desirable real estate. Owners can enjoy solitude without isolation, knowing that they and their island are only minutes away from the mainland by boat.

We enter the narrow channel between the islands late afternoon and anchor with just enough room not to swing into one of them, or into another boat. We are enchanted and dine in the cockpit enjoying the view, and a blazing red sun sinking behind the trees on one of the islands.

We should like to linger here for a few days, but first our weather radio warns of thunder storms and then the Coast Guard issues severe weather warnings on the VHF of 50-knot-plus winds, damaging torrential rain, poor visibility and possibly hail. We decide to head for somewhere with more room for boats to swing and possibly drag. And after being quite hot and humid the temperature goes to the other extreme, becoming so cool that we dig out body warmers and long trousers for the journey.

Martha's Vineyard

Another must on our visiting list is Martha's Vineyard in Massachusetts. The first English settlers arrived here in 1642. By the late 18th century the island had become famous for whaling. Nowadays, its visual charm is a lure for residents and visitors alike.

The problem with places famous for their eye-appeal is that often their reputation is such that they are doomed to disappoint – not least because of the sheer number of tourists. The harbour *is* very crowded and we set off in the dinghy expecting the town we're heading for, Vineyard Haven, to be likewise because the island's population increases five-fold with summer visitors.

The town *is* busy, but buy a 75-cent ticket and the Number 1 bus will take you across the island - through a rural landscape, a scatter of hamlets and the State Forest - to Edgartown, which is a delight.

Edgartown's harbour was the focus of the island's whaling industry in the 18th and early 19th century and money was spent here on buildings of quality which have stood the test of time. Its main street is lined with historic cedar mansions built by whaling ship owners along with the impressive whaling church where their captains received a blessing before setting off on their latest voyage. A great part of this little town's charm is that so far it has not been primped and prettified but simply allowed to mellow over time.

A sandy path leads down to an equally unspoilt seashore with a small 19th century cast-iron lighthouse and, above the dunes, a few white-painted hotels with dovecotes and small summer houses in their luxuriant gardens. A couple of hundred yards offshore is the tiny island of Chappaquiddick.

After a pub lunch we head back to *Voyager*, this time on a bus winding its way along the coast road. The crowds have thinned by the time we get back to Vineyard Haven, so having had a rest on the bus journey across the island we do a walking tour here as well.

Martha's Vineyard may be no slouch where conspicuous consumption is concerned and housing prices reach into the stratosphere. Yet it is not the in-your-face sort place I was expecting. Nor are the visiting boats. In the harbour, on our way back to *Voyager*, we observe a couple anchor their aging but serviceable sloop under sail.

They have none of the equipment modern yachtsmen take for granted. They have no echo sounder, or even an engine; only wind in the sail and a lead weight on the end of a long piece of string. The woman at the bow swings the lead to measure the water's depth and when the string shows a suitable level she signals to the man at the helm. He drops the sail and she releases the anchor. Just two people in harmony with their boat, the environment and each other.

Nantucket

Nantucket, 28 miles away, was settled by the English in 1659 and began whaling in 20-foot open boats several decades later, after a Grey Whale swam into the harbour and they caught and killed it. They began building special ships and going further afield after 1712 when a local man was driven 20 miles offshore in a gale and discovered Sperm Whales.

The sperm oil, or spermaceti, stored in their massive heads once lit the lamps of the world as well as lubricating its machinery, and for nearly 100 years Nantucket – little more than fourteen miles by three - was its whaling capital. At its height, there were 150 whale ships sailing out of the harbour where we are currently anchored.

Herman Melville featured the town in his 19th century whaling epic, *Moby Dick*, although his foreboding description of it is not only a winter one, but also invented since he had yet to visit Nantucket when he wrote the novel.

Ultimately the Atlantic's sperm whales became so depleted that ships were having to sail to the Pacific in search of them, on voyages taking several years. The great whales were only saved from extinction by the distillation of paraffin (kerosene) and lubricating oil from crude oil in the mid-19th century. These days Nantucket's commercial fleet offers whale-watching tours instead.

I had come expecting kitsch but both Nantucket and Martha's Vineyard are gorgeous, with their cobbled streets, brick sidewalks, ancient trees, old cedar houses, secluded gardens and low white picket fences with old-fashioned cream-coloured roses trailing across the top.

Prosperous sea captains and ship owners built their mansions on these islands from the proceeds of their brutal and bloody trade. Some have a walkway at chimney level called a widow's walk where, it is said, a wife went to gaze out to sea in the hope of spotting the topsails of her husband's returning ship. The more prosaic reason is that these rooftop walkways allowed chimney fires to be extinguished quickly – by dropping sand down them – essential where wooden houses are concerned.

After a walking tour of Nantucket we settle at a table on one of its restaurant balconies, overlooking a tree-lined street with old-fashioned sunflowers, and indulge ourselves with a whole lobster each. And melted butter. Although why anyone would need all that butter is a mystery to us since all it does it blur the incredible flavour of the lobster.

Back in the harbour *Voyager* is spinning like a whirling dervish thanks to wind over tide. A little later, as we settle in the cockpit, David says of a boat formerly well off to starboard, 'Goodness, he's drifted a bit!' But it is we who have drifted - a lot – and are rapidly approaching a nasty-looking buoy. We are by now in very shallow water, but fortunately on a rising tide. David sits up until the tide changes towards midnight. I don't know how the whaling ships got on but the holding here is rather uncertain.

13
Maine

If variety truly is the spice of life then we have spice in plenty as we leave the pretty towns of Martha's Vineyard and Nantucket for the rugged shores of Maine. By late July we are in this most northern State on the USA's east coast and the one Americans go misty-eyed about when you say you're headed there. It is where many of them spent summer holidays as children and is about as unspoiled as it gets. They also never fail to mention the cheap and plentiful lobster.

Maine's two-and-a-half thousand mile coastline is broken by hundreds of deep bays and thousands of small, rocky, pine-clad islands. Some have a scattering of houses on them. Some a lighthouse. Most are uninhabited.

To sit in your cockpit in glorious isolation and drift through such beauty is pure happiness. It is Eden. But every Eden has its snake. Maine's famously cheap and plentiful lobsters come at a cost - every available bit of water is littered with lobster traps attached to a plastic buoy by a long length of rope which is just waiting to wrap itself around your propellers. The result, for David, is a dark descent into extremely cold water to remove it.

A commercial licence in Maine at this time allows 1,500 traps per harvester which, multiplied by the number of licence-holders, means in excess of five million plastic buoys bobbing on the surface of the water.

Lobster Pots and Big Tides

Maine is somewhere we had wanted very much to visit last year but both the weather and the expiry date on our visas had been against us. One thing we knew about Maine was its impenetrable fogs. What we had not been prepared for is the sheer number of lobster traps. They are *everywhere*. Our first encounter coincides with our first sortie inland as we leave the coast and venture up the New Meadows River.

Our first anchorage here is to be Cape Porpoise Harbour but its entrance is filled with buoys; multi-coloured - like hundreds-and-thousands if you are British or sprinkle chips if you are American. We've done fishing buoys before, in lots of places, especially Chesapeake Bay with its ubiquitous crab pots. But this is ridiculous. Initially we can't even see a route through them. And this is a harbour entrance!

They are particularly difficult for a catamaran, given *Voyager*'s sixteen and a half foot width. And with her two propellers widely spaced, as we attempt to keep one of them away from a buoy we inevitably put the other one at risk.

A visiting monohull would navigate this density of buoys more easily, and local boats have what is called a 'bonnet' fixed to the bottom of their hull protecting their propeller so they can simply ride over the top of them.

This is not an option for us so I stand on the bow and direct David this way and that. With my extended arms and circling motions I am reminded of the traffic policeman in Nassau, except that my performance is far more frantic because of the speed with which you come upon the next buoy.

David, concentrating all his attention on following my directions, will suddenly find himself on the wrong side of a navigation marker and far too close to rocks and have to lurch back into the channel.

At last we are through the entrance and anchor in the first available spot. Finally at rest, and freed from our intense scrutiny of buoys in the water, we are able to appreciate the sheer beauty of our surroundings and congratulate ourselves on getting to Maine at last.

There is a bigger tidal range here than further south, continuing to increase the further north you go and requiring greater attention to anchoring because if you fail to put out enough scope you are going to drag. For instance, at Kittery Harbour, Maine's most southern point, high tide is nine feet/2.7m whereas at Eastport, its most northern extent, it reaches twenty-five feet/7.6m.

There is wildlife here, too, that we haven't seen further south, such as seals and species of sea birds which, like lobster, prefer colder water. For instance, in an area the chart says is clear of obstructions we see a long line of foaming water and think we're heading for unmarked rocks. A little closer and it looks more like fish engaged in a feeding frenzy.

Closer still and it turns out to be a long line of black and white razorbills taking a bath in formation. Like sparrows in a puddle, these small birds hurl water over themselves with abandon, although swimming at high speed in a long straight line while they do it.

Coastal Towns

Maine's small coastal towns are friendly and very pretty, with traditional houses and gardens vibrant with the colours and scents of sunflowers, lilies, roses and night-scented stock.

The town of Boothbay also provides a small, open-sided town bus complete with a brass bell to announce its arrival and velvet cushioned seats with hand-embroidered antimacassars. Its friendly driver provides visitors with a welcome commentary on past history and present delights.

For instance, the local boatyard – which we wouldn't have thought to visit - currently contains the wooden ship made for the film *Mutiny on the Bounty*. Found in a state of neglect, it has been hauled out and is being restored. Built for MGM in 1960, using the original 1787 ship's drawings from Britain's Admiralty archives, its waterline was extended to provide for film-making and production crews. Its beam and rigging were also enlarged to scale, but the resulting ship was fully equipped for sailing. The refurbished *Bounty* will be used for charter.

A stretch of Boothbay's waterfront is graced with 19th century sea captains' homes. Most of these lovely old wooden houses, with their front windows overlooking the harbour, are now Bed & Breakfasts.

The Tug Boat Inn incorporates an old tug which, according to our fount of all knowledge - the bus driver - sank in the harbour twice before being hauled ashore and made into part of the restaurant.

And you quickly find that there is a vast amount happening locally, as you might expect where the summers are short and the winters long and inhospitable. Even August is often foggy, as the warm air of the Gulf Stream travelling north meets cold Canadian air coming south.

Sometimes the lobster traps defeat us. We head for Christmas Cove on the Damariscotta River. But as we get close the buoy clusters get thicker and thicker and when we eventually get to the mouth of the anchorage we simply can't find enough space between them to pass through. At Permaquid we end up reversing for a mile and a half – unable to find room even to turn around.

Other places are not only accessible but magical. Peabow Island lies at the top of Johns Bay, where it narrows, and there is forest all around you, reflected in the still water. The sheer beauty of it is captivating. You find yourself just standing on deck, gazing out at it.

In the meantime, the natural world gets on with its daily life around you as if you were just part of the scenery. An osprey hovers in a bright blue sky, spotting up its lunch. A line of Canada geese swim majestically past. A family of seals feed nearby. Cormorants bathe and fish.

Camden, where we spend our wedding anniversary this year (enjoying some of that cheap and plentiful lobster) seems to have the best of all worlds - a beautiful coastline for summer sailing on one side, and a small winter ski resort on the other. We dine on clam chowder followed by one-and-a-half pound lobsters. The town also has an old-fashioned deli, with a real soda fountain, that serves delicious ice cream.

And so we thread our leisurely way - generally in a north-easterly direction – through Penobscot Bay and Jericho Bay and myriads of small rocky islands with a scattering of trees on them and every once in a while a small picturesque lighthouse.

And if we can't always avoid a pot – especially those abandoned ones below the surface, we learn to at least shed it by putting the engines into neutral so that as *Voyager* slows the pot will hopefully float free. Although sometimes there is still no option but for David to go over the side and unravel it or, in extremis but rarely, cut us free. Despite our best efforts, one afternoon alone we pick up three.

Little Cranberry Island

From Cranberry Harbour we dinghy out to Little Cranberry Island. It turns out to be one of those places that linger in the memory. Different from the more tourist-oriented places like Boothbay and Camden, it is the kind of wistful place where you could imagine yourself creating beautiful artefacts. And sharing warm, sociable winter evenings in clapboard houses enveloped in fog while from outside there comes the mournful clang of a navigation buoy heaving and plunging on a stormy sea.

We land at the dingy dock by the Fisherman's Co-operative. Like islanders everywhere, Maine's do many jobs - lobster catcher, coastguard, ferryman, painter, potter, mail boat skipper, fireman.

The islanders here are friendly and cheerful and our first stop is the tiny art gallery, with its polished hardwood floors and white painted walls. Its owner is one of the artists as well as supporting his family by fishing. As for the paintings, by local artists, I could happily have taken them all home. Their subjects are simple – a stretch of shoreline or an inlet - but they are riveting.

Very soon you understand why. From the wharf we walk inland. The tarmac disappears and in no time at all you realize that what the artists have captured is the essence of the island itself. It is a place of grasses and wildflowers contrasted against dark pines. The colours are luminous. And there is a particular clarity to the light.

Back on the waterfront there is a pottery to visit and a small museum. In the island's small store we buy fresh bread and orange juice and discover that, on an island with a fisherman's cooperative, you cannot buy fresh fish. As we dinghy back to *Voyager* fog begins to spread across the water and gradually the islands disappear until only the mountain tops remain visible.

We wake next morning to a real Maine peasouper and, despite having intended to move on today, decide to stay where we are. The forecast for next day is good and we set off, but out at sea the fog returns.

With visibility barely 100 yards we are glad of the radar. Sitting in the pilot's chair, the right lens of your glasses constantly mists up while the left stays clear, so you end up observing a foggy world from a cock-eyed perspective. With the fog comes a dramatic drop in temperature and, on what had begun as a hot early August day, we go in search of extra clothing. But within twenty four hours we are back in summer again and spend the days drifting gently through this rugged landscape and anchoring in fishing villages, small harbours and coves for the night.

Mistake Cove and Roque Island

At Mistake Cove our only neighbour is a grey seal on a tall rock. It sunbathes there for hours as the tide rises. Eventually the water reaches the seal and when the rock is finally awash the seal floats away. When the tide rises sufficiently, the seal re-appears and settles back onto the rock again.

It is hot and sunny and despite all the rocks around us we feel quite comfortable with our position. I'd done some laundry days ago but the fog had arrived shortly afterwards and it has been lying around wet ever since. Hung out in the cockpit, it is drying nicely.

Around 4.30 the sky goes black and we hastily take the laundry indoors and have the last hatch closed when we are hit by a vicious squall. Visibility disappears and we wait and hope the anchor holds as we are swung violently.

The sound and fury is soon over and we are left in that unnatural calm you get after a squall, as if everything is holding its breath. We re-anchor, as we have dragged a little, and are below deck cooking a meal when the air is filled with the sound of a very powerful engine and our port windows by a very large hull. It seems about to collide with us and we rush up on deck to find the US Coast Guard beside us. They are checking boats following the squall, seem surprised to find one like ours here, ask us if we are OK, then go on their way.

Roque Island, along with some smaller ones, form a lagoon. The island is very beautiful with fields and woodland and a long, curved, white sandy beach over a mile long so that gazing at it from your deck you could almost believe you were back in The Bahamas. The island is privately owned and the land a family farm but you are free to walk on sections of the beach. So we do.

Back on board we listen to the weather forecast and find that they are now predicting strong winds from the south-west and *not* the west which is why we anchored where we have. So we pull up our hook – along with a mass of seaweed - and move down to the other end of the beach.

There is a lot of seaweed up here. Like the sargassum off the Florida coast, it keeps settling round your rudders and props and for days now we've had to keep stopping and reversing to get rid of it.

In addition, the lobster traps are offering an additional hazard. This far north many of them have a second plastic fishing buoy attached to the first by a long piece of rope. It means that if a particularly high tide pulls the first buoy under water the fisherman can still find his trap with the second. For us it just means another rope to wrap around our props. And it is not the weather for spending long periods on the foredeck on lookout nor, indeed, going underwater to prise it loose.

The cold and wet intensifies, and storms are forecast. It is blamed, as always, on cold fronts sweeping down from Canada colliding with warm air travelling up from the south. For months now, from The Bahamas to Maine, we've been hearing about cold fronts sweeping down from Canada. And if Canada is expelling all its turbulent weather down here, maybe it is currently quite nice up there.

We decide to go and find out.

And let's be honest, we've become greedy for another trophy on the belt, another name to add to the list. Our 17th country in three years. And, after all, we *are* only 30 miles from the border.

We start lifting the anchor just after 5am, an early start which should enable us to get under a low bridge between us and our destination. The Lubec Bridge is either 43.5 feet/13.2m high, or 47 feet/14.3m, depending on which source you consult. Either way we hope to be able to squeeze our 53 feet/16.1m under it between low and mid tides.

Heading North

Before doing so our plan is to head for Lubec to re-fuel and Eastport to shop for Canadian charts, a courtesy flag and a cruising guide, and clear out with US Customs. We arrive in the Lubec Channel well within our deadline and treat the bridge with extreme caution. This is because charts normally give bridge clearance heights at high tide, when the clearance is at its least. However, our chart doesn't use high tide. Instead, there is a note alongside the bridge saying that water depths for this small area are given at minimum low tide.

As we approach it David puts the engines into reverse, allowing *Voyager* to continue forward but so slowly that, even if our topmast does connect with the bridge, it will be the lightest touch possible; it being quite difficult to judge your masthead's relationship to a bridge from on board until you are just about to hit it. With *Voyager*'s bow sliding under the bridge and the mast getting close I can see from my position amidships that we shall, in fact, clear it. We start breathing again and David puts forward power back on.

We are now off Lubec Marina and radio up to locate its fuel dock but it does not have one, says the man who answers the VHF, 'But Eastport *probably* does.'

We had rather assumed that the location of fuel docks would be common knowledge in an area like this, but motor on to Eastport anyway and try to get into its harbour, which our chart tells us is an anchorage. It is very small with no space available at all. We talk to a monosyllabic harbour master via the VHF who tells us that there is no fuel available. With nowhere to tie up or anchor, and no fuel to be had anyway, we decide to head straight for Canada - and some of the nicest people we have ever met. Including ones in uniforms.

CANADA

14
Bay of Fundy

For the first time in our sailing career we are totally unprepared for a new country. We have no charts and no cruising guide. Not even a courtesy flag. The only information we do have is a brief reference in our US cruising guide that New Brunswick is the next area to the north after you leave Maine and that the nearest Canadian Customs and Immigration dock is on Campobello Island. Similarly, the top couple of inches of our US chart for Maine has the southern tip of New Brunswick on it along with the location of Campobello Island.

So we raise our yellow quarantine flag and sally forth. The trouble is, we don't know where on Campobello Island the dock is likely to be. David thinks it might be Head Harbour, but before we can put his assumption to the test we notice an official-looking RIB behind us. We wave it down to ask directions. They turn out to be Canadian Police. They are very pleasant and helpful and offer us a freephone number to call up Customs, saying it can probably all be done on the phone. One of the officers calls the number up to us, reading it off the back of a small cigar box.

I dial the number and tell the person who answers that we are two people on a catamaran. I think my accent defeats her because she asks if we are a cruise ship. Assured we're not, she tells us to tie up at Head Harbour and contact them again. So we set off down a really nice inlet with trees sloping down to the water. Suddenly another RIB appears behind us containing three Canadian Immigration & Customs Officers.

I don't think they get many catamarans up here, because the officers are concerned that given our width we may have difficulty turning round to leave the jetty afterwards. So they find us a suitable place to anchor, off a beach on which a couple are sunbathing.

Then they raft up to us and one of the three crew members comes on board. He calls his office on his cell phone and hands it to David who gives the operator our details.

Seeing so many people in uniform milling around a foreign boat seems to unnerve the couple sunbathing on the beach because they rapidly gather up their clothes and flee. Our man laughs softly to himself. He then gives us a clearance number and we are officially in Canada.

With the Immigration part of his duties completed, the officer turns his attention to Customs and asks to see our liquor store – currently two bottles of wine and a six-pack of American beer - and has a general look around. I am glad I tidied up a bit as we came in. Although he is probably more interested in the importation of hard drugs than the state of our galley.

With the formalities completed the men recommend St Andrews harbour as a safe overnight anchorage as well as somewhere to buy food, charts and a cruising guide. We are knocked sideways when they even offer to lend us a chart to get there.

'You can leave it with the Harbour Warden,' says one of them, 'and we'll pick it up later.'

On our way to St Andrews we skirt the southern tip of Deer Island and cross the entrance to the massive Passamaquoddy Bay. Thus far we have seen no fishing buoys of any kind but are now greatly disappointed to find this great mass of water *covered* with them as far as the eye can see. We groan, but as we get closer the 'buoys' rise up and fly away - the biggest flock of seabirds we have ever seen - leaving behind a blissfully pot-free stretch of water. Nor are there many other boats about. In short, this looks like cruising paradise.

It is 5.30 pm as we enter St Andrews harbour. The Warden is waiting for us in his boat. He is very cheerful and takes us to an ideal spot with good holding and away from sunken obstacles, where we can anchor safely, and in as shallow water as possible. There are very high tides here. So if you are not careful you can simply run out of chain at high tide, pull up your anchor and float away.

David calculates that we need to let out at least 75 feet/23m of chain. This is a slight problem as we possess only 55 feet/17m but he unhooks the bitter end from the chain locker and shackles it to a length of rope to provide the extra.

The Warden, who appears to go by the name of BB, says we probably won't be able to get a cruising guide in town but if we see him in the morning he will give us what information he can. Tired but happy we go to bed early, very impressed with Canada.

St Andrews

Mid-morning we go ashore and set foot in Canada for the first time. BB meets us at the dock and tells us to help ourselves to information leaflets from his office.

A lovely old town, St Andrews was founded in 1783 by Loyalists and retains many of its original buildings. In fact, the Loyalists even brought some of them with them - by barge from Maine - when they were driven out of what would become the United States of America at the end of the Revolutionary War.

An explanation of terms might be useful here. What Americans call The War of Independence of 1775-1783, many British, Bahamians and Canadians call the Revolutionary War, since the upheaval was seen at the time, and since, as a rebellion by nationalists attacking the legitimate government in the form of militias. Loyalists, by definition, were those who remained loyal to Britain and King George. Many of them, driven from their homes, fled to Canada.

One of St Andrews' historic buildings is a War of 1812 blockhouse. It is said that travel broadens the mind and, until we reached North America, 1812 had meant only Napoleon's retreat from Moscow as celebrated in a very lively overture by Tchaikovsky.

In fact, the War of 1812 lasted two and a half years and came about when James Madison, the fourth President (1809-1817) of what was by now the United States of America, decided to extend his holdings by taking over Canada. It was deemed an opportune moment as the British had their hands full fighting Napoleon at the time. It also seems that the Americans believed that Canadians would welcome the opportunity to 'join a free country'.

Since many of these Canadians were the very people the emerging American nation had driven from their homes in the first place, causing much suffering and many deaths, they resisted the American invitation with an energetic call to arms. St Andrews' blockhouse was built as a coastal defence structure during that war between the US and the British Empire but never saw action.

The town also became Canada's first seaside resort when a hotel was built here in 1889. It is a popular holiday town still, not least with whale-watchers thanks to the Humpback, Fin and Minke, along with a lot of very appealing seals, to be seen in Passamaquoddy Bay.

Over the next couple of days we find a dive shop which sells charts although, as BB had warned us, we are unable to buy a cruising guide. We fill several washing machines at the laundrette, post our immigration cards back to the United States since we were unable to clear out in person, and buy a phone card so that David can call our insurance company to tell them where we are, as we had not included Canada in our coverage.

We find a wet fish shop and buy fresh salmon and mussels. And the supermarket is surprisingly good. It is also in the centre of town, unlike many south of the border which are on the outskirts and require a long walk or a bus ride.

On the way back to *Voyager* BB lends us his pilot book, in lieu of a cruising guide, and we take it back on board with us. David studies it after dinner and thinks the St John River will suit us very well.

He hauls up the anchor from 26 feet/8m next morning, clutches his back, groans and we head for the wharf. Although we are dead on time as arranged, BB looks at us a little oddly but says nothing. We fill up with water, return his pilot book to him with our thanks and then head back across the entrance of Passamaquoddy Bay and out into the Bay of Fundy. We are glad to have a detailed chart. This part of the coast is littered with small rocky islands.

It has been estimated that during a 12-hour tidal period around a hundred billion tons of water will flow in and out of the Bay of Fundy. Its spring tides, at the northern end of the bay, are 48 feet/14.6m but at their extreme can reach 54/16.5, giving it the highest tidal range in the world.

Our anchorage for the night is Beaver Harbour. We are the only vessel in it. This is the thing we will discover about Canada. Space. You have the same rugged shores and stunning islands as the northern US but there is no pressure on space. The harbours are uncrowded, anchorages are not filled with mooring buoys and there are virtually no fishing buoys to keep dodging. Seals pop up their heads to peer at us - just nose and eyes exposed – then disappear again. It is our kind of cruising: unhurried, uncrowded and very beautiful. The weather is delightful, too – all the cold fronts having moved south.

15
The Reversing Falls

There is just one impediment to be overcome before we can enter the desirable cruising ground of the Saint John River System. It is called The

Reversing Falls and navigating it requires careful planning. Time, as the saying goes, is of the essence. Which is why, at our final anchorage in the Bay of Fundy, we are to be found heaving up our anchor just as it is getting light to make sure we reach the Falls at the appropriate time.

The Saint John River rises in Maine before winding its way into Canada where it forms the Canadian/US border in two places. At the end of its 450-mile journey it empties into Saint John Harbour and the Bay of Fundy. The river bed is higher than the sea bed. The entrance to the river is a narrow, rocky gorge. At low tide the river water, rushing downstream, forces its way through this narrow gorge sending a waterfall tumbling down into the harbour.

However, as the tide in the harbour rises, there comes a point where the river water and the incoming tide are at equal heights. This lasts for approximately one hour, although actual slack water may last as little as ten minutes.

As the tide continues to rise - to its maximum here of 28.5 feet/8.7m - the sheer volume of so much seawater forcing its way upriver through a narrow gorge creates a situation where the sea is higher than the river and its entrance now becomes a waterfall in the opposite direction. Hence the name, The Reversing Falls.

In essence, if a yachtsman tried to enter the river when the sea is at high tide, he would end up surfing down a waterfall into the river's swirling eddies, rocks and cross-currents. Should the yachtsman try to enter when the sea level is at its lowest, he would find himself trying to sail *up* a waterfall.

Navigation in or out of the river is, therefore, possible for only around one hour four times in every twenty-four. The rest of the time its entrance boils and seethes in a series of rapids and whirlpools.

Fortunately as we make our way to the river through the busy commercial port of Saint John, dodging tankers and cruise ships in shifting morning fog, we see a number of yachts casting off from a public quay and making their way in the direction we want to go.

By our calculations we have arrived much too early, our plan being to allow us to hang around and judge the timing of The Reversing Falls visually. But as all these leisure boats are flying the Canadian Maple Leaf ensign we assume they have local knowledge and decide to follow them.

The route takes us left into a deep gorge; then sharp right round a blind corner and through a narrow rocky gap, both of them spanned by bridges – worryingly without any height gauges on them. Bringing up the rear we can't see the Falls ourselves yet, but the leading boat puts out a call on the VHF to say that the currents are still quite strong. This hardly surprises us as according to our calculations we are an hour ahead of time. All the boats slow and wait a while but not for long and soon we are off again.

We are the last to go through and still confused by the disparity between our calculated times and our entry into The Falls but we enjoy a safe and comfortable passage through and are grateful for the boats having been there. The only disturbing part has been the row of tourists lined up on a viewing platform above our heads waiting for something interesting to happen.

Navigating the rocky narrow entrance to The Falls, all your attention is focused on getting through it without hitting something. Once inside, and with leisure to look about you, the Saint John River reveals itself as wide, wooded and very beautiful.

We head up-river and on to a fuel dock, where a very helpful young attendant ties us up and after filling our tank waves us off with a very helpful leaflet on the area. After the enormous depths of the Bay of Fundy, in places we are now sailing in water as shallow as five feet/1.5m.

16
Canadian Hospitality

After a while we see a number of boats on moorings and anchor nearby. They turn out to be part of a small yacht club, and we have no sooner dropped our hook than club members begin to row out offering us lifts to the Co-op, or the supply or loan of anything we need, followed by the Vice-Commodore, Steve. He offers to lend us charts and then says the club is having a race today followed by hot dogs and soft drinks and a wine and cheese party this evening. Would we like to be the club's guests?

It is a warm, sunny afternoon. The race goes off earlier than we had expected but we have a prime view from our deck anyway. And after the finish signal and the appointed time we go ashore for the post-race party.

We meet Steve's wife, Lisa, along with Jeff and Laura, Richard and Joanne, Robert and Paula, Carla and Sonny, plus lots of other members, founding and otherwise, guests, friends and family. It is a very jolly occasion.

The men want to know about our Atlantic crossing while the women hover anxiously in case it gives their husbands ideas. We are presented with a club burgee and, before we return to *Voyager*, there are invitations to dinner and car trips and Richard offers to drive us to the supermarket next morning to stock up. Canadians are very hospitable.

Jeff and Laura give us a tour of St John the following afternoon, including a view of The Reversing Falls at its wildest - untenable by anything at this stage of the tide except a couple of white water fanatics in kayaks paddling like madmen to stay on the spot. And a small flock of cormorants taking an almost childlike delight in being dragged backwards by the violent current, paddling furiously until it gets too strong for them, then flying back to the beginning to start again. So not much different from what the two men in the kayaks are doing. Apart from the flying bit.

And then on to a quiet suburb to meet Tom and Barbara who are building a 45ft power catamaran in their back garden and making a fabulous job of it. How they had the courage to start I find hard to believe. The hulls are built, the engines in place and now the cabins are going on. So far it has absorbed 5,000 hours. They plan to launch it next year – once they've found a way to prise it out of the back garden - and hope to see us in The Bahamas next winter.

On another day there is a marvellous road trip north, up through the wooded hills along the Fundy Trail, reaching its end at the scenic Big Salmon River in its rocky, tree-lined valley. And on the way, pretty St Martins Harbour which has two of the area's covered bridges, like the ones made famous in the Meryl Streep/Clint Eastwood film, *The Bridges of Madison County*.

Although picturesque they were built to be practical, the barn-like superstructure protecting the bridge from the weather. An unprotected wooden bridge will last 10-15 years, apparently; a covered one a hundred. They are also safer when there is ice and snow on the ground. In the year 1900 New Brunswick had 400 of them, but only 62 remain. Vandals set them on fire.

We also stop off at a beaver dam. There are no beavers in sight, of course. Not in broad daylight near a busy road. But their handiwork is awe-inspiring. Their purpose in life, as they illustrate here, is to dam streams and rivers using mud, grass - and tree trunks up to 10 inches in diameter which they fell with their teeth - to create large ponds and the habitat beavers need to flourish.

In the process they also produce highly productive wetlands that support many other life forms — mammals, fish, frogs, turtles and birds. People, too, for beavers can turn arid areas into verdant ones when their ponds preserve water which would otherwise evaporate. The dam also keeps the pond at an optimum level with regard to the winter freeze, enabling the beaver to gather food all year round.

And then back through Fundy National Park and along the coast road. After a long time spent looking at the world from sea level it is wonderful to be driven high up into the hills above the Bay of Fundy, among the pine trees, and gaze out across this vast expanse of water.

On one particular morning Steve has arranged to take us out. We are to meet him ashore at 10am. At about 8.50am he comes by in his dinghy and asks us if our 10am collect time ashore is still OK. We say yes, fine, and go and make coffee while we wait. He must have gone and had a word with Jeff because at 9.30, still with 15 minutes before we need to think about closing up the boat and climbing into our dinghy, Jeff rows out to us and asks if we have a problem.

'No,' we say, surprised. 'Not at all.' We still have 30 minutes before we are due ashore to join Steve. Jeff looks at us strangely for a moment and sighs. And then, as if the scales suddenly fall from his eyes, his face brightens.

'You do know, don't you,' he says, 'that Canada is an hour ahead of the US?'

We didn't.

The US mainland arranges its four time zones from east to west, so we had been on Eastern Standard Time all the way up the Atlantic coast from Florida to Maine. A time change at the Canadian border had simply not occurred to us. Nor been mentioned by anyone.

We are aghast at how ill-mannered we must have seemed. For over a week we have been late for everything — the sailing club's race meeting, its barbecue, meals with Laura and Jeff, and lifts to the shops with Richard hanging around for an hour. How patient they have all been. How forgiving.

I remember the puzzled face of BB, the Harbour Warden at St Andrews, and cringe. There he was, expecting us to tie up at his wharf for water at 7.30am as arranged but watching us pottering negligently about on our deck for a further hour. At the first opportunity I send him a postcard to apologize. Only at the end of a long and embarrassing catalogue of hourly lapses does the Big One occur to us.

I read somewhere that the world is divided into people who think that arriving up to thirty minutes late is being on time, and people who believe that arriving on time constitutes being late and so are always early for everything. David and I fall into the latter category. Although we had intended to arrive at the Reversing Falls an hour before the proper time, we were still early ... to be an hour early. But if we hadn't been there in time to see those other yachtsmen in Saint John Harbour, and followed them, we should have been an hour late attempting the Reversing Falls. We both shudder at the thought.

We apologise to Jeff and, already more than half an hour late for our appointment with Steve, scramble to close up the boat and get into our dinghy. Over a family dinner table that evening we apologize again to Steve and Lisa, Jeff and Laura – and especially to Richard who has so kindly given us several lifts to the supermarket. He dismisses it as nothing. Later someone else tells us, laughing, that Richard had waited half an hour for us yesterday morning, taken his wife Joanne to do their own shopping, dropped her off at home and returned to find us just then dinghying ashore - and gave us our lift.

On the way home from dinner we catch a whiff of a terrible smell and are told that it is skunk. On a road, that will usually mean a dead skunk. The biggest threat to this small and rather beautiful animal is its attitude to life. Its survival technique is the appalling odour it launches via a jet of liquid from a gland at the base of its tail. So confident is it that this will repel any predator, no matter how large, that it fails to recognize that an approaching juggernaut will not, in fact, be deterred. That its driver will not even *notice* the little, predominantly black skunk in the darkness.

Picture the scene. There is the skunk on an unlit road. The truck or family car is bowling along towards it. The skunk has the option of getting out of the way: of moving to the side of the road or into the undergrowth. Instead, while still keeping its eyes on the approaching headlights the skunk bends its flexible body so that its rear end is aimed at the coming threat. At the appropriate distance, and with touching confidence, it ejects its noxious fluid. And ... splat!

The vehicle driver opens the window to let out the mind-blowing smell coming in through his ventilation grille and roars on with only a revolted twitch of the nose. But the poor skunk is reduced to a furry pancake on the tarmac, just a lingering odour for subsequent travellers to grimace at.

Our oven stops working. Jeff drives David to the chandlers. They don't have one in stock that will fit the space left behind when the old one is removed and will have to order one.

Our outboard has packed up, too. Things usually go in groups. Back in Jeff's workshop they set to work on it. It takes about two hours to fix it and even then only because Jeff just won't give up.

With several weeks until our new oven's delivery date, we embark on our original plan to explore the Saint John River. We are waved on our way with charts, directions to the best places to cruise, the nearest anchorages to the best supermarkets and where to find the club's own mooring buoys for the night, thereby saving us the trouble of anchoring – we *are* flying the sailing club burgee after all!

17
The Saint John River

Coming days will find us exploring coves and creeks among spectacular scenery whilst being spoilt for choice as regards sheltered anchorages each night. The wooded river banks are rich with evergreens, but also a wealth of deciduous trees – many of them the scarlet-turning maple. Autumn here, must be mind-blowing.

In places, getting the dinghy ashore means pushing your way through tall grasses or reed beds to reach solid ground on river banks fringed with maple trees and scattered with wild flowers.

This is a time of soft misty mornings, bright breezy sailing days, solitary anchorages and hot afternoons spent in the cockpit's shade with your feet up. Ours the only boat in sight. Places like Whelpley Cove behind Catons Island and a walk ashore through the edge of woodland. Lawson Passage by Upper Musquash Island. And the delightful little Gagetown offering all that's needed by people like us – a general store, a post-office, a bank and laundrette.

At Flowers Cove on Grand Lake one morning a resident dinghies out to offer us the use of her washing machine, which we say is very kind but we did it all at Gagetown yesterday. Mid-afternoon a man and his daughter, out on a pedalo, attract our attention to our rear steps where a fluffy young cormorant stands, taking the air. Unusually for a cormorant, it shows no fear and doesn't even move when the man ties up to our stern for a chat.

On the afternoon we reach Douglas Harbour it begins to rain. Unusually, a motor around the anchorage reveals it so full of mooring buoys that there is no room to anchor between them. Visibility is rapidly diminishing so we pick one up and find it bears the name Flood.

As if it were an omen the heavens open and the rain becomes torrential. It is still quite early but we tuck up for the rest of the day anyway, hoping that the bad weather will not drive Mr Flood home and wanting his mooring buoy back tonight.

Next day, with the rain gone, Douglas Harbour township reveals itself as a scattering of homes and a venerable general store. Its shop furnishings and equipment border on the antique, with old signs on the walls advertising products that went off the market in the 1950s. The man himself sits contentedly in an ancient armchair and says he never has enough time to do everything since he became semi-retired although nowadays he only sells ice.

Back out on the Saint John River the banks become meadows, with secluded farmsteads, neat, wooden and painted white. Beside them, huge, old, sun-bleached and wind-weathered barns with traditional red doors. Barns big enough to get livestock through a long, bitterly-cold winter – of the kind our Canadian neighbours in The Bahamas were all escaping. By mid-October it will be below freezing here and not warm up again 'til May. We are already discovering for ourselves how cool the nights are becoming despite the daytime heat.

Because of this, and despite the fact that it is only the tail end of August, the Canadian sailing season is nearing its end. So as well as its beauty we also have this blissful cruising ground mostly to ourselves. Muskrats dog-paddle across our bows, one with a youngster clinging to her back. Golden eagles, bald eagles and the occasional osprey fly overhead. Coyotes howl in the night.

By the end of August we have arrived at Fredericton, the capital of New Brunswick. There is a city at each end of the navigable section of the Saint John River. The one called Saint John – where the entrance to the river and the harbour meet at The Reversing Falls – looks as if it *should* be the provincial capital. It is modern, thrusting, brick-built and high-rise; its modernity partly the result of a fire that destroyed much of its historic business district in 1877. The *actual* capital, Fredericton, has more the look of a genteel county town and retains intact a number of buildings that typify early New Brunswick.

A good deal of Fredericton took its inspiration from England. Its little Anglican cathedral is a replica of the 14th century St Mary's Church in Snettisham, Norfolk, on the edge of The Wash. There is some domestic architecture, as well as the early 19th century barracks, guard house and officers' quarters of the military district. And it is surprising that even all the way up here, more than eighty miles from Saint John, the effect of the Reversing Falls can still be felt in the river's current.

After a night at anchor off Fredericton we are up early under a clear sky, the sun not long risen. To our right, a small creek emerges from under a small bridge, the low sun illuminating the water's passage into the river. On this still, cool morning a mist rises from it in wisps, turning two cormorants perched on the branches of a dead tree, half-submerged in the shallow water, into a detail from a Chinese painting.

Voyager is covered in small (happily non-biting) insects and all our spiders have full webs. You really do wonder where all the spiders on a boat come from. They are a yachtsman's constant companions and on mornings like this one their dew-laden gossamer glistens in the early sunlight. A few of ours even survived a trans-Atlantic crossing. We have no idea what they fed on. Each other, probably. An example of survival of the fittest, like people shipwrecked for a long time.

Labour Day Weekend

Two weeks on, and with the weather still perfect, the yacht club's members join us up-river for Labour Day. A public holiday celebrating Canada's workers and labour union movement, it takes place on the first Monday in September and is seen by many as the last long weekend of the summer. We arrange to meet up at Colwells Creek behind Killaboy Island. Laura and Jeff arrive. And John with the lobster boat that he and his wife Annie are planning to convert into a cruiser. Larry with wife Amy and their two kids. Steve and Lisa.

As with any group, there is a lot of discussion about where best to go for the prevailing conditions, much calling up with other club members still heading up-river, and opinions exchanged. The final decision for tonight is Foshay Creek.

It heralds three days of activity, sociability and occasional hilarity as our large catamaran is accommodated among the smaller, more manoeuvrable club boats. The days are spent sailing in company, the nights settled into a sociable raft-up. Ten boats in two rafts.

Truth is, we're a bit big for the members' usual haunts but it gets sorted. With someone in a dinghy pushing *Voyager*'s bows towards a thickly-wooded shore, while we anxiously watch our genoa connecting with tree branches. Nosing into mud banks, getting shore lines entangled, slipping and sliding and barking shins. Our stern anchor lifting in a strong current and, as by far the biggest boat, *Voyager* leaning on smaller ones. Or her bow anchor giving way, going aground in the mud, and being dragged off again.

The early morning air is filled with the smell of frying bacon as people sit around in the sunshine enjoying the last trip of the year. The phrase on everyone's lips is that summer is nearly over. There are dinghy rides down creeks, many of them with no marked depths on the charts and never surveyed, but probably navigable by yachts. On afternoons and evenings there is much socialising on one another's boats.

Labour Day weekend reaches its end and those with jobs to go back to on Tuesday take their leave. Several others plan to head back down river too, because strong head winds are forecast and they have fairly small motors. Jeff and Laura stay on for a few more days.

We head for Washademoak Lake. Once into it, with headsails set, we enjoy a leisurely two-hour sail up the lake before rafting up on one of the club's buoys, savouring a beer and the view. In the evening we go ashore and walk to a diner run by Jeff's sister and niece. Jeff has friends and relatives everywhere.

All the way up the east coast of the USA we have revelled in the scenery but seen little agriculture. Here on this river system there are gently rolling pastures, fields with great round bales of recently mown hay, grazing cattle – often accompanied by young calves – and the occasional sheep. Bullocks stare out at you from muddy river banks, paddle in the shallows or stand up to their knees in water with their rumps to the sun.

Finally, an unbreakable appointment takes Laura and Jeff down-river too. But, before they go, they tell us where – if we are prepared to anchor precisely, get up early and stay out of sight – we might see a beaver.

It has been claimed that the beaver is the reason why North America was explored and exploited in the first place. In the late 17th and early 18th centuries the European fashion for top hats made from fur required beaver pelts. Explorers were dispatched to trap and trade with Native Americans. And for a period the Hudson Bay Company viewed it as its major source of revenue.

Before the demand for beaver fur began, the beaver population was estimated at six million. At its peak, 200,000 pelts a year were being sent to Europe. Fortunately, before the species became extinct, the fashion changed to silk top hats.

Beavers weigh in at about 45 lbs but can reach up to 75 and live for 20 years. They mate for life and produce two to four kits a year. The young will remain in the family for two years, with the yearlings babysitting the new litter.

To be honest, we don't have any great expectations of seeing one. A beaver lodge has its entrance under water so that the animals can come and go in safety. This is a particular benefit in protecting their young, but may mean we see nothing of the creatures themselves. Nevertheless we anchor across from the large, untidy tepee of mud and saplings anyway and tuck ourselves in warmly for another cool, early September night.

18
Beavering Away

We rise before dawn and take up a position at a window each, gazing out at the lodge just as it gets light enough to see. A boat makes an excellent hide. As well as being warm and comfortable while you wait, you can also make a hot drink.

At first all we can make out is something moving about in the water but cannot identify what it is. Suddenly there is a beaver climbing up the side of the lodge inspecting its condition. Obviously, like anyone with a waterfront property, there is the perennial problem of erosion.

After a time we can see that there are *two* beavers and, having assessed the damage, they start work on repairs. They fetch sticks, hold them in their front paws and gnaw them to the required length before pushing them into the holes that have appeared in the fabric of the lodge. Then they vanish.

In a while we see a large clump of grass moving upstream, its seed heads bobbing about a foot above the water. As the grass draws alongside us we can see a beaver pushing it – only the top of its wedge-shaped head, round eyes and small, neat ears visible.

At the lodge, this building material rises out of the water and it soon becomes apparent that it is not the grass itself which is important to the beaver but its tangle of roots and the generous amount of mud clinging to them. These will dry and harden around the sticks wedged into the holes earlier and make the lodge weather-proof again.

Accordingly, this clod of river mud is pushed up the side of the lodge in a single, smooth movement and laid over one of the damaged areas. But it is what happens next that is most surprising.

A beaver's hind feet are webbed for powerful swimming, but its front feet resemble the four fingers and thumb of a human hand. And we watch in fascination as a long, skinny 'arm' reaches upward and this very versatile 'hand' spreads the muddy river weed over the damaged section and pats it flat.

The two animals work companionably; swimming down river, returning with a clod of mud and grass roots, pushing it into place and patting it down. Having completed the repairs to the lodge's circular wall, they begin work on its roof - designed, it should be said, to let CO_2 out and fresh air in. It is a most wonderful display of teamwork and continuous industry which only stops when the rays of the rising sun edge toward the lodge and they disappear inside.

Still with time to spend until our new stove arrives, we set off up Belleisle Bay. These are magical days and unruffled nights, sheltered and incredibly beautiful. Heavily wooded with occasional high meadows of surprisingly green grassland, dotted with hay bales and the odd farmstead. At Anderson Point we anchor close to shore, stroll along its narrow, pebble beach after dinner, then sleep undisturbed on a mirror lake.

Jenkins Cove, well-protected and shallow at its margins, is an ideal anchorage. A few houses, one with a seaplane. Water like glass.

Hatfield Point, at the top of the bay, was once the last stop for the stern-wheel paddle boats up from Saint John, and the boiler of the final one, which caught fire in 1907, is still visible in the marsh grass.

Ashore for a walk and a visit to the convenience store we discover Brenda's, a small diner reminiscent, in the nicest possible way, of a typical North American family kitchen.

The village also has a post office and a Pentecostal outreach church and a lovely old cemetery. Since *Voyager* is tied to its public wharf it is easy to go ashore to Brenda's next morning for a large fried breakfast overlooking the lovely, sunny bay. And then a leisurely sail all the way down Belleisle Bay and back into the Saint John River.

19
The Calm Before The Storm

It is now the ninth of September. I always know the date because of filling in the Log. I wake in the night and cannot return to sleep. Finally I get up, pad into the saloon, put on the earphones and tune into BBC World Service. World news. None of it ever good. Corrupt governments, famine, mudslides, drought, refugees, war. Each time you tune in to world news the Four Horsemen of the Apocalypse ride out. And with increasing vehemence these days, or so it seems. In Afghanistan tonight, the report is of a single death, yet the horsemen seem to rush through with greater menace even than usual. News of this man's death rivets my attention.

There has been a lot about Afghanistan on World Service for some time now. Among the names most prominently featured - Taliban, al-Qaeda and Osama bin Laden - is the country's peace and power-sharing agreement known in the West as The Northern Alliance and a beacon of hope in a troubled part of the world. Heading this Alliance has been Ahmad Shah Massoud, Afghanistan's Minister of Defence. He rejects the Taliban's fundamentalist interpretation of Islam and has recently resumed arms to resist their siege of the capital, Kabul. Today, General Massoud has been assassinated by a suicide bomber.

I know that this is the beginning of something bad. And big. How big, I could never have imagined.

Two days later we are back near Jeff and Laura's house. It is a Tuesday. Even by the standards of this uncrowded waterway, today is even quieter than usual. In fact, we see no-one at all. We are low on food but don't want to put anyone to the trouble of taking us shopping. So we search the shore for a road up from the beach that we estimate will be walking distance to the shops. We spot one at last, drop anchor and dinghy ashore; climb a steep little hill, cross a railroad track and are soon on the main road.

After about a quarter of a mile we arrive at a supermarket. We are surprised at the atmosphere. We are the only customers there, yet the staff are uncommunicative. It is unusual. All the Canadians we have met have been friendly and helpful. We make an attempt at cheerfulness but their responses range from downcast to resentful. So we buy enough food for the next few days, return to *Voyager*, set off and give Laura and Jeff a call to say we're back.

Soon after we are anchored, Jeff rows out to us in his dinghy. David and I chatter on about beavers, how much we have enjoyed the trip and crack three beers to celebrate our return and the arrival of our new stove.

Steve motors past in his yacht. He is on his way to the boatyard to have it lifted out for the winter. He calls out 'Hi', but is very subdued, makes a reference to 'America's troubles' and passes on. We ask Jeff what he means.

Jeff looks at us and says slowly, 'You haven't heard, have you?'

'What?' we say.

'America's at war.'

'Who with?'

'They don't know,' he says and proceeds to tell us about an attack that morning on New York and the Pentagon and a hijacked plane that crashed into a Pennsylvania field before it could reach the White House.

His voice is flat. We are having difficulty understanding him, not sure if we are supposed to believe him or not. We've been travelling all day and haven't turned on the radio since first thing this morning, nearly two hours before the attack. We blink at him. He shepherds us into his dinghy and takes us home to Laura.

We sit in front of their TV for hours, the four of us, with that awful loop of film playing, of the two planes endlessly hitting the twin towers of Manhattan's World Trade Centre, and wait with the rest of the world for someone to explain who has done this, and why. Instead there is only media speculation apart from one commentator admitting, 'To be honest, we don't have a clue.' In the meantime, President Bush circles the sky for hours and on television the two hijacked planes repeatedly crash into the two buildings. No wonder the staff at the supermarket had been so offended by our cheerfulness.

By evening there is increased television coverage. The eyewitness reports of firemen running past them up the stairs of the Twin Towers to their deaths are heart-breaking.

And I remember those good-tempered policemen at New York's Fourth of July fireworks celebration - with thousands of us swirling around them on FDR Drive and ducking under barriers we weren't supposed to – and wonder how many of them are among the missing.

20
Returning South

We arrive at the Reversing Falls at the due time and our friends – except Lisa who is at work - line the viewing park to give us a final wave. Naturally, as we set off across the falls a massive tug appears from the opposite direction and fills the horizon, but we pass in good order and leave the river.

At Saint John, Lisa is waiting for us at the public dock. We hug her goodbye and she goes back to work. David walks up to the office to clear out. There have been many rumours in recent days, of US Immigration tightening up after the terrorist attacks on New York and Washington. Some people, it is said, have been turned away.

Naturally enough, after what has happened, speculation is rife. And, if we are refused entry back into the USA, we could end up making the entire journey down the Atlantic coast, a long way offshore to avoid the treacherous Gulf Stream, and most likely in some difficult conditions. So we are keen to complete our paperwork properly, and get our passports stamped.

We have a little difficulty getting off the dock afterwards, thanks to a brisk offshore wind, but some passing teenagers give us a hefty push - a last act of kindness from our Canadian hosts.

We had stumbled into Canada like debutantes but, the people there had scooped us up and welcomed us in, fed and entertained us and showed us much beauty; then scooped us up and seen us safely out again before the bad weather could set in. We have been most fortunate that this year Canada has been enjoying an Indian summer.

Before we'd left, Robert had come to fit our new stove. Paula had sent with him gifts of homemade wine and strawberry jam and what proves to be the most delicious mustard pickle I have ever tasted.

Robert is a craftsman. His mantra is: measure twice, cut once. And all his saws have shields on them so their teeth don't get damaged in the tool bag. He has made the most beautiful job of the stove. It might not have been quite the same depth as the old one, but by the time he had finished, and with an inspired contribution from Jeff and Sonny, you would think it had been installed when the boat was new.

They have all been generous, thoughtful and very, very kind. We shall never forget them.

UNITED STATES OF AMERICA

21
Maine

The Bay of Fundy has one last treat for us before we leave it. Between Maine and the large Canadian island of Grand Manan, we come upon a couple of Right Whales. They are easy to identify from the white patches on their faces and their lack of a dorsal fin. The species is rare, after being hunted to near-extinction over a period of three centuries, and collision with vessels nowadays because they are such slow movers. Populations also grow slowly since a female is ten years old before conceiving her first calf and pregnant for a year. These two are well exposed on the surface, relaxed, and observe us minutely before sinking.

Jonesport

Our objective now is to find an Immigration dock so that we can clear into the USA. We head for Sawyer Cove and the afternoon is well advanced when we call the Coast Guard to announce our arrival at the crowded little harbour of Jonesport. They take a while to answer and then tell us to wait while they contact Customs. We hover between lobster pots and mudflats on an ebbing tide, as time and visibility evaporate. Eventually, someone calls us and tells us to tie up on the floating pontoon in the harbour, which delights us because it means we will be able to stay the night there. There is no way anyone will expect us to leave and anchor now, among the lobster pots, in the dark.

Around 8pm US time, an amiable, very large, very polite young Customs officer is cheerfully persuaded to throw himself fast from the cockpit into the unlit saloon. It is a desperate measure on our part to avoid becoming full of the local oversize mosquitoes that had gnawed our hands and faces as we'd tied up.

Although we had expected difficulties, and not a little suspicion in the circumstances, he did both Customs and Immigration in the blink of an eye. And then he obliged us by blasting out of the saloon at the same speed he had entered, although by now I was aware that he was slightly wider than our companionway doors and initially feared for him.

Afterwards we realize we had thrown this very good-natured and helpful young man out into utter darkness. It had been a long day and having turned out the saloon light to keep the gnawing beasts at bay while we opened the doors to let him out, we had forgotten to put on the cockpit light, or even shine him onto the pontoon with the torch. Bone weary, we fall into bed as soon as he has gone and feel very ashamed of ourselves next morning when we realize how badly we treated him.

Mistake Cove

Within an hour of leaving Jonesport next day the fog closes in and the wind changes from south-east to south. As a result, we bang into the sea to the point where all the loose objects aboard change position and everything fixed creaks and groans remorselessly. After a long day yesterday we are finding these conditions tiring and decide to turn into Mistake Cove where we had sheltered earlier this year and the Coast Guard had come looking for casualties after a particularly vicious squall.

By the time we approach the main channel into Mistake Cove the fog is so thick we have to depend on the GPS and the radar until we get close enough to see the rocks on either side of the narrow entrance and its smooth, sandstone-coloured shore.

Once inside the jumble of pine-clad rocks which makes up the cove we are in calm water and the fog is less. We zigzag through the lobster pots to the far end, where we anchored before. And just like last time, a seal basks on an exposed rock. Only this time it is a spotted seal. It turns its head towards us as we work, blinks heavily several times, then turns away again. The tide comes in and the next time I look the rock is invisible but the seal is still balancing on it, shaped now like a banana with its head and tail up, and giving every appearance of hovering unsupported on the surface of the water. In no time the water covers its back and, after flicking its head and tail together briefly, it floats off and disappears.

We have a lazy afternoon, reading *Madame Bovary*, unmoved by her self-inflicted plight but surprised at the depth of Flaubert's intense hatred for the rather benign bourgeoisie with which he has surrounded her. When the tide drops sufficiently to leave the rock opposite awash, a different spotted seal swims over and settles onto it.

Staying here for the night proves to be a good move because by next day the adverse winds have fallen away to almost nothing. Although the fog remains and we continue on down the coast still using the GPS and radar. In fact, from now on fog will be our companion throughout our journey south.

Northeast Harbor

After nearly 40 miles, in visibility which is never above half a mile and often far less, we edge our way into Northeast Harbor, with me on the foredeck blowing our foghorn, as we carefully pick our way through the fishing buoys from one navigation marker to the next. We do it quite naturally now, yet a year ago we should have baulked at even the thought of trying to sail through such conditions. It is surprising how easily you get used to things.

Once in Northeast Harbor we try to contact the harbour master on the VHF and fail. A couple in a fishing dory say they will alert him for us, but suggest we take any buoy we fancy.

We wake dreamily after a long and refreshing sleep. Meanwhile, the fog has lifted to reveal a very pretty shoreline, with many of the trees already turning yellow and red. We fill our tanks at Beal's Lobster Pier and with the sun out and the fog gone, set out for Provincetown. Once clear of land, however, visibility drops to less than 100 yards and stays that way for most of the day. There is also a fair bit of timber floating in the water, including part of a jetty.

Late afternoon the fog suddenly rolls back like a carpet, revealing a sparkling sea and bright blue sky. It is glorious after such a gloomy day. Seals pop their heads up to watch *Voyager* go by and a dozen shearwaters sweep around us, one wing dipped almost into the water. At 8pm the fog returns. David does a long watch, from now until 2am when it lifts again.

It is unpleasant sailing at night in fog. Usually there are lights from the shore and other boats so that even on an overcast night there is always something to give your world some sort of definition. But in fog, you stand in the cockpit, growing increasingly damp from the moisture in the air, and stare out into nothingness. All you can do is listen, and keep one eye on the radar. Tonight it shows only two fishing boats and a ship.

David wakes just after 5am to find me concerned about one of the fishing boats with which we are now on a collision course thanks to its constant sharp changes of direction. We move well over to starboard, to pass him port to port, and are closing slowly. When we are almost abreast he suddenly turns into us.

Then he calls us on the VHF to complain that we are not following the rules of the road and giving way to a fishing boat trawling. We are too busy avoiding him, and looking for his net, to go inside and pick up the VHF's receiver to point out that the rules of the road don't include allowing a fishing boat to intentionally steer at another boat at very short range on a whim and simply expect it to get out of the way in time. Or that he isn't actually showing the requisite lights that would have told us he is trawling anyway. If indeed he is. Fishermen don't own the ocean, but some of them think they do. The rest of the journey is uneventful apart from being hit several times by something solid floating in the water.

22
Massachusetts

Provincetown

At Provincetown the fog becomes so thick that, despite radar, the next day is not one for moving on. Even the local terns that colonize our front rail in large numbers look fed up. In the circumstances, what better than a hearty meal? I christen our new oven with roast chicken and vegetables.

We are half way down the Cape Cod Canal next day when the overheating light on the starboard engine comes on and David shuts it down. He investigates but can do nothing while we are on the move. The Canal is not a place to stop but once out of it we turn into Onset, anchor, and David sets about finding a solution to the problem.

The cooling of our engines uses the raw water system: sucking in sea water, circulating it around the engine and then ejecting it along with the diesel fumes. Its inlet is absolutely choked with weed and quantities of it have managed to get well into the system. This is not a problem we encountered last year, but have done so several times lately. He clears it all out but with 1,500 miles of rivers, lakes and canals still ahead of us we go to a boatyard and book *Voyager* in to have water strainers fitted. These can then be easily checked daily, even on the move.

Mattapoisett

It is October now and we are eager to get south as quickly as possible but in Buzzards Bay the chop is so uncomfortable that we give up any attempt to reach Newport, Rhode Island today. Eventually we bounce our way into Mattapoisett Harbour, which is not so much a harbour as a very large bay, and drop anchor in a sheltered corner. It is such a relief when all the banging and hobby-horsing stops.

The weather forecast now warns that a gale is on the way and since we are well dug in and protected we decide to stay put. But with the day still sunny and bright we go ashore, although not expecting much as very little is visible from the water.

Instead we find a very pretty town with many of the houses built in the early 1800s. They have plaques on them, each one bearing the date on which it was built and the name of the original owner. Men called Seth and Lot and Jeremiah.

Mattapoisett, it turns out, was a famous ship-building centre in the 19th century, constructing around 400 whaling and trading ships. One of them was the *Acushnet*, the whaler on which the young Herman Melville sailed out of New Bedford, just a few miles along the coast from here, on a voyage that would provide the background for his novel, *Moby Dick*.

This small stretch of Massachusetts' coast, it seems, is a veritable treasury of sailing history. For between Mattapoisett and New Bedford is Fairhaven where, in 1892, Captain Joshua Slocum arrived at Poverty Point to rebuild a derelict 36-foot oyster sloop named *Spray* that had been given to him. Between 1895 and 1898 Slocum sailed the *Spray* around the world alone - becoming the first person to accomplish such a feat and the instigator of the blue water cruising so many of us enjoy today.

Our fridge has defrosted and we don't know why. David thinks it might either have lost its gas or the thermostat is faulty. In what is for me an unusual bout of optimism concerning anything electrical, I suggest it may be having a frozen valve moment, something to which it succumbed once before; and that left to defrost overnight the unit may refreeze tomorrow. If not, we have a problem. Not as big a problem as it would be in hot weather, but still another time-consuming visit to a boatyard.

There is a magnificent sunset. The sky clears partially an hour or two beforehand, leaving a vast rippling cloud to the west. The last rays of the sun catch it and turn it gold, then orange, then a hypnotic red. A long, straight vapour trail from a long-gone plane cuts through its western edge and looks for all the world like a sword blade dripping blood. The sky around it is azure, faintly greenish, the way it is sometimes after bad weather, and backlit in gold. Glorious.

We wake to a cold morning, the windows dripping with condensation. Not helped by toasted muffins and the last of Paula's homemade jam. David mops the windows. I dry out the fridge and suggest we do the deed that has been depressing David since yesterday. We start the engine and breathe a sigh of relief as the plate begins to freeze. We still have a fridge.

The sun rises higher and begins to warm the cockpit and finally we open the companionway doors and let in the outside air which is now far warmer than inside. The sky is the most wonderful blue with just a few tiny wisps of cloud. The trees on the harbour's southern shore are an even deeper red than yesterday.

According to a free newspaper we picked up on our trip ashore, this is the time of southern Massachusetts' wine harvests, and you can join in if you wish. Also the cranberry harvest.

Cranberries are wet-harvested. The vines grow in bogs. Growers flood the bogs when the fruit has ripened and use water reel harvesting machines to dislodge the berries. These then float on the surface, creating a brilliant crimson lake before the fruit is pumped into waiting trucks.

There are lots of things to do around here if you have a car. We are particularly intrigued by the Lizzie Borden Museum. What do they have to put in it, we wonder, apart from an axe?

Today is Sunday, October 7, the eve of Columbus Day, and the event occurs we have both been expecting but hoping wouldn't happen. As history students we both know that attempts at invasion or occupation of Afghanistan have proved disastrous, thanks largely to its mountainous terrain and an unconventional approach to combat. Both Britain and the Soviet Union tried it at various times and failed. Britain three times. But when we turn on the news this evening we learn that a US-led coalition has launched a bombing campaign on Taliban-controlled Afghanistan.

23
Rhode Island

There is a wide entrance to Newport Harbour and we fishtail our way in, because the tide is coming out and the wind is on our port quarter. Fort Adams, on the right-hand corner as you approach the anchorage, has a turf roof. It dates from 1824 and although active in five major wars the fort has never fired a shot in anger. Since the 1980s its grounds have played host to the annual Newport Jazz Festival.

Our anchorage is a good distance from the town and, although we would make it in the dinghy without difficulty, the weather forecast makes us wary about getting back. So we take the Oldport Launch into Bowen's Landing and fall in love with Newport with its picturesque waterfront of wharves, small jetties, old ferry buildings and 19th century pubs.

The town itself sports small houses with window shutters and large clapboard shops, many with window boxes. The combination of colours - bright red geraniums or burnt orange chrysanthemums against dark creosoted timbers or white painted clapboard – and shop windows filled with luxury clothing and soft furnishings is delicious. A canvas-covered cushion, in red, white and blue squares, is offered for a king's ransom. Best not enquire the cost of the luminous red sailing jacket even if it could transform your life.

We stumble upon the International Yacht Restoration School where people learn how to restore old wooden boats. A young man painting the railings tells us how best to view the work - from an interior balcony. It is fascinating to watch the restoration work in progress from a vantage point we should have thought an intrusion on our part had we not been invited. At the same time, it keeps visitors safely away from the planing elbows and swinging hammers of those in ear protectors who may not be aware of your presence.

As we leave the workshop, the same young man invites us to go and take a look at the old yacht tied to a wharf at the rear of the building. Her name is *Coronet*, a 131 foot schooner built in Brooklyn in 1885. She had sailed the world as a luxury yacht and for many years was the flagship of the New York Yacht Club. She is now a little tired and run down, but her former glory – especially her gorgeous interior - is still plain to see.

With no shortage of chandlers in a place like this, we purchase the few things we need for *Voyager* and continue to wander the town, breathing in its textures, colours and affluence before setting off for the Stop and Shop supermarket to fill our rucksacks and heading home.

With the weather still unsettled and not ideal for moving on we hail the Oldport Launch again next morning for a tour of the Old Town. At Trinity Church we find a lecture to school children going on so we settle into a very comfortable cushioned box pew across the aisle and listen.

The original Trinity Church was destroyed by fire but this one, consecrated in 1879, was built in the early American style and remains much as original examples would have done if the modernisers hadn't got at them.

A three-hour sermon was central to the worship of the time and accordingly the pulpit was built in the centre of the nave. This one is still there, obscuring the altar, whereas most have been moved to one side. It is a wonderfully *massive* three-tier affair with the bottom one for the clerk to tell everybody what happened in the parish during the week, the middle one for the reading of the lessons and the top one for the sermon. Above that is a sounding board, a wooden canopy ensuring that the preacher's voice carries down to the congregation instead of up into the rafters.

At a time when America, Britain and other European countries are embarking on a war in Afghanistan, not to mention all the other more long-standing wars around the world which also have roots in religious conflict, this small State's early history has a particular resonance.

Rhode Island's religious freedoms were founded by Roger Williams (c.1603-1683), a Londoner educated at Cambridge. At odds with England's theology of the time - which he saw as a hard-line, High-Church Anglicanism leading to a return of Catholicism - he was attracted to Puritanism. And in his early thirties emigrated to the Massachusetts Bay Colony which, 60 years in the future, would become infamous as the site of the Salem witchcraft trials and of religious bigotry. However, Williams wasn't there long, having been quickly expelled for his opinions on freedom of worship, and in 1636 founded a settlement on Rhode Island.

He named it Providence Plantation after what he called 'the Providence of God' in allowing him to find the place. The word 'Plantation' had no connection with slavery. Williams was an abolitionist.

With a talent for linguistics, Roger Williams soon learned the language of the native population. Not only did he use it to help them prevent too much of their hunting grounds and arable land from being absorbed by settlers, but he was so impressed by their culture that he proudly admitted to never having converted a single one of them - much to the disgust of fellow-ministers. In fact, he declined to convert anybody. He practiced what he preached – freedom of worship. Ultimately, he came to believe that all formal religion was invalid.

As with any name, I am curious why a State is called an Island, when it is part of the US mainland and the name Rhode does not appear on any of the islands on either of our charts. The name Rhode Island, on which the famous town of Newport stands, was bestowed on it after the colonists arrived in 1638. This may be the result of a perceived resemblance to the Greek Island of Rhodes. Before that it was called Aquidneck, the name that local people still use and which causes a little confusion for unsuspecting visitors.

Although the smallest State in the Union, it has the longest name. Rhode Island's full moniker – and the scourge of small envelopes everywhere until they abandoned its regular use - is State of Rhode Island and Providence Plantations.

We lunch on seafood at The Black Pearl, an old wooden building on the waterfront and then walk to Touro Synagogue, since Jews were among the many who found a place of safety in Rhode Island's tolerant atmosphere.

Built by Englishman Peter Harrison and dedicated in 1763, the Touro Synagogue is a beautiful building and the only surviving synagogue in America from the colonial era. It was following a visit here by George Washington in 1790 that he penned his famous letter to the congregation pledging that the new nation would 'give to bigotry no sanction, to persecution no assistance.'

Sadly the armed guard who asks permission to search my bag before we can enter it replies to my question, 'Is this because of 9/11?' that unfortunately the precaution has been necessary since long before then.

24
Colours of the Fall

Something we have very much wanted to see is a New England Fall. And what better place to do that than Connecticut.

At Newport Harbour we wake to a cool and misty morning, set off at sunrise and after a leisurely sail down Long Island Sound in bright sunshine turn into the Connecticut River late afternoon. A mile or so on, we have to wait at the railroad bridge for the new high-speed train – apparently capable of 150mph – to go through. And that's pretty much the last noise and bustle we will encounter for a while.

When the last carriage has disappeared the bridge opens, we pass through, and the bridge and the river close behind us like a cocoon. To anchor for the night we nose our way up a narrow channel and tuck in between Goose Island, with its tall rushes and birdsong, and a stretch of riverbank with some fine houses on it.

Just after sunrise we edge our way back out into a warm sunny morning that turns into a very hot day. The river is wide and often fairly shallow but has a dredged channel winding through it. The only small difficulty is that, at a distance, green and red navigation markers can be difficult to spot against a dense backdrop of green and red foliage since the markers blend in perfectly.

The river's banks are lined with trees as far as the eye can see. They are also steep, providing a perfect setting for what is commonly known as 'leaf peeping' – a description used with enthusiasm by the visitors who do it, but disdain by locals who have to deal with all the extra traffic on their normally quiet roads and waterways.

I have to say that I had come expecting a richness of colour, but in shades of red and gold. What I had not been prepared for is the sheer range of colours we encounter as we drift upriver. Scarlet, crimson and gold certainly but also orange, apricot, peach, salmon pink, mauve, purple and bronze; all highlighted and contrasted by a dazzling variety of yellows, greens and browns. Even the marsh grass is at its best, tall and straight with big feathery seed heads. It is stunning.

You can look at a photograph of something like this, although it is only a glimpse. A giant flat-screen will offer more. But to stand on deck, with the trees rising up the hillsides on each side of you, and reflected in the water below you, is breath-taking. And in a couple of places this long winding river turns back on itself to provide a panorama, a full 360° that just blows your mind.

Adding to the experience is the unspoilt nature of the river. There is little evidence of human activity, a few houses only, here and there, traditional and mostly painted white, which gives an added focus to all the colour and texture surrounding them.

Nor are there any other boats. In fact, the only other thing moving is a vintage steam train running along the bank, its smoke white against the trees. Fortunately, for mid-October, we are blessed by unseasonably good weather.

The only people we see are those at the swing bridge at East Haddam. The Godspeed Opera House on the river bank has a small park in front of it and as we approach we can see a re-enactment involving redcoats and militia. The redcoats then board an old wooden schooner called *Quinnipiack* and sail downstream. They leave behind the militia, and civilians in period costume, who all look rather shifty when we wave and point to our flying Red Ensign.

From our growing experience of these historical re-enactments we assume they have just routed the British. *Again*.

Our chart book for Long Island Sound has got us this far upriver, but by Middletown we have reached its limits. The river's navigable channel twists and turns so much that we need another chart if we are to continue. Spotting the Yankee Boat Yard we phone and ask the man on the other end if he has such a chart and if we can tie up to his fuel pontoon while we buy it. He says yes to both.

This very nice man turns out to be the owner of both the yard and the marina next door. As a cruiser himself who winters in The Bahamas, he is considerate to fellow-cruisers. So, when David asks the whereabouts of a grocery store, he suggests we take *Voyager* out to one of his moorings and come back in our dinghy. After which he gives us directions to the supermarket and the keys to his spanking new, fire engine red, very powerful pick-up truck. It looks expensive. And not a mark on it.

'Are you sure?' we ask him.

'Yep,' he says. 'But you should've been here yesterday. I came to work in my Porsche.'

We have a really good shop-up and return with the back of the truck loaded to its rim and think it is just as well we missed the Porsche.

At Hartford, the State capital, low bridges prevent yachts going any further up the river. Our arrival also coincides with a drop in temperature. Despite a bright morning there is a lot of condensation when we wake, and old towels are unearthed to dry the windows.

Cold itself is not the problem on a boat. You can always put in heat of some kind. The problem is condensation. When the outside temperature drops below a certain level, and depending on its moisture content, sometimes you only have to breathe inside your boat to make the windows steam up. Add actual heat, plus the effects of cooking, and the place will soon be streaming.

So you cook your main meal of the day at lunchtime when your surroundings are at their warmest and you can have the galley hatches open to let out the steam. You give up late evening hot drinks and litter your living and sleeping areas with small plastic containers filled with granules that absorb damp. And if you opt wherever possible for warm clothing and a rug over your feet of an evening, instead of a heater, quite soon you become adept at staying dry while still being warm, well fed and comfortable.

All the anchorages have been beautiful but a couple are particularly memorable. David chooses Middle Haddam when strong winds are forecast because it offers protection but, as we prepare to anchor near sunset, a most beautiful waterfront with a small group of houses reveals itself. Our galley faces it and though I am supposed to be preparing a meal I spend most of my time staring out at the view.

Dressed in full wet weather gear against the cold, after breakfast next morning we set off downriver. David had originally planned to anchor off the town of Essex this afternoon. But given the latest forecast – for 30 knots of wind – we shall end up with a very turbulent night of wind over tide out in the river. So instead he opts for the shelter of Hamburg Cove, a mile and a half north of Essex, and a quieter night.

Since we have begun our return downriver it is very noticeable that the autumn colours are far from static. Trees that we observed only a few days earlier have changed, some of them into colours you can't rightly give a name to. Words like 'peach' and 'orange' simply don't do them justice any more. You just gaze in awe. You feel drunk on colours. Such glories, indeed, that were it not for the chill wind blowing through the cockpit you could believe at times that this was late spring and they were trees in blossom.

To get into Hamburg Cove's anchorage there is a well-marked, very narrow channel through the cove and then sharp left into a little basin full of mooring buoys. According to our cruising guide, the HM advises you to pick up a buoy but be prepared to vacate it if the owner turns up. Most of the buoys are vacant, and with not much chance of too many owners turning up on a blustery Tuesday afternoon in October.

On September 21, 1938 a hurricane hit this area. The boats sheltering here all survived, whereas those in Essex were destroyed. Ever since then, the locals have called this Timid Cove. 'Prudent Cove' seems a more appropriate choice to us, but there you are.

It is very pretty, with small jetties, old houses - and resplendent trees, of course. Also a dozen or more swans, with their heads underwater grazing on river weed, and, when we first emerge from the channel, at a distance we mistake their upended bottoms for mooring buoys. Late evening a flock of Canada geese make our rigging rattle as they pass overhead. They make so much noise the wonder is they've survived as a species at all - every man and his gun knows they're coming from at least half a mile away.

It is another cold morning with condensation. David checks the engine oil and the weed filters after which we motor the mile and a half down to Essex, anchor, and then dinghy ashore. We set off for the dinghy dock at The Chandlery but tie up at the Corinthian Yacht Club by mistake.

We take a walk around the town which is picture postcard stuff, old homes built by ship builders and whaling captains in the 19th century and all framed in exquisite foliage. We find the post office to send cards and letters home and to Canada, then pick up a fresh loaf and a few other things at the convenience store.

At the far end of town we find the Essex steam train station, or to give it its proper title, The Valley Railroad. There is a working engine, a couple more awaiting restoration, some Pullman rail cars and a handcar – also known as a pump trolley – familiar not least from clips of that frantic chase in a Buster Keaton movie where the hero uses one to rescue the heroine from the villains aboard the train.

There is also a caboose, a word that echoed through the black-and-white Westerns of my childhood, although I never did find out what one was. It turns out to be the small wagon once hitched to the end of a freight train. Painted red, and carrying a red tail light, the caboose identified the end of the train while providing accommodation and cooking facilities for the crew on long journeys. Just as we are about to leave, the train we had seen skirting the river bank on our way upriver steams majestically into the station.

The Essex anchorage is still not a comfortable one, given the wind, and we return *Voyager* to a mooring buoy in Hamburg Cove for the night, only just making it before dark thanks to a two-knot current against us. It still needs fifteen minutes to six o'clock but the sun has already set by the time we reach the entrance, with dusk lasting about half an hour at present.

It is also getting close to low tide and the water emptying out of the cove and meeting the two knots in the river creates considerable turbulence in the very shallow entrance to the very narrow channel. And for a few moments we seem doomed to end up stranded on a mud bank. It is a very cold evening and despite sleeping bags on the sofa we go to bed more for warmth than tiredness.

At 6.30 next morning it is positively Arctic in our cabin and the duvet damp to the touch. The windows are dripping and even the linings are wet. David, who has been listening to the forecast under the bed clothes on our little weather radio, says that considering the poor long-range forecast, today is likely to be the best we can expect and that we should go.

The bad news is that given the strength of the current in the river, if we are going to go, it has to be now. It is an effort to abandon a very warm bed. But when we step out into the cockpit to raise the anchor, and our feet go from under us on a layer of ice, we accept that it really is time for us to leave.

It is sometimes the case that the most beautiful surroundings present themselves in the most physically uncomfortable conditions. And so it is now, with our breath crystallizing on the freezing air and fingers numb with cold. The sun rises just as we begin to leave Hamburg Cove. Its soft, pink-and-gold radiance transforms everything it touches, adding even greater lustre to the everyday glory of the trees reflected in the still water, making everything look warm and inviting despite the cold. The heads, backs and wings of two low-flying swans glow with it, while its warmth accelerates the mist rising from the narrow channel so that by the time we reach the exit, it is spiralling up in slender white plumes eight feet high.

At its edge, the water is so shallow that a swan has grounded on mud and is pumping its feet frantically as it pushes itself forward into water again. Across the river, a patch of dense, low-lying mist turns such a deep red that at first glance the opposite bank appears to be on fire.

We pass back through the railroad bridge that carries the super-fast train and a short while later re-enter Long Island Sound. We have spent seven days on the Connecticut River.

25
A Wounded New York

Within a couple of days we are back within sight of New York. From our City Island anchorage, Manhattan looks ethereal in the diffused light. The buildings are all soft blues and greys and seem almost transparent. But once you set off for the city you are facing the New York skyline and become acutely aware of the two missing buildings. You don't want to but, in spite of yourself, your eyes become transfixed on the place where the twin towers of the World Trade Centre used to be.

David telephones around to find a suitable place to buy diesel as some fuel docks are not wide enough for a catamaran to get into; or, if you do manage it, it's a nightmare getting out again. The World's Fair Marina can accommodate us. It is at Flushing Meadow – such a restful name - where the US Open Tennis Championships take place.

The fuel dock has a raised freeway behind it, and the flight path of La Guardia Airport directly over it, making it impossible to communicate with the attendant unless the two of you stand inches from each other and shout into one another's ear. It is a far cry from the tranquillity of the Connecticut River.

Going through New York Harbour a boat's passage times are dictated by the state of the current at Hell Gate, where the Harlem and East rivers meet. The narrow one-mile stretch of water is a dangerous mixture of cross-currents and whirlpools and reaches speeds of four or five knots at its peak. This tidal race is currently at its gentlest, and even has a man in a small boat drifting about in the middle of it, fishing. However, we do hit some underwater debris and our log stops.

Once we are alongside Manhattan, and the buildings around us prevent us from seeing where the World Trade Centre was, we are struck by how normal everything seems. Except for the Coast Guard behind us telling a speedboat owner through a loudhailer that the limit through here is 10mph. And the fact that you can now only navigate the river between sunrise and sunset, and must stay a minimum of 25-yards away from bridge supports. The fear is sabotage. If someone brought the bridges down, notwithstanding the carnage, the city would grind to a halt.

Then somebody ashore spots our British Ensign and shouts have we sailed all the way from Britain? Yes, we say, and a little group of people give us an undeserved round of applause, as if we are doing something brave in being here instead of simply making our way south for the winter. But we are carried on down the East River and there is no time to say anything except that we are sorry for what has happened to their city.

We had enjoyed our stay in New York in July so much and when we left we had promised ourselves another few days here on the way back. But we don't stop. We feel it would be inappropriate. Disrespectful to the dead, the injured and the bereaved. Our earlier trip had been light-hearted and happy. How could we flit about enjoying ourselves in the shadow of Ground Zero? Such sentiments, shared by many, will have a negative impact we later discover - depriving the city of much-needed tourist income at a time when its costs are astronomical.

From the three times we have already passed through here this has always been a polluted river – and heaven knows why anybody would want to fish in it - but now it is worse than ever. And several times more we are hit by something in the water, once quite violently.

As we round the southern tip of Manhattan Island we see a barge being filled with debris from the twin towers and the other buildings demolished by their fall. It is particularly poignant, as this is where we used to see visitors boarding the tourist boats for trips around New York Harbour. There are no tours now. Only trucks delivering tons of shattered masonry to a fleet of barges for disposal.

A little further on we can look back at the area where the towers had stood. There are two very tall red cranes in the unnatural space where the towers used to be and a massive mound of rubble. We can't find words to express our feelings. We just push on down the harbour in silence towards Sandy Hook Bay and an overnight anchorage.

Yesterday they had forecast winds from the north then changed it to the south-west (on the nose). This morning they have given light south-west, going to the north and then to the east. Tomorrow is back to south-westerlies. We decide to just press on.

As we haul up the anchor, a lobster boat drifts past. A vast rising sun, deepest red and matt-finished in the gauzy morning light, silhouettes the boat and the solitary fisherman, lowering his pots and oblivious of the glory behind him.

A little further along the New Jersey coast the sun, higher now, metallic and bouncing off the water, lights the undersides of a long skein of geese flying south, making them glow like stainless steel.

Out in the Atlantic the wind fails to follow the forecast but happily it is also never on the nose. Although sometimes it dies away completely. We reach Manasquan Inlet, and given the fact that we expect strong headwinds tomorrow, decide not to stop here but press on through the night as far as we can.

26
Trouble Strikes

Just before dark, about five miles off the coast of New Jersey and approaching Atlantic City, there is a bang underneath us. *Voyager* shudders violently and lifts slightly in the water. Then exactly the same thing happens again. We do not see, and shall never know, what hit her undercarriage – twice. It could have been one of the many submerged steel containers routinely washed off the decks of cargo ships; old telegraph poles traditionally dumped at sea off the New Jersey coast; or debris from 9/11.

We stop and search as best we can. When we set off again David is sure we are travelling slower than we should be and the steering doesn't feel quite right. Nor does the starboard engine seem to be producing the power it should. However, deprived of the log and its ability to measure our speed through the water - lost in collisions with the detritus in Hell Gate - we are unable to resolve this issue. There is nothing else to do but press on. David checks the bilges to make sure we are not taking in water. Though anxious, we a just glad that *Voyager* wasn't holed and sunk.

By three in the morning we are off Cape May Harbour and spot fishing buoys in the water. The last thing we need is rope around a prop and with the moon almost down we decide to anchor by the breakwater into Cape May and wait for dawn before carrying on.

As we anchor, a thick fog descends. One moment there are red and green navigation lights on the harbour walls and a well-lit coastline. Next moment - nothing. We are relieved to be at anchor and at the same time very glad to be away from the harbour entrance. We can hear vessels rumbling in and out in zero visibility while knowing that, although we have our anchor light on, none of them would have been able to see it anyway.

Come daylight we make the decision to head for Annapolis which, given its reputation, should have the facilities we need to lift and repair *Voyager*, and also friends who will direct us to the right places. So, despite the fog, we edge our way towards and around Cape May's notorious headland of rocks and shoals and make our way into Delaware Bay.

By now it is quite apparent that we have damage to our starboard rudder from yesterday's collision. It has begun to squeak and the steering is now very stiff. The fog remains until early afternoon, when we are abreast of the nuclear power station and a brisk southerly wind gets up. So we roll out the genoa and, with a strong current behind us, get over eight knots.

It is a lovely run down the Chesapeake and Delaware Canal. The trees along the banks are very pretty colours in the late afternoon sunshine and there is yellow honeysuckle, even in late October. Just before dark we anchor at Chesapeake City. We both sleep for nine hours solid.

After such grey, dreary days we wake to a bright blue, clear autumn morning with a forecast for the 80s. In fact, so changeable is the weather just now that while Philadelphia – just to the north-east of us - is forecast to hit the record books for heat today, two nights from now it can expect a sprinkling of snow.

Before we leave the anchorage David inspects the log. Something has hit the transducer paddle hard enough to bend its spindle. He is able to straighten it and now when we leave here we will be able to check our through-the-water speed and judge if there is any propeller damage.

The log works and confirms David's suspicion that the starboard propeller is not working properly and that we are down a knot or more on speed. Initially it doesn't matter much and we plod along at about 5 knots with a light headwind. But it rises steadily through the morning. By 11 o'clock we are getting gusts of 35 knots, taking a lot of water over the bows and averaging just over 3 knots.

It is too uncomfortable and we go into Still Pond Bay near Kinnard Point to anchor and shelter. We have lunch and listen to the forecast. It says 20 to 25 knots, falling this evening to 15 or 20 from the west and to expect the same mixture of conditions for the next three days.

However, the wind moves to the west early, David checks the chart and thinks that although it will be uncomfortable for a time it is worth attempting a run for Annapolis – and the solution to our problems - rather than kick our heels for three days in Still Pond Bay.

Each headland we go round puts the wind a little further off our nose until about 5pm when it drops to 15 or 20 knots and we can unfurl the sails. It soon shifts back towards the nose again but we are determined to get to Annapolis. Radar helps us after dark and we pick our way cautiously to our destination.

At last, in Spa Creek around 9pm, we pick up a mooring buoy in the darkness and collapse.

27
Annapolis, Maryland

The weather in Annapolis next day is bright and sunny; not cold enough for the rasping oilies we have been wearing at sea, but cool enough to require a light coat. I have just the thing at the back of the wardrobe.

Everybody has a favourite piece of clothing that not only suits the weather conditions perfectly but is also cosy, comfortable and ... rather attractive. I lift out my old red coat with a smile of pleasure. It's been a while – since before we first set out - but it was one of those things I couldn't throw away. I instantly recall its weight and texture. It's perhaps a little shabbier than I remember, and there's a touch of mildew on the collar, although that soon brushes off.

Next day we get a diver to go down and assess the damage. He returns within minutes with two pieces of information: 'The skeg of the starboard rudder is broken in half,' and 'That will be 85 dollars.'

Annapolis is known – not least from a little self-promotion - as The Sailing Capital of America for its large amount of yacht brokers, marine goods and services, marinas, boatyards and boat shows. Even so, there are only two yards able to lift a catamaran - one using a cradle (which we prefer) and the other a crane.

We ask the advice of someone we met last year who was very kind to us and who lives and works locally. Joe's Shipyard is the one with the cradle and it is Joe also who is recommended for the work we need doing, along with the proviso that he is weird – and pricey.

Small and hyperactive, with shoulder-length hair streaming out from under a tall knitted hat, Joe roams his cluttered yard and narrow berths on a small scrambler motorbike. At first it doesn't look as if he will take us on, as he is much exercised by today's date – there are only 24 hours left before the Internal Revenue Service amnesty expires. Paperwork, as we will soon discover, is not something he does. However, with a little persuasion he directs us onto the end of a pontoon until the morrow.

We are lifted out on Halloween. There is a long gouge on the port keel boot, both props are damaged and the loose half of the skeg falls off as *Voyager* is lowered onto the hard. Our next job is to get Joe to put a quotation together and fax it to our insurance company, together with a report from us as to how and where the damage occurred. Our part is already done. The problem is getting Joe to do his.

Since we are going to be here for a little while, until repairs are complete, we decide to get some other odds and ends done ourselves. So we head into town. David is off to a chandlery for various items, and a sailmaker to get a quote for a new sacrificial strip on the stay sail. I am heading in a different direction to buy groceries and get some films developed. On our way to the bus station we call in at the office of the friend who had recommended Joe.

'I gave him a call,' he says, 'and told him to do a good job for my friends. He said he would, because you are so poor.'

We both look mystified. Then, in the warmth of his office, my nose twitches at a slight mustiness. 'Must be my coat,' I murmur.

'Let him think it,' he says laughing. 'It may keep his prices down a bit.'

At the supermarket checkout I am given a 5% reduction on my current bill and a voucher for future purchases. And when I collect our photographs the cashier tells me that the store is selecting certain customers to receive a discount on all purchases until the end of November. I glance uncomfortably down at my coat. After I've deposited the shopping back on *Voyager* I collect some bags of washing and set off for the laundrette, in easy walking distance of the boatyard.

Even by American standards this is an affluent town. Built around a stunning harbour it is home to the State Legislature, a thriving marine industry and the nation's premier naval academy along with many historic waterfront homes, expensive restaurants and a vibrant social life.

Less noticed perhaps are the people from the projects, the renters, those on minimum wage or welfare and the occasional foreign cruiser without the laundry facilities that come as standard on American leisure boats - in short, the patrons of this laundrette. Machines loaded, I unzip my old red jacket, settle into a plastic chair and blend right in.

First an unsteady, dishevelled man swings in, looks around, sees someone he doesn't want to see him, and swings right out again. Somebody unseen holds an animated one-sided conversation on the public phone around the corner beyond the last dryer. A very tall, completely silent man strides the length of the place, sets his laundry circling in the furthest machine from the door and strides silently out again.

A large couple, dressed all in black, clatter in carrying a large basket of washing each. She throws her basket heavily onto the floor by the door, then snatches the one being carried by her enormous but sheepish male companion and hurls that on the floor too, all the time telling him *very* loudly she just *doesn't* believe him. They go out and come in again. There is more slamming of washing baskets as her litany of disbelief rises an octave. Her indignant voice diminishes as they go back out into the street several more times – I assume for more laundry baskets - but when I next look up from my book there is no laundry and no couple, so they must have changed their minds and taken it all away again.

The animated phone call behind the dryers ends and the caller lopes out in a disconsolate sort of way. All is quiet for a while, until a slender, vibrant man very neatly dressed in a crisp shirt and tie, tweed jacket and twill trousers explodes through the door and booms a question at me.

I blink up at him. He has a voice like an evangelical preacher and so loud it makes the tinny doors of the dryers rattle. I am so startled I have difficulty understanding him initially, until I realize he is asking me if I have enough coins for my wash as sometimes, he says, the change machines run out.

I'm not surprised; people keep pulling up in cars, rushing inside, and feeding in $5 notes for parking meter money. At the same time I assume this is a scam against the unwary. Assured I have plenty, he folds up a newspaper that a previous customer has left open on the table, tucks it into his pocket as though his attention is really elsewhere, and departs.

The gap between us denizens of the laundrette and other social groups is nowhere better expressed than on the way home with my bags of clean laundry. On the pedestrian crossing I pass a designer-clad couple. As the three of us draw level, I hear the woman saying forcefully to the man beside her, 'I *read* it in an *etiquette* book! You *can't* have a Bloody Mary *before* 3pm.'

When I reach the pavement on the other side I pass the local bag lady. Observing me, and my bulging plastic bags, with a wry little smile she nods to me as to one of her own. I really must get a new coat.

Back on Voyager, David has returned. We still have no quotation, he tells me, but while we have both been occupied elsewhere Joe has started work on *Voyager* without waiting for our insurance company's permission – which it won't give without a quote. Joe has promised one tomorrow.

Something we have been intending to do before our Atlantic crossing is get our life-raft serviced and while we are here it seems an ideal opportunity. We got it new before setting off, just over three years ago, although when you buy one you can't know how long it has been sitting in a storeroom.

The inside of your life-raft is something you don't normally see until you have to use it. You buy it sealed, strap it down on your deck and forget about it because nobody believes they will ever need it anyway. And after some Swedish neighbours we had in the Canaries told us, over several glasses of wine, about the course they had attended on the art of getting into a raft from their boat, we decided we didn't even want to *think* about it. They had found it difficult enough under controlled conditions, they said. The thought of having to do it in the dark (bad things usually happen at night), on a storm-tossed sea, horrified them.

Like lots of other subscribers to yachting magazines we have, of course, read stories of panic-stricken yachtsmen launching their raft - without first tying it to their stricken boat while they get into it - and watching the wretched thing hurtle away in a storm-force wind. Also those who *have* remembered to tie their life raft to their yacht while they struggle into it, only to discover once inside that they have forgotten to bring a knife with them to cut the rope tethering them to their sinking vessel.

However, since we intend to embark on some serious offshore sailing soon, it is time to do something about ours. Accordingly we contact a company that services our type of life-raft and are given an appointment to take it in for an overhaul.

The man who is going to service the raft for us begins by asking if we have ever seen inside ours and if not, would we like him to take us through how it works and what is inside. We are delighted with his offer, and the tips he gives us should we ever need to use it.

His inventory reveals that the flares are out of date, the drinking water has evaporated, the torch batteries are flat and the manual pump - which would be needed to re-inflate the raft should it begin to sink - doesn't work. He replaces what is necessary and reseals the unit. We are impressed with both the raft and especially the manner in which it has been dealt with and demonstrated. And much more confident about ever having to use it.

Although acknowledged locally as a first-rate and highly-respected practical engineer, Joe will do anything to avoid paperwork - be it looming tax returns or a quotation for an insurance claim. Nor will he employ anybody to do it for him.

Shortly after arriving here we had been offered the use of a small flat across town, but had quickly realized that getting our work done before the winter sets in requires us to remain on board. Two days on from the last 'Tomorrow' there is still no quotation.

With the days passing David begins following Joe about until he is able to manoeuvre him in front of his desk. Once there it takes hours, given Joe's antipathy and frequent interruptions. One of them is an attractive 30-something blonde antique dealer with a hideous broken lamp. Joe joyfully abandons his computer to repair it. The two of them have never met before but her ex-husband has suggested she come and see him. David lends a hand with the lamp repair to get her on her way and Joe's mind back on the quote.

Today is Friday and we had hoped to fax the quote before noon so that our insurance company would receive it before close of business for the weekend and we could hopefully get the go-ahead to begin the work on Monday. But we run out of time and David telephones the claims department to say he will send all the details over the weekend. They say they will give it their speediest attention.

Saturday morning dawns and the yard is deserted so David changes *Voyager*'s engine oil and filters. Late morning there are signs of life and David continues pursuing the all-important quotation. Joe eventually finishes hand-writing the final details and David types the quotation onto Joe's computer. He prints it out and by the end of the afternoon has managed to get Joe to fax it to our insurance company along with our own letter.

It's a small victory and we feel like celebrating but there is not much to hand. We've been on the wagon for weeks and Saturday evening television is devoted to sports. Tonight a baseball World Series in which only North America participates, and a lengthy National Football League discussion about Cornelius Wortham's Flop.

Nevertheless, the range and quality of foods here is sumptuous so during our stay we eat well and, television being what it is, we read a lot: the final chapters of Dickens's *Little Dorrit* are followed by Evelyn Waugh's *Scoop* and a Patricia Cornwell crime novel.

In terms of expertise *Voyager* may be in the best place for her but what's good for a boat in special circumstances is not always best for her crew. I'm talking here about bathroom facilities. The one at the boatyard is like the aftermath of a hurricane and also has a large, resentful-looking cicada residing in the sink. *Voyager* has a holding tank, but not large enough for the length of our stay and with no way to empty it up on the hard.

Given the cicada in the wash basin, my real concern about the boatyard's bathroom lies in what might reside unseen among the fallen tiles and crumbling concrete. Accordingly, today I forgo the imperative learned in childhood - to always go before you leave home - and decide to hang on until I get to the big supermarket up in the town with its excellent restroom.

Instead of numbers above the bus windscreens as in most places, the excellent free transport service in Annapolis uses colours. And getting where you want to go is simplicity itself since each route on the bus map is shown in a particular colour. All you have to do is look for an approaching bus saying, 'Red', 'Green', 'Brown' or whatever, on the front. The colour may be qualified with a letter of the alphabet. I've done this before. I know the route. To get to the supermarket I need a Brown A.

I board one. However, to the initiated - which as well as the driver appears to include all the passengers except me - it is really a Brown C (the Brown B now being the Brown CC) although for some reason we follow the Yellow Route for a time, visiting neighbourhoods I've never seen before. Then it takes a dive down the Orange Route and possibly a bit of the Red. All the passengers on the bus seem perfectly relaxed about it, except me, until the person in the neighbouring seat kindly explains it to me.

Unfortunately it means that I keep seeing the supermarket – and its increasingly desirable restroom - hoving into view, only for it to hove out again immediately as the driver surges off down another byway. In the end I rush in through its doors barely in time.

The trees around the boatyard are stunning in their late autumn colours. There are three in O'Leary's car park that are a deep salmon pink in sunlight and simply magical in the evening with a streetlight inside them.

Naturally, with all these trees there are so many leaves covering the sidewalks that the local authority doesn't bother employing people to sweep them up. It sends round a vehicle shaped like a fuel tanker with a 'City of Annapolis Leaf Recycling' sign on the back and its driver vacuums them up.

High winds during the night bring in the forecast cold front on Monday morning, although thankfully not the promised freeze. David telephones the insurance company at 6am Eastern Standard Time. The quote is agreed and David hurries off the boat to tell Joe as soon as he spots his motorcycle and discuss how soon work can start. Joe goes off ostensibly to check their faxed confirmation but as it turns out has disappeared somewhere else entirely. It is like shovelling feathers. David, without a jacket, and having stood about expecting him back any minute, returns to *Voyager* with his lips turning blue.

We should have liked to have anti-fouled *Voyager* and polished her topsides here, but Joe allows only his own men to work on clients' boats. The rate per hour is only $10 less than the most expensive mechanic we ever employed. We watch the guy who will do the work, known to his colleagues as Mack the Mouth, talk about himself to a young woman for two hours without a break while he washes a nearby boat, which is not encouraging. Especially when the boat's owner, arriving on Sunday, apparently sees no difference in its condition and sets about washing it himself.

On the other hand, if we don't get the work done here, we shall only have to pay for another haul-out later on. It will therefore end up cheaper – and quicker - to have her anti-fouled here and then do her topsides ourselves when she is back in the water and somewhere warmer.

With no chance of work being started today, David goes off to try once more to get a refund from AT&T for money we paid them last year for a telephone service in The Bahamas that they subsequently accepted they were in no position to supply. Unfortunately he only succeeds in being given the address of their head office. But he comes home with a copy of James L Stokesbury's *A Short History of World War II*. A Professor of History at a Canadian university, he has the remarkable ability to write a coherent history of complex events in lucid prose in a single volume. We have already read his books on World War I and the American Civil War and have been looking out for this one for ages.

David also returns with glue for the teak strip on the foredeck and a new ink cartridge for our computer printer. He has also contacted the manufacturer of the new stove we bought in Canada about a burner which has stopped working and we are being sent a replacement part.

Work finally begins on *Voyager*. The rudder comes off and the shaft is straightened in a hydraulic press.

Joe is of Sicilian descent with a weathered face, a pronounced limp and a problem with his left side which is why he uses the motor bike. His voice has a rasp like Marlon Brando's, perhaps from his habit of breaking the filter tips off his cigarettes before lighting them. He likes to talk while he works and David is more than willing to listen if it keeps him focused on our boat.

He sang and played in pop groups when he was a youngster, he tells him, even missing out on eighth grade to cut records. As to the Sicilian background, he says, his uncle drove around in a Cadillac although no-one knew what he did for a living. His father was a musician in bands until a three-year illness and a lost lung left him unable to play. His brother raced hydrofoils and two of his old boats are hanging up in the workshop.

Joe says he is a cousin of a famous Hollywood actor and that many years ago he and some of the family travelled for several days to visit him in California. They knocked on his front door but the butler wouldn't let them in until he had consulted his employer. After a wait, the butler returned with a handful of dollar bills and told them to go away.

He is also an equipment freak with a most wonderful range of tools that he is constantly adding to. On one occasion David is invited into the inner sanctum where they are kept; many still in their original packaging. He also appears to work seven days a week, often late into the night.

Meanwhile, I compose a letter to the CEO at AT&T's Head Office – everybody else having ignored us - about the fact that nearly a year after being relieved of an $800 deposit - for a service they do not provide - we are still awaiting the promised refund.

David prowls around constantly, trying to keep everyone's mind on the job. The skeg goes back on. The following day, Mack the Mouth disappears. Woman trouble, apparently. Eddie, the quiet one, begins rubbing down Voyager's old anti-fouling instead. He ends the day blue from head to foot.

Progress is slow but in the coming days Joe fills the skeg with a compound he announces will make it even stronger than it was before. And a man called Mike arrives and works into the night on the gear box.

There is a problem with the rubber gaskets which seal the space between the hull and the propeller housing. The ones the manufacturer has supplied don't fit, so between them Joe and David cut new ones out of a sheet of plastic on Joe's band saw. While David makes a couple of spares for future emergencies, Joe completes the antifouling. They finish around 10pm Friday.

Monday everything stops. Mack has gone missing again. Car trouble, it is said. Another woman, it is muttered. But the replacement part for our stove arrives. And a cheque from AT&T for $830.34 proving the famous maxim: forget the monkey; go straight to the organ-grinder.

On Wednesday work starts on the rudder and by nightfall it is back in place and looking good. On board we hear Joe putting the final coat of paint on it around 10.30pm.

Next day there is some flutter and urgency about pressure of time regarding another boat, and talk of its imminent lift-out. But there is plenty of room in the yard so we are surprised to return from a trip into town to find Voyager back in the water.

The challenge now is to get Joe to produce invoices because we cannot leave until the insurance company pays for the repair work, and that will not happen until it receives an invoice.

Our hope is to get an invoice from Joe and fax it by mid-day Friday Eastern Standard Time at the latest so the Insurance Company receives it before everybody goes home for the weekend, the UK being five hours ahead of us. Of course it doesn't happen.

On Saturday David corners Joe in his office and finally types up the two invoices himself from Joe's dictation and notes. He faxes the one to the insurance company and settles the other himself.

It rains in the night, the wind gets up and it is *very* cold. The unseasonably good weather has finally broken, making us more aware than ever that we should be a long way south by now.

On Monday David rings the insurance company. On Tuesday it confirms the money has been sent to Joe express. We have not made a marine insurance claim before but have heard horror stories from people who have. Given our situation, the process could have become an utter nightmare. Instead, Pantaenius have been prompt, courteous, helpful and understanding throughout.

Ready to go first thing next morning, David sets off to get Joe to move the boat blocking our exit from his yard. He is nowhere to be found. We eventually get away mid-morning - with Joe thanking David for helping him with the paperwork.

Spa Creek Bridge opens on request. As we pass through, the tender leans over the rail, grins down at us and calls, 'Happy Turkey Day!' - a popular name for today's national holiday through which he is having to work. For, appropriately enough, this day on which we have been released from our incarceration is Thanksgiving. We have been in the boatyard for three weeks.

28
Thanksgiving

Thanksgiving can be something of a mystery to non-Americans, who are not always sure what is being celebrated. Even Americans can be a bit vague sometimes. In fact, two important moments in US history come together in this event.

One of them occurred in the middle of the American Civil War when, in 1863, Abraham Lincoln proclaimed that a national day of Thanksgiving would be held on November 26 that year for all those blessings Americans still received from the Almighty despite the present carnage. Its purpose was to direct people's minds forward, toward a future unity and national healing. The fourth Thursday of November subsequently became fixed as an annual federal holiday.

For many Americans, however, the focus of the day is what is commonly called the First Thanksgiving, celebrated in 1621 by the Pilgrims off the *Mayflower* at their Plymouth Colony which they founded just across Massachusetts Bay from our recent Provincetown anchorage.

The link between these two apparently diverse events is survival. That early 17th century harvest feast at Plymouth, Massachusetts is a central part of America's creation myth. It represents the founding of a nation, and without that harvest – made possible by the generosity of Native Americans in showing the English settlers how to propagate alien crops in unfamiliar soil – they would not have survived.

What is particularly significant, however, is that prior to first going ashore in 1620 a group of settlers signed the Mayflower Compact – essentially a social contract but also the first system of government to be written and enacted in what would become the United States of America.

Two hundred and forty years later America was tearing itself to pieces in a civil war, northern States versus southern, while its President strove to preserve the Union and enable this new nation to survive. It was a large land mass with a small population and divided it would become two weak countries constantly working to undermine each other while leaving both of them prey to attack from outside forces.

If Abraham Lincoln's vision of uniting the States of America was to prevail, there had to be unity between the two halves. Hence his Thanksgiving proclamation, his invitation to reflect on the bounty and the greater good that this extraordinary country had to offer but which was in danger of being thrown away because of differences which *could* be reconciled. And that sooner, or later, they would have to learn to live together. Of all the differences between North and South which were undermining unity and nationhood the most intractable was slavery.

Unity is what the monument in Washington, which we visited on our last trip up the east coast, is all about. Lincoln's triumph was not only to preserve the Union and consolidate a nation but, in the process, outlaw slavery. And his massive marble figure, rising 30 feet from the floor, requires the visitor to look up to him physically, as well as in the sense of recognising his monumental achievement.

Thanksgiving nowadays is a gathering together of family and friends for a traditional turkey meal based on some of the foods – such as the pumpkin in the Thanksgiving pie - which were served at that first harvest celebration in 1621. It may also include a fir tree, festive wreathes, greetings cards and presents under the general banner of The Holiday Season. Because only a month later they do it all again – for Christmas. Nice if you're one of those seated once more at the big roast turkey dinner and opening presents but for working moms ... kinda tiring.

29
The ICW

Virginia

Once out of the Severn River we have a good wind behind us and put up the genoa, doing 8 knots and delighted to be out on the water again. There are almost no other leisure craft now. The snowbirds – retirees and others heading for warmer climes each winter - are two months ahead of us and most local sailors have already had their boats hauled out.

We need to get south quickly, not just because of the weather but there is a date on our visas which must be respected. To this end we sail for as long as possible each day. With the hours of daylight growing less, we set off as soon as there is light enough to see by, and continue until dusk. Accordingly we sidle into the first anchorage of our newfound freedom - Little Choptank River - just as the sun sets.

Next morning we see pelicans for the first time in months. Also A10 ground attack planes which rise from the western shore beyond our stern every half an hour or so. Things might have seemed back to normal in the heart of Annapolis but, out here on the margins, the world's most powerful nation is flexing its muscles.

Our immediate objective is the mouth of the Intracoastal Waterway and after a couple of days' sailing down Chesapeake Bay we are within reach of it. Once inside, we shall head for the familiar anchorage at Hospital Point but, before we can approach it, we first have to pass through the naval dockyards of Norfolk, Virginia.

We are late arriving, sailing the last hour and a half in the dark, and can only make out the shore by the lights that residents have put up around their homes for Thanksgiving and will now leave up until after Christmas. It looks very festive but unfortunately makes it impossible to spot vital navigation lights against such a background and one good reason why leisure boats are not supposed to sail the ICW at night. Roof lines drip electric icicles, small deer cavort on lawns between giant candy canes and garden trees become red triangles from the hundreds of tiny lights festooning them.

It's been a long day and we are both tired. David, peering through the darkness across a black river for sight of a navigation marker on the starboard bank, says optimistically, 'I think I can see a red triangle.' And I tell him irritably, 'That's another flaming *tree*!'

Fortunately we are the only vessel going south; what few tugs and barges are about are mere voices on the VHF, reporting their movements going north.

There are not nearly as many warships in the docks as we have seen at berth here previously. But there are some Navy RIBs patrolling those that remain. We expect to be challenged, blundering as we are through America's premier naval dockyard in the dark, after the worst terrorist attack in the country's history, but nobody bothers us.

That doesn't mean no-one is watching. Throughout our journey the military is aloft, whether it is low-flying Navy F18s circling above us, or twin-rotor helicopters on manoeuvres and periodically discharging parachutists.

It is thus a concern to us, as a foreign vessel at such a time, to appear to be showing a lack of respect and moral support as regrettably the USA courtesy flag up in our rigging is now in unrecognisable tatters. This is because, since September 11, a Stars & Stripes in any form cannot be bought for love nor money. The US national flag has always flown from government buildings. Now it flies from every house and commercial premises as well. Also car aerials, for which the small marine courtesy pennant that yachtsmen hoist up their masts is the ideal size and shape.

We are now regularly encountering fog. Some mornings we have to delay our departure until the impenetrable greyness lifts sufficiently. But we can't afford to linger. At this time of year the weather can only get worse.

So, increasingly, as the dark grey fog of dawn gives way to the light grey fog of morning we set out. Past shadowy banks and trees. Sometimes with the opposite shore visible, sometimes not. But, after all, we did do an advanced fog course in Maine and Massachusetts recently and with a combination of careful chart work, eyes and ears, a foghorn, the GPS and the radar we make good, safe progress.

In the worst conditions one of us is always on the foredeck while the helmsman keeps one eye on the radar. We also keep close to marker buoys and as we slide by them are grateful that each one is numbered, making it easy to identify our exact position on the chart. We are also using anchorages familiar from previous journeys so that we know what to expect - sometimes, having run out of daylight, with me on the foredeck with a torch and frayed nerves seeking unlit marker buoys.

North Carolina

One afternoon on the Pungo River, with visibility so poor we are following the waterway entirely by radar, two elderly men in a small fishing boat materialize alongside out of dense fog. We slow, assuming that since they are clearly locals they are about to tell us we were heading for some uncharted disaster.

We both lean anxiously towards them. The one at the helm looks suddenly sheepish and asks directions. Disorientated by the fog, although too proud to admit it, he has lost his way home. David looks carefully at the chart and points very precisely towards the harbour requested, which is less than a mile away. The helmsman looks unconvinced, says crossly, 'Are you sure?' and when David says, 'Positive,' shoots off in a different direction entirely.

Sometimes, quite suddenly, after days of cold, damp greyness, conditions will change. One morning in particular we get up to a deep red sun rising into a clear blue sky and a forecast temperature in the 80s. Pelicans dive around our hulls and a dozen dolphins come to investigate us, energetic and interested, swimming between our bows in twos and threes, nature's original synchronized swimmers.

On a beach a man exercises two Labradors. He drifts along in his boat, parallel to the shore, while the dogs race along the sand together. We've seen people exercising their dogs by bicycle – even on one occasion by car - but never by boat before.

Tucked up one Saturday evening in the sheltered little basin at Carolina Beach, watching a video, strange noises send us out on deck to investigate. The anchorage here is bounded by family homes and it seems the little waterside community is putting on a show.

A dozen boats glide past, lit up with fairy lights. First a simple sailboat, its mast, rigging, sail and hull all edged in shimmering light against the darkness. Then, imagination and creativity. Motorboats, trawler yachts and fishing boats transformed into a steam engine, a steamboat, even an early Santa and his reindeer. It is all very jolly, with lots of cheering from the shore, horn blowing and applause. It is also beautifully done, must have taken many hours of work and is even nicer for being so unexpected.

On the Waccamaw River we are woken in the night by the sound of tug boat engines and see two pass by us side by side as one overtakes the other. Then the one overtaking stops a few hundred yards past us and the other continues. We can't work out what is going on and the cold soon drives us back to bed.

Morning arrives cool and clear and we pass one of last night's tugs high and dry. It obviously stopped because it had run aground as it tried to overtake. It leans to starboard now, and the crew looks dejected. A mile or so further on we come across the other tug, also aground. Both crews are in for a long wait. The waterway here is silting up and it will take time for recovery vessels to re-float them.

South Carolina

Although December now, the further down the coast we get the more amenable the weather becomes. Here we may still begin the day in foul weather gear, woolly socks and deck shoes, but by mid-day we are barefoot in shorts and T-shirts.

For our pleasure, pelicans abound. And the welcome warmth means that we can go back to our old cruising habits out in the cockpit – one reading, one steering - currently *Treasure Island* interspersed with Shakespeare's *Sonnets*. There is the odd tug around, and now and then a trawler yacht, but mostly the ICW is abandoned except for the occasional man in combat fatigues and an aluminium dory, fishing or duck hunting.

Early December is clearly the time for parades. After the delights of Carolina Beach's night-time water pageant, Beaufort's day-time parade follows the road along the waterfront, parallel with the anchorage. It is led by a military band followed by political worthies, local services such as Police, National Guard and Water Board, then the Scouts, a dance academy and a local band which is far enough away not to clash with the military one at the front. Bringing up the rear, and as if somehow keeping everyone in line, is the Sheriff's tracker team of bloodhounds. This is the Deep South after all.

It is also a hot afternoon and the no-see-ums are out in force, so there is a deal of swatting and scratching going on aboard *Voyager* until we can locate the insect repellent we haven't needed in months. Unperturbed by our frantic flailing against the invisible foe, a sandpiper stands on the stern seat of our dinghy tapping lightly at its own reflection in our chrome davits. Disheartened by the lack of response it is getting from this 'other' sandpiper, it flutters to the bow seat and tries its luck with the other davit. Failing to get a suitable response there either, it gives something like a sigh and flies away.

Georgia

The ICW in Georgia has a lot of short canals between inlets from the sea. The land is mostly salt marsh, an occasional town and has lots of pelicans. A young one – uniformly brown - floats about, its wings partly raised, as if practising a manoeuvre while bobbing placidly. Pelicans are very placid. An adult with the characteristic white head shares a marker post with a cormorant. The cormorant, a naturally nervy bird, is as always ready to bolt at our approach, feet shuffling, rocking back on its tail. But the imperturbable presence of the pelican is so soothing that in the end the cormorant doesn't bother, merely eyeballing us warily as we pass.

Near the mouth of the Savannah River, a fast little picnic boat overtakes us but, like a true southern gen'leman, slows alongside us so as not to send so much as a ripple of wash. Once clear of us, it roars away.

A Whaler – a type of boat most often used for fishing or water skiing - and called *Law Enforcement*, overtakes us with rather less consideration than the picnic boat. And we laugh at the cheek of its name as we bounce in its wash until a blue light, appearing suddenly, begins to flash and whine. The driver of the picnic boat is ordered to pull over and then set to filling in lengthy forms on a clipboard.

It seems odd somehow that in all the high-speed frenzy of sports boats during the summer, we didn't see one police attempt at speed restriction the entire length of this waterway. Yet now, with barely a handful of leisure boats abroad each day, they are out fining people.

I suggest this might be a great idea for us to add a little revenue to our budget but David says even with the addition of a flashing blue light he didn't think our small aluminium dinghy and its little sewing machine engine would fool anybody into forking out on-the-spot fines.

Anchored for the night, just inside a creek off St Catherine Sound, as we settle into bed three shrimp boats anchor out in the Sound and begin work. We can see them from our cabin, eerily beautiful in the darkness, their deck lights turning their nets and rigging into gossamer and the water, lapping around their hulls, into a quivering pool of silver.

Inevitably, after a clear day or two, we will hit fog again. It will arrive suddenly after a clear morning start, changing our surroundings into something other-worldly. Shrimp boats, with their nets up, loom slowly out of the greyness like dancers holding out their skirts in a ghostly *pavane*. Pelicans, looking even more like tiny pterodactyls than usual, float silently through the gloom.

One day it arrives dense and protracted, but with nowhere to pull off the waterway for miles there is nothing to do but carry on. Gradually, as happens in these conditions, we begin to close up and form a line with other vessels, grateful for someone to follow. Directly in front of us, in the lead, is a tug called *Ariadne*.

Three other leisure boats call up on the VHF asking what's up ahead, and we say we are a sailing catamaran behind a tug and intend to stay here. They decide to do the same, and pretty soon we are a convoy of two yachts, a power boat and a sports fish chugging through the fog behind the tug. Although just to make life interesting a fisherman begins darting about dropping pots with plastic buoys beside the marker posts we are all following. Dropping pots at navigation posts means they can easily be relocated, but simply provides yet another hazard for everybody else using the waterway.

After an hour or so the fog lifts considerably and when *Ariadne* falls in behind another, much slower tug, it is arranged that she will overtake it. The skipper of the slow tug's final comment is, 'You got a string goin'!' So he knows we are all here. But when we begin to overtake him too, he speeds up, then slows again and when we try to call him up to determine his intentions and arrange to overtake, he doesn't respond - unless you count a crew member stepping out of the wheelhouse, glaring at us, spitting into the water and going inside again.

We get past it safely anyway, it is going so slowly. So do the other leisure boats, except the last one. At the crucial moment the tug turns into it and drives it towards the far bank. Tug drivers are notorious for not acknowledging leisure boats when they call up on the VHF, even when the latter are trying to be courteous and safe, but this one's behaviour is unprecedented in our experience.

The fog thickens again.

Law Enforcement roars past, clipboard and penalty clauses at the ready, but is probably the only vessel exceeding the speed restrictions on a day like today.

Meanwhile, we catch up with *Ariadne* and settle behind her again, her stern hatches like two great eyes staring benignly down at us. To paraphrase one of Shakespeare's sonnets (No.116), this tug is the star to our wandering bark whose worth *is* known and even when her driver slows mightily - trying to locate his leading marks after the river widens and the marker posts disappear in the murk - we stick with her.

A little after 2 pm and back in the narrows, *Ariadne* goes aground when a tug and barge coming from the opposite direction force her into the starboard bank. There is an anchorage just up ahead. And though it seems a mite thankless, we all overtake and carry on. It is the only thing to do. The tug captain needs room to shunt his way off the mud bank and our presence is an unnecessary hazard to him and to any other boats approaching from behind us.

Florida

And so we continue down the coast, sometimes in bright winter sunshine but often in fog. We have had fog in every state from Maine to Georgia and surprisingly there is even some at the northern tip of Florida when we arrive. But soon we are into constant clear weather and free to enjoy the scenery.

Our route now takes us down canals and rivers between wooded banks of pine and palm. Large flocks of white pelicans glide over the river, dividing their time between small lagoons. Dozens of ibis, with their long curved beaks, perch in trees with their backs to the sun. Dolphins arc out of the water and slide below again in a single, svelte movement.

We see our first osprey in months. And as if to alert us to the fact that we are back in God's Waiting Room, the turkey vultures begin circling. Floridians, of course, prefer to call it The Sunshine State, and it really is nice and warm here after the damp and chill further north. We have also left the marshland of Georgia behind and now have waterfront homes and gardens to admire, their orange trees heavy with fruit. And, with all the clear skies, the nights are full of stars again.

We are currently on the northern section of the Indian River. This morning, two fishermen in a dory twirl white, circular nets above their heads for a few moments before sending them spinning into the water. Half a dozen dolphins circle them.

There are large colonies of white pelicans, looking so pristine, their beaks and legs the colour of fresh apricots. Where the river is at its most shallow, a white-haired man stands up to his chest in the water harvesting shellfish from the river bed with long-handled grabs.

Someone asked us recently to name our favourite place and we couldn't because there are so many. But this morning as we drift along, somewhere between New Smyrna Beach and Cocoa City, this has to be one of them. A microcosm of the Indian River itself, its banks are lined with feathery pines and secret sandy places favoured by anglers, herons and egrets. The water is as flat as a mirror, there are brown pelicans on the rocks and manatees in little side pools. Even the bridge tender has the bridge open ready for us as we arrive.

Another memorable place for us is Addison Point Bridge. There is nothing especially noteworthy about the landscape here. But this is the site of Cape Canaveral and on the bridge's eastern bank is NASA. We anchored here last year, the first time we came up this waterway, and were treated to a private viewing from our cockpit of a Delta rocket launching a satellite into space. It had been serendipity. We had not known there was to be a launch that evening until a fellow-cruiser had mentioned it.

Today we touch lucky again. And just as unwittingly. We had stopped for fuel, otherwise we should have sailed on past and missed it. But as we approach Addison Point Bridge, two loud bangs attract our attention. And as our eyes are drawn up towards the sound we see the *Endeavour* space shuttle flying just above the horizon on its flight path back into the NASA complex.

Endeavour had been launched twelve days earlier, making the 4.8 million mile trip to deliver a replacement crew and around three tons of supplies to the International Space Station. It is now bringing back those crew members who have completed their tour of duty on the space station as well as the results of experiments conducted in space on behalf of institutions around the world. Some of them are for school science projects, providing inspiration for a new generation of scientists.

Beside us a pelican sits with a full beak resting on the water, pausing briefly before sieving and swallowing its catch. A small gull sits on the pelican's head waiting for any scraps that may escape the process. In the cockpit above them we lunch on our own seafood - with a glass of chilled Chablis. Mondays never used to be like this.

S. F. Travis

Supermarkets had still to be invented when I was small. Locally there was a butcher, a baker, a fishmonger, a grocer, a greengrocer and a haberdasher. For all other domestic needs there was the ironmonger.

Though now mostly transformed into massive gardening and hardware chains, in those days the local ironmonger was an Aladdin's cave to a child. Cramped, poorly lit and aromatic with wax candles, creosote and coconut matting, my visits there were two-fold. My Mother and I deliberated over a new teapot, washing-up bowl or doormat. While Dad and I sorted through various sizes and grades of tap washers, rawlplugs or sandpaper.

Old fashioned, independent hardware shops do still exist throughout Europe and America and I become nostalgic at the mere sight of one. So neither the lack of urgency for a new tin of varnish, nor the threat of imminent rain, will stop me going ashore at Cocoa City to visit S. F. Travis and Company, reputed by aficionados to be the best hardware store on the US east coast. It does not disappoint.

Begun in 1885 as a single store, over time it has gradually taken over neighbouring buildings, although there has been no real attempt to integrate them. You wander out of what must have been the back door of one building into what was once a yard but now has a roof over it, to be confronted by various other buildings going off in different directions. At some of them you end up facing unmarked doors which you think might be reserved for staff, only to find behind them the paint department or timber supplies. The rope section includes old reels of genuine hemp (oh, that evocative smell!); there are arcane tools whose purpose is known to very few; boxes of every possible size of nails, and screws, plastic tubes, small generators, rubber boots, stepladders ... And of course we come out loaded with stuff.

30
North Palm Beach

A few days before Christmas we reach North Palm Beach. David's brother, Tony, has forwarded our Christmas mail there and we collect it from FedEx. We do our food shopping at the big Publix supermarket, but as this is our first Christmas in America we feel it would be incomplete without a Christmas Eve trip to a shopping mall.

Outside the morning temperature is already in the 80s. Inside the mall, artificial snow is floating through the air conditioning. Beneath the snowflakes, on a dais just off the main concourse, you can have your photograph taken in a sleigh with Santa. Two highly-photogenic parents – she with cascading honey blonde hair and celebrity smile, he with boyish good looks – are ready to record a family memory picture for the album.

Unfortunately their three young children will have none of it. The baby, held aloft by its smiling mother, stares resignedly off stage left. The eldest, prevented from escaping by Papa's iron grip, glares belligerently off stage right. While the middle child, round-cheeked and a natural for cuteness, gurns and squints and drags down the corners of his mouth until he resembles a mutant form of Cabbage Patch doll. A crowd begins to gather.

The parents toss their heads more gaily, smile ever more widely, and generally behave like actors in a toothpaste commercial. Meanwhile the photographer and her assistant shake cuddly toys and rattles in a futile bid to get the baby on their side at least. But all three children, as if embarked on a pre-planned act of sabotage, studiously ignore the adults.

Since the happy snap is clearly going to take a while we set off on a relaxed stroll through Macys, Sears, Bloomingdales and The Pottery Barn. The mall is huge and uncrowded, it being too late for most buyers and too early in the day for last-minute panic-shoppers. And we have no shopping list at all to tax our nerves. We are here simply to enjoy the Christmas decorations, the piped carols, the festive mood - and the air conditioning.

Our final visit is to a shop called Things Past featuring a brown leather lounge suite, in an upright shape reminiscent of the 1930s and impossible to sit on comfortably. It appears to have been artificially distressed and bears a monstrous price tag. There is also a fish slice with a sprung handle so when a lever is pressed your fried egg flips over without you having to move your wrist. It occurs to me that food landing this way would probably send hot fat flying everywhere, which might be why it never caught on and became a collector's item instead.

We return home, via the Barnes and Noble book store, clutching a famous biographer's latest tome, which is unavailable in Britain, and settle down to a thoroughly delicious trawl through all the scandalous stuff we would not be allowed to read about at home. What better way to spend a hot Christmas Eve, out in a shady cockpit, along with a glass of chilled wine.

Christmas Day – in stark contrast - is chilly with lots of rain, which is to say not that unlike a British Christmas. Still, it makes cooking the festive roast easier than soaring temperatures. Although its aroma does set a flock of turkey vultures circling overhead. At least we hope it's the poultry that is attracting them and not us.

31
Miami

Given the opportunity, anyone who ever watched Bugs Bunny cartoons as a kid would *have* to visit Miami Beach. Bugs was forever looking for Miami Beach. I'm not surprised he had trouble finding it. Like many people on a first visit, you tend to assume that the beach is the coastal rim of the city.

It is, in fact, a long strip of land separated from the City of Miami by Biscayne Bay which, around here, is two miles wide. The beach is joined to the city by three long causeways, each made up of a system of man-made islands and bridges. We are anchored, somewhere between beach and city, off the one called Venetian Causeway.

Miami Beach, when we get there in the dinghy, is a very long tourist resort with a lot of multi-storey hotels and a very long sandy beach. It is also a suburb which is convenient for shopping and also a dentist who won't even embark on so much as a clean-and-polish without a local anaesthetic and antibiotics.

Miami City is a sprawling metropolis and walking anywhere is not an option. Getting about requires the use of the bus service and automated overhead railway. It is a mixture of typical modern American strip malls and streets lined with traditional shops run mostly by the pre-dominantly Hispanic population.

As we wait for some stable weather by which to set sail again we enjoy several delightful anchorages; meet up with a number of yachtsmen encountered during our travels – including one lovely couple we met in Canada - and see in the New Year on a deliciously warm night with spectacular firework displays going off all around us.

With Miami's afternoons now in the upper-80s we make our visits ashore as early as possible. We also have the opportunity to observe the Miami lifestyle. For instance, if car drivers find a car park full they will simply drive up over the kerb and remain on the sidewalk until a parking space becomes free. Sometimes great lines of them. As a pedestrian you get used to weaving in and out of them, dodging oncoming traffic as you go. Although when we reach the head of one such line of drivers we find a handwritten sign promising, 'The best hand car wash in Miami'.

'Why,' I ask David, 'sit in a queue for hours in a hot car waiting for someone to wash it for you by hand when you could do it yourself in a fraction of the time?'

'So you can visit a gym and work up a sweat?' he says.

This is Miami water frontage, where people are affluent and labour is cheap. You pay someone to mow your lawn, wash your car, walk your dog, shop at the supermarket and do your housework so you can engage a personal trainer and stay fit. We see them exercising before a huge wall mirror as we pass the gym on our way into town.

You can also defy the elements to make a fashion statement. By sprinting through a searing carpark from your vehicle's air-conditioning into thermostatically-controlled stores, you can wear the latest woollens.

On one of the days, our own special focus is the purchase of new batteries for *Voyager*'s domestic power supply. Fortunately, we have a small trolley to wheel them from the marine store to the dinghy.

*Un*fortunately, when timing our trip ashore to coincide with the coolest part of the day, we forgot that it would be low tide. And that we should be lowering two 75lb batteries into a dinghy which by now is a *long* way down.

A fellow-yachtsman's dinghy, tied up behind ours, carries a large printed notice - 'Need Lady for Bahamas' - followed by a phone number. And I'm thinking, 'Before you sign on as crew, Lady, find out about the state of his batteries.'

Once back on board David works up a sweat hauling the old ones out of their confined locker space and heaving the new ones in. We also need to take the old ones back to the store to dispose of them. But this time we make sure we catch high tide because, lifting two 75-pound batteries up onto a dock above your head out of a rocking dinghy, is a lot harder than lowering two down into it.

Our long journey south has made us think about where we spend next summer. When we set out on the cruising life we had decided that it was sensible to do the long hauls - such as an Atlantic crossing to the Caribbean and the USA – sooner rather than later, while our energy and physical strength was at its greatest. And then decide where to go after that.

There are so many attractive options on this side of the Atlantic, including the Pacific and South America. But for us, several things militate against them, including some enormous distances and extreme climates.

So we have made a decision – to head back to Europe. It offers a temperature range to suit all seasons with so many varied countries and coastlines to be explored without the need for long-distance travel or entry restrictions. An enormous pleasure in the past year or so has also been inland waterways. We should very much like to wander through more of them, as well as spend some time in Britain.

Our plan, then, after a second winter in The Bahamas, is to return across the Atlantic via Bermuda and the Azores. But before we leave the USA there is one last place we should like to explore - the Florida Keys.

32
Florida Keys

When we leave our Miami anchorage we continue following the ICW south. On our port side are two Atlantic barrier islands. The most southerly is Key Biscayne, known to many as the home of Richard Nixon.

A mile and a half to the south of it, there is an area known as Stiltsville. The water is very shallow here and in the 1930s people drove piles into the coral reef and put a wooden building on top. Naturally, they had no water or electricity and the only access was by boat. But since no-one owned the seabed they could build a house, or business premises, without buying land or paying property taxes. As well as homes, one was an elite, membership-by-invitation-only club and another a gaming establishment, since at the time gambling was only legal a mile offshore.

Local government passed laws after World War II preventing any more buildings and tried to get rid of the existing ones. They failed, but fires and hurricanes gradually did the job for them until, though once numbering around thirty, only seven now remain.

If you continue on south from Key Biscayne and Stiltsville you pass a string of coral shoals and islets which gradually get bigger until they become the islands of the Florida Keys.

This chain of coral and limestone islands forms a gentle arc in a south-westerly direction around the tip of the Florida peninsula. From Elliott Key at the top, to Key West at the bottom, the chain is around 125 miles long, with Key West just 90 miles from Cuba.

These islands are the visible part of a long reef, with the Atlantic Ocean on one side and Florida Bay on the other. Many are very narrow - some only a quarter of a mile wide - and low-lying. Even their highest point, at Key West, is only 18 feet/5.5m above sea level while others are as little as four feet/1.2m, making them vulnerable to stormy weather.

Elliott Key

Our first stop is at Elliott Key. It is heavily wooded with a rocky shore and, after tying up the dinghy, we follow a nature trail through its woodland. The trees are pine and palm, the climate sub-tropical, and we see frigate birds for the first time since the Caribbean. The roads are unmade and the only habitation a scattering of tents among the trees, where a small group of teenagers are camping.

The one downside is the mosquitoes, but we have visited enough places by now to always carry insect repellent with us. And after the bustle of Miami the tranquillity of an undeveloped island is delightful. The next ones we shall visit will be habited and we have heard much about their delights. After a restful couple of days here, swimming and wandering through maritime forest - containing plants not seen elsewhere in the US - we set off south.

Key Largo

Further down the island chain is Key Largo and the change is dramatic. Key Largo is joined to the Florida mainland by the Overseas Highway, usually referred to as Highway 1, and which connects the major islands all the way down to Key West. Its 133 miles include 42 bridges, one of them seven miles long.

One of the attractive things about islands is that their isolation from a mainland, and from each other, produces individuality and variety. When accessible only by boat, they offer a sense of privacy or escape that can be very seductive to the weary city-dweller or troubled soul.

The downside in terms of daily practicalities is that goods and services carry an increased cost and an element of delay when they have to be transported by sea; although the need to make do and mend has produced many an island population which is both inventive and resourceful, not to mention a unique environment.

Despite being very attractive, relaxed and friendly it is with regret that we find the islands disappointing. Perhaps it is the fault of those old Humphrey Bogart movies, or maybe it is all down to your perspective.

Travel writers eulogize over the drive down Highway 1 for providing a panorama of sun-sparkling sea dotted with small islands and, best of all they point out, are the spectacular, uninterrupted sunsets and sunrises.

For a yachtsman, whether at anchor or on the open sea, sunsets and sunrises usually *are* uninterrupted except when there's a blooming great bridge in the way. And to us they seem omnipresent, looming over the islands and the sea spaces in between. At sea-level, rather than highlighting the beauty of the islands, the bridges seem to have turned them into mere stanchions for themselves; while the highway itself slices the islands in two as traffic rushes across them in straight lines between the bridges.

Its other effect has been to turn the islands into Miami suburbs with all the familiar building styles, roadways and consumer outlets - Publix, Home Depot, K-Mart, and fast food franchises. In short, they are not islands as we have come to love them. They are also quite crowded. Their population, according to the 2000 census is 80,000 which naturally increases greatly with holidaymakers.

However, the development is hugely convenient and makes for a relaxed life-style for residents and visitors alike, in a sub-tropical climate listed as warm and dry in winter, hot and humid in summer. Anchored off Key Largo as we are, one evening we dig out the Humphrey Bogart movie of that name and watch it in situ. In the shopping mall next day, in some sort of *homage* presumably, David sucks his teeth and hitches up his pants with his wrists but happily nobody notices. We later discover that only the title scene was shot here, the rest was filmed in Hollywood.

In sailing terms, the water around the Keys is mostly shallow with only about five inches of tide, while the holding is often poor. And, in a world of changing weather patterns, the traditionally warm, dry winter is surprisingly hot and occasionally very wet – one day alone produces two inches of rain – making for rather high humidity levels as well. It also gets very windy at times, with constant changes of direction making it difficult to find a secure anchorage. For example, in one 24-hour period it goes from SE to S to SW to W to N to NE.

We drag some, although so does everybody else. But torrential rain does act as a very effective power wash on a boat instead of having to heave up buckets of sea water. David's brother telephones. It seems the UK has had storms and flooding for the past week. A friend calls later and says they are in the midst of a flu epidemic. Suddenly a little heat, humidity and a day of rain don't seem much of a hardship.

During our time here we encounter tarpons for the first time. These saltwater game fish are not only prized for their size but also the fight they put up when hooked - leaping dramatically out of the water. They grow up to eight feet long and 350lbs. A bony, inedible fish, they are usually thrown back afterwards. Tarpon-catching tournaments are very popular and the Florida Keys attract a lot of anglers. In fact, one visitors' guide describes fishing as more of a religion here than a sport.

Boot Key Harbor and Marathon

We particularly enjoy Boot Key Harbor in the well-sheltered area between Vaca Key and Boot Key, which has the town of Marathon on its north side. The facilities here are especially generous. For instance, the Marathon Municipal Marina has a huge community room which I take advantage of while David pursues some replacement switches for our control panel, a new propeller for our dinghy's outboard engine and checks our emails at the library.

At the Municipal Marina there are two washers and two dryers in this cavernous building (originally a fish dock, a fellow-yachtsman says) and the rest is effectively a community centre for cruisers, with two enormous TVs - one showing movies (Buried Alive and its sequel Buried Alive II) and another behind a room divider with a news channel on. As a recovering claustrophobic I opt for the latter, although not without a certain curiosity as to how somebody having escaped live burial once would get into the same situation a second time.

The section airing the news programme has a couple watching with a pushchair beside them draped with clothing. I assume that, like me, they are taking advantage of the washing machines. Then I see two little feet in ankle socks sticking out the bottom and wonder if it is the parental equivalent of putting a cloth over the parrot's cage for a bit of peace and quiet.

The huge table in the room, for folding laundry or anything else a cruiser needs to do, is mostly taken up with a cheerful young man cutting a complex cockpit hood out of canvas. There is also a workshop with power tools, a book exchange and *very* comfortable chairs.

Apart from a sheltered anchorage and a friendly town, something else that endears us is the dinghy ride between the two. It takes you down a long line of wooden jetties. Each jetty is fixed on piles and there is a pelican on every pile. There they perch, defying splinters and the rocking from constant wash, as if no more comfortable billet could be found should you search the world over. Dozing. Grooming. Drying their flight feathers. Or simply gazing into the middle distance in that mellow, contented way they have, as if blessed with the wisdom of the ages. Small sentinels at their posts, they observe you benignly. An honour guard to your passing. There can be nothing nicer.

And after the chores are done another dinghy ride, down Sisters Creek, takes you to Sombrero Beach. The birdlife here isn't bothered by humans any more than the pelicans in the harbour.

Busy little sandpipers rush about only feet away as we paddle through the shallows while black skimmers stand about in groups on the water's edge, on very short, red legs. But in flight they are stunningly beautiful, their four-foot wing span, on a body only 18 inches long, giving them a particular grace. The 'skimmer' part of their name comes from the way they forage for food, swooping down to skim the shoreline with the lower half of their beak just below the surface of the water.

The most developed and populated islands are from Key Largo down as far as Marathon with its airport. The islands south of Marathon are much quieter. Until of course you get to Key West, which is the most densely populated of all. But we don't go there as other cruisers have warned us that the holding is extremely poor. And besides – after what has been quite a long period of erratic weather and high winds from the wrong direction - the forecast promises good conditions for crossing the Straits of Florida for a second winter in The Bahamas – only for longer this time.

33
Back To The Bahamas

The passage to the Bimini Islands will take too long to complete in one daylight stretch. So the sensible thing to do is spend the hours of darkness at sea where there is deep water and we are well away from reefs and fishing buoys.

By setting off from Marathon in the afternoon and sailing through the night we can expect to get to Alice Town on North Bimini by late morning the following day. So even if anything untoward should happen, there will still be plenty of daylight left in which to navigate our way in.

We begin our journey by following the curve of the Florida Keys up the Hawk Channel until we get to Alligator Reef. From there we can set a direct course across the Straits of Florida for Alice Town.

However, far from decreasing, as the forecast had predicted, the wind is getting stronger and our progress through the reefs into open water becomes very slow. Beyond the final reef we find still more pots and continue pushing further out into deep water to avoid them until around 7pm by which time it is pitch dark and we just have to hope for the best.

We also begin getting a strange, high-pitched whine from the starboard engine. On inspection there appears to be no reason for it and it disappears when the revs are altered, so David decides it is harmonics and ignores it.

Around 8pm the wind shifts to the east. This had not been forecast either and is not at all good for our crossing. Despite our destination being to the north-east, we are having to aim for a point 30° south of Alice Town to compensate for the strength of the Gulf Stream – that miles-wide current running through the Straits of Florida - which is trying to push us north. This change in wind direction means that we are now sailing close hauled. And because of the wind direction it is now very bouncy and also extremely noisy with the bridge deck slamming into every wave.

Unfortunately it is too late for us to head back to one of the anchorages off the Florida Keys. That would mean groping our way through reefs and fishing buoys after dark. So there is nothing for it but to grit our teeth and continue.

By 10pm the wind has risen to 27 knots, sending wave after wave crashing over the foredeck. *Voyager* keeps burying her bows in the Gulf Stream's largest ones as if intent on becoming the world's first submarine with sails. We put two reefs in the genoa and press on.

It is so turbulent that David has a rare bout of seasickness. As soon as he is actually sick he feels much better. I just wish he hadn't insisted on doing the gentlemanly thing and hanging over the stern to lose his supper because he is in danger of going overboard at any minute. The one consolation is that by around 2am we are making good progress, often reaching 8 knots, which means the journey will be shorter than feared.

Because we are sailing so close to the wind we have kept the engines on at low revs to keep our bow pointing in the right direction. Sailing this close to the wind is not something catamarans are very good at and we are concerned that the Gulf Stream could sweep us straight past Bimini altogether.

At about 5.40am the starboard engine gives a high-pitched scream. David shuts it down and a quick inspection reveals that the alternator is hanging off. It has apparently seized and the pivot pin has come undone.

Gradually the wind begins to lessen. When it settles between 18 and 20 knots we let out the reefs, and with only the one engine still manage to hold our course. During my final watch, around 6am, I am joined by a family of dolphins with at least a dozen of them in sight and more around the bows. I have no idea what species they are. Small and brown, with distinctive beaks and dorsal fins, they are fast and exhilarating. They clear the water effortlessly while four of them repeatedly surf down towards our starboard hull inside rolling waves.

They remain alongside for a quarter of an hour before disappearing forward and I want very much to go and hang over the bow rail so that I can continue watching them. But, with David asleep in an aft cabin, I feel duty-bound not to. We are pitching a lot, and he and I made a pact when we first began sailing that whoever was on watch would never go outside the cockpit while the other was asleep. It would be hard enough to locate someone under averagely turbulent conditions. In the Gulf Stream, with its relentless surge north and without even knowing how long ago I fell overboard, the likelihood of even my body being found is small.

And it isn't just about putting oneself in danger either. In the beginning I asked my sailing instructor, also a professional delivery skipper, what was important in a crew member because I wanted to be a good one. *I want somebody*, he had said, *that I can trust to still be there when I get up. Not doing something stupid and falling overboard while I'm asleep and leaving the boat and me at risk.*

THE BAHAMAS

34
Alice Town, Bimini

We arrive off North Bimini around 8.30am. It is typical Bahamas: transparent water in blues and greens, surf flying off a shoal, and no visible navigational markers anywhere. There *are* some, according to the chart. But even staring relentlessly through binoculars into the morning sun's piercing silver-white glare, I still can't spot them.

We try calling someone, anyone, on the VHF but get no response. We had thought to wait for the inter-island freighter behind us to overtake so that we could follow it in. Unfortunately we have arrived on low tide and its captain, with a far deeper hull than us and not about to risk it, drops his anchor noisily out in deep water.

Finally we spot the flying bridge of a sports fishing boat making its way inside the shoal, very close to shore, and in the latter stages very, *very* slowly – which is *most* unusual for a sports fish. We follow its course as best we can, never at any time entirely sure whether we are in the channel or not. At its lowest, the water is 1.1metres/less than four feet deep.

Our biggest problem, however, is getting into the marina given the loss of our starboard engine. Running on one engine is effective and economical on a straightforward passage. But a twin-engine catamaran is designed to manoeuvre with two. Using only one, the response is slower and less precise. In particular, making a sharp turn to port with only the port engine working is difficult. Especially in a strong wind.

There's no answer on the VHF from Bimini Blue Water Resort on Channel 16 – we discover later they listen only on 68 - but we turn in anyway. A strong wind combined with only one working engine results in a minor crash-landing, but now that typical Bahamian characteristic - cheerful, polite, helpful people – comes into play.

'Which way would you like to face?' one of them asks grabbing ropes.

'This one!' we reply, not about to attempt any change – just grateful to have staggered in. And they haul us onto the dock and tie us up in such a way – using nearby piles - that will prevent the wind from endlessly driving us against it.

When we go to book in, the marina manager hands us customs and immigration forms. We fill in the same questions as last year, about having plague, cholera, yellow fever or smallpox aboard, and about the mortality rates among *Voyager*'s crew and rodent population.

The only difference from last year is that yachtsmen need no longer book into a marina to clear in. However, we are more than happy to be tied up securely in one, given the strength of the wind and the poor holding in the nearby anchorage which is so shallow that most of the boats appear to be aground.

There is no possibility of getting an alternator locally so David spends some time trying to organise for one to be sent from Florida but without success. The carrier companies don't deliver here, and the seaplane company will not carry cargo. Late afternoon we take a walk along the west side of the island, paddling along a very lovely beach of palm trees and pale sand.

Ask a local what there is to do here and the proud rejoinder is, 'Fishing, fishing ... and more fishing.' For although the water around these islands is very shallow, the deep surrounding ocean provides the kind of high-octane pursuit of marlin, tuna and swordfish beloved by deep-sea fishermen and most famously by Ernest Hemingway, inspiring his book title, *Islands of the Stream* – the Gulf Stream.

The waterfront, meanwhile, is lined with anglers. Their constant companions are brown pelicans. Pelicans everywhere - on jetties and pilings or bobbing patiently on the water - waiting for fish entrails to be tossed to them as the fishermen gut their catch.

Opposite the marina is The Compleat Angler, a three-storey, wooden hotel with balconies around it and a very attractive garden. It was built in 1935, from the planks of old rumrunners left behind when Prohibition ended and was one of the first fishing clubs in The Bahamas.

For the first two years of its existence it was also home to Ernest Hemingway. Visitors can rent his old room. Each morning, it is said, he would swim, breakfast, retire to this room to write a few pages of *To Have and Have Not* and then go deep-sea fishing for the rest of the day.

We drink Kalik - a local beer which is very good - in the hotel's bar and vibrate to the very loud music coming from the room next door. The room has a vast sound system in it but no party people at this time of day. Like the Caribbean's buses, in Bahamian bars the choice of music, and its decibel level, is adjusted to the taste of the youthful male staff rather than the age of their clientele or how much they would simply like to be able to hear themselves think.

We haven't heard anything quite this loud since our last trip on a Caribbean bus. Interestingly, there was an item on World Service the other day about curbing the volume on these buses. During our time there we found that the people aboard, mostly middle-aged and elderly women, didn't seem to mind. Although they might simply have had impaired hearing after so many years as passengers.

The bar is all dark varnished wood – walls, floor, ceiling and furniture – the walls covered in pictures: framed photographs of Hemingway and other deep-sea fishermen posing with their huge catches hoisted up by their tails. Also framed drawings from *The Old Man and the Sea,* the book which won Hemingway both the Pulitzer Prize for Fiction and the Nobel Prize for Literature and made him a celebrity. The hotel has quite a collection of memorabilia, including signed copies of his work.

The barman gives David a very useful travel guide to The Bahamas. 'Here you go, Buddy,' he says cheerfully, sliding it triumphantly across the bar to him after a gallant fight to breach its almost impenetrable polythene wrapping.

We decide against staying for a second beer as we're both getting a headache. Outside an elderly American guest about to enter asks how we are. 'Fine,' we say, 'how are you?'

'Fine,' he says in a tense sort of way, 'I'm on holiday.'

His female companion, equally elderly and a little frail, recoils in the doorway as if from a blow, shudders, ducks her head slightly then strides purposefully into the music.

The only way to get a replacement alternator is to have one shipped from America to either Nassau or Freeport and then go and collect it. In the meantime, David decides to take the one from the port engine and put it on the starboard. This will at least allow us to run the starboard engine which is the one that keeps our refrigerator working. If you are able to use only one engine, it might as well be the most useful one.

As he starts to remove the port alternator he feels unsure how one set of wires should be disconnected. So he decides it would be better to experiment on the faulty unit first and when he does the wires come off easily. He continues to remove the unit and in the process discovers that it has not seized at all. It is while he is re-assembling it that he discovers the cause of the problem.

In order to fit the refrigerator compressor to the engine, the engineer had made up a non-standard bracket. The slot on the bracket which holds the alternator in place is too wide for the screw and if the tension on the screw eases, there is just enough movement for the fan part of the alternator to rub against the bracket. This had been the cause of the high-pitched whine. David's recital reminds me of nothing so much as the childhood rhyme, *Because of a nail, a horse was lost.*

As a separate problem the pivot pin, which puts tension on the fan belt, had come undone – probably due to the vibration - and the alternator fan had then jammed against the bracket. The solution to the problem is to buy a lock washer for the pivot pin for a few cents at the nearest chandlery and keep an eye on the bracket in future.

It is a great relief on all counts. Firstly, we do not need to go to the considerable expense of a new alternator and air-freight. And secondly we shall now have both engines with which to cross the Great Bahama Bank to Nassau instead of only one.

Bimini consists of three little coral islands and some islets. Even its major one, where we currently are, is only seven miles long by 700 feet/213m wide. But its proximity to the Florida coast – just fifty miles away - caused it to become a centre for the illegal rum-running trade after the United States instituted laws prohibiting strong drink in 1920.

One of the Americans using the islands to ship Prohibition-busting alcohol to the US mainland was William S. McCoy, believed to have been the inspiration for the phrase 'the real McCoy' because, although illegal, his product was at least the genuine article, unlike much of the hooch being distilled at the time. Some of the stuff people were drinking contained ingredients more commonly found in antifreeze or ancient Egyptian embalming practices, and which were resulting in blindness, madness and even death.

Nowadays Bimini's capital, Alice Town, is a tranquil village of wooden houses with a few shops, bars and market stalls along a modest little main street called The King's Highway. There is also a white wooden church and a small cemetery with its back to the sea and its gravestones set into the sand.

The people here are very sociable and more than happy to engage with visitors. One of our morning walks finds us overlooking the entrance we navigated only a few days ago, and some local people stop their electric golf cart alongside to have a chat.

The golf cart is the preferred form of transport for most people on the island's narrow roads. They come in several models: the four-seater, which is family-friendly and has a shady hard top; the two-seater sporty, which isn't and doesn't; and a stripped-down version without any seats at all.

As we talk a large yacht starts heading in, rolling and plunging very close to shore. David and I watch in horror, but the boat carries on safely and the people with us say that it is a local boat with a helmsman well used to the conditions and knowing exactly where the channel is. We mention our own inability to spot the range markers intended to lead people in. The driver of the golf cart, a yachtsman himself, tells us where to locate them but admits they *are* invisible in the early morning light.

In the afternoon a Canadian couple stop by to introduce themselves. They are from a boat in the anchorage and the only one not currently aground. This explains the solitary boat facing a different direction to all the others. It is a 1960s wooden boat with regular engine trouble but that doesn't seem to restrict them much. They tell us of a small island off Haiti they visited, which was desperately poor but one villager was beginning a library for a populace eager to read. At the time the library was a shelf with seven books on it until they had asked schools back home for contributions. The response has been 120 boxes.

Other fellow-travellers include an American couple and their cat on *Happy Days*. The Bahamas is not what they had anticipated. It is neither as easy nor as convenient as the Florida Keys or the US mainland. And an assortment of things have gone wrong, the latest of which is that they have picked up some dirty fuel.

Meanwhile their cat, not a natural sailor at the best if times, is so stressed out by the whole experience that it can only be allowed free rein at anchor. It has to be restrained when they are dockside to prevent it going AWOL, and afloat is permanently stoned on catnip.

The entry into Alice Town had proved the last straw for all three of them and the couple is seriously considering quitting the cruising life. We offer moral support and some empty containers into which they can drain their contaminated diesel. They can then refuel at the marina.

A Norther arrives in the night – heavy rain followed by high winds – with David up on deck several times checking mooring lines. But it is nice to be securely tied to something solid in these conditions. And after consulting the forecast we decide to remain where we are. It rains on and off all day, very heavily at times, with strong winds throughout the night.

We wake to what seems a calmer day. In fact the wind has simply shifted to the north-west and the trees and marina buildings are sheltering us from its 25 knots. On a walk to the western side of the island the wind nearly lifts us off our feet. Waves crash onto the beach and the salt spray from them reaches us even up on the road. We are more than happy not to be out at sea in this.

In the distance we can see the inter-island freighter out at anchor again, waiting for a chance to come in, and rolling quite violently. On the rocks near the southern end of the island, where you approach the entrance to Alice Town, lies the beached and rusting wreck of one of the freighter's predecessors, *The Gallant Lady of Belize City*. With that as a constant reminder you can see why the captain of the current one decides to stay put and not risk the passage into harbour until conditions improve. It is another noisy night, with *Voyager* straining at her mooring ropes, although caused more by the surge from the sea than the wind now.

Finally, things seem quiet enough for us to set out on the next stage of our journey. We untangle the mass of mooring ropes which we had put out to various pilings as protection from winds from different directions. And though our leaving is more graceful than our arrival, the long winding channel out to sea, between the reef and the shore, is chaotic thanks to the high winds of the previous days.

There is a point where the depth of water is at its shallowest and the water rushing off the reef at its most violent. A big roller breasts the reef, hits our starboard quarter and pushes us onto one hull. The depth gauge, when we settle again, shows 3.5 feet/1.1m. *Voyager* grounds at two feet three inches (0.7m). And I wonder what the jolt would be like should a wave lift Voyager's eleven tons and drop it onto the unrelenting sand. Better than rock perhaps, but that begins looming up at us as well, as our next lurch drives us toward the shore.

I look back and see *Happy Days* behind us, and being hit as we were in the shallowest place by the strongest wave. The yacht heels to port alarmingly, its starboard hull and part of the keel clearly visible. I wonder how the ship's cat is coping. And hope the catnip is working.

35
Great Bahama Bank

We are not planning to go far today, just 14 miles and then anchor off a tiny uninhabited scrap called Gun Cay. We arrive about 11am. The holding isn't brilliant and on our first attempt we drag a bit. Nor is there any real shelter here either. But the forecast is north-east and only ten knots so there shouldn't be a problem, although being so exposed it is a bit bouncy. However, timing is the important thing now and these few miles will shorten the distance enough for us to get across the Great Bahama Bank in daylight.

Tomorrow also appears to be the only good weather window in what threatens to be a continuing pattern of turbulence. Another cold front is expected in two days' time, with high winds and rough seas, so we need to be tucked up somewhere secure by then.

For now, however, we enjoy a delightful afternoon on deck. Perfect temperature, no insects, a light breeze and the awning up. I love days like this. At sunset we sit in splendour, under a glowing red mackerel sky.

We want to make the earliest start possible and set off next morning with just enough light to see by. An apricot-coloured sun begins rising half an hour later. There is little wind, most of the time just a gentle breeze.

Last year, en route for the Berry Islands, we had travelled around the top of this enormous, vaguely U-shaped bank. On that occasion we had sought the deep water, off the northern top of it, for a safe night passage. This time we not only relish the experience of sailing across the Bank itself but, given the approaching bad weather, it makes for a shorter journey. Just 61 miles, whereas going around the northern edge would be twice as long.

The Great Bahama Bank bears the geological name of 'a carbonate platform' - a build-up of sediment that includes limestone, coral, the tiny skeletons of long-extinct marine creatures, microbes, fossils and seashells. But it still wouldn't have happened without the right conditions including temperature, turbulence, light and the salt density of the water. It may have begun forming sixty-six million years ago or perhaps even earlier, during the Jurassic period when dinosaurs walked the earth. It is part of the seabed and the islands we visit merely its surface projections.

It is a green and blue world out here today: the sea jade green, the sky powder blue. Shading us from the sun's brightness we have one of our side awnings down, turning the cockpit into a cool blue grotto.

One of us is at the helm at all times, keeping a careful watch on the depth gauge, while the other one settles among the cockpit cushions and reads aloud - *Claudius the God*, Robert Graves' sequel to *I Claudius* – in between serving regular cold drinks, snacks, meals and cups of coffee.

The need for caution during this day-long journey is because there is often as little as 18 inches, or less than half a metre, of water under our keel. It is a strange experience. There you are the whole day, miles from anywhere, out of sight of land in any direction, yet in places the water is so shallow you could get out and walk. Your boat would also be aground, of course, so despite what the chart might say, you need to keep a constant eye on the depth gauge.

We also need to complete the journey in daylight so that, when we get to the navigation markers that will lead us safely off the Bank and into deep water, we shall be able to see them. This is no small matter given that the water at the edge of the Bank is only a foot deep in places (0.3m) and it would be easy to run aground within sight of the deep water to which you are heading. Our chart says that the navigation markers' lights are unreliable, which is why sailing after dark is not an option.

By mid-day, with the temperature in the upper 70s, there is a kind of shimmer over our world. The sea is quite transparent, with grass, little shrub-like plants, starfish and large sea slugs visible on the bottom. When a breath of wind ruffles the water, its shadow on the seabed turns the water into patterned green glass. We do not see another vessel all day.

Sunset, when it arrives in this vast emptiness, seems to be putting on a show just for us. It is stunning. Although even more so than we at first realize. There is a phenomenon - sometimes visible in clear, stable air - called the Green Flash. It occurs just as the sun is first sighted above the horizon, or just as it disappears below it, and lasts only seconds. We have heard of it a few times. Long-time cruisers sometimes mention it but we have never seen it. This evening we do. We aren't even looking for it. Just admiring the sunset.

It happens, just they describe it, a bright spot on the top of the sun's rim that flashes luminous green at the very moment the sun disappears. As a special bonus the moon opposite, already well-risen, has green streaks on its upper edge.

36
Frazers Hog Cay

Happily we reach deep water just before it gets dark, arriving at the westernmost end of Frazers Hog Cay two hours later in moonlight so bright we can watch our anchor settling 10 feet/3 m below. It is so clear we can see the individual links in our chain, lying among the sea grass and rocks. The seabed actually glows in the moonlight. We have never seen anything like it before. The water is so still and so clear that it disappears from sight, as if *Voyager* is floating in air and only prevented from drifting away by the chain attached to her bow at one end, and to the anchor dug into the luminous sand at the other. We hope it will be as still in the morning so that we can take a photograph of *Voyager* appearing airborne. It is not to be. By morning the wind has risen and the water is choppy.

With the weather due to deteriorate, and this anchorage's holding described in the cruising guide as 'fickle', we set off for the eastern end of the island and Berry Island Club Marina. It is famed for having very secure mooring buoys equal to the most difficult conditions.

We tie up to one of them and go ashore mid-afternoon, walk the road around the north-east point and along a very lovely beach. During the walk we investigate a long-abandoned house – its ruins beautified by hibiscus and other luxuriant flowering shrubs running wild.

It isn't really something you should do, as we discover when we enter what was once its large workshop. In among the rubble left by some distant hurricane is a sunken rainwater storage tank with a broken cover. And although I manage not to fall into it I do nearly have a heart attack when I look down into the black hole and see a white face staring back at me. Mine, reflected in the water.

We stop off at the attractive little clubhouse with its small bar and pretty dining room, have a beer with the marina's owner and pay the rental on our buoy. We mention the coming bad weather and he assures us the buoy is quite secure. He and his brother, who run the Berry Island Club along with his brother's wife, bought some very large old generators which they lowered onto the seabed to anchor the buoys, so we have something like 50 tons of metal holding us in place. The brother and his wife have taken their trawler yacht to Nassau to buy supplies. Their habit is to sail there one day, shop the next and return on the third. They are due back tomorrow, weather permitting.

Observing the darkening sky we resist the temptation to remain for a second beer and set off back for *Voyager*. We barely have time to get on board before the rain starts.

Although we shall be kept on board for the next five days - the sea state being too rough for the dinghy - the only things we are deprived of is the beach and a chat with the owner in the bar. Apart from that we have everything we need: plenty to eat and drink; books, chess, Scrabble and backgammon; SSB radio to stay in touch with the outside world and since our wind generator is keeping our batteries well topped up we are able to watch videos each evening. In fact, David notes that our 12-volt batteries are still registering 13.8 volts - the maximum charge – even after we'd watched a two-and-a-half hour movie.

On the evening of our fourth day here, we notice a commercial vessel anchored in deep water to the south of us. With a lull in the weather next morning, we watch it thread its way through the shoals and anchor just off a beach-side house. It turns out to be a small tanker carrying diesel fuel.

In all but the largest islands everyone has a generator because on the small ones there are no services at all, and electricity is needed even to pump water up from a well. The only difference between this delivery and that of a supply of heating oil arriving at a house in rural Britain is that the tanker is 150 feet long and has been hanging about for many hours offshore.

Once near the house, the crew lowers a large dinghy and tows the delivery hose ashore for connection to the house's storage tank. Half an hour later, the process is reversed - the hose floating behind the dinghy like a huge black sea snake - and the tanker sets off back through the shoals and out to sea to its next customer.

Later in the morning, while a dinghy ride is still tenable, we go ashore to pay our dues on our mooring and stretch our legs. The man at the marina is still waiting for his brother and sister-in-law to return. With a well-loaded trawler yacht they have been wary of the current conditions and remained at Nassau until the worst is over. If they do not arrive soon, however, this could easily become the pub with no beer. Food supplies are also running low.

The Club's dog, Jenny, decides to join us on our walk. She obviously has a Dalmatian lurking somewhere in her family history. A feisty breed, they were used to protect Britain's horse-drawn carriages and coaches in the days before the railways.

In the late afternoon the wind gets up to 30 knots again and the Club's yacht has still not arrived. With more bad weather predicted it will be at least two days more before the bar and restaurant get relief.

The latest cold front arrives next day and hits hard. We wake to a grim morning and an insight into what life living on a small, exposed island is really like. Where your fuel arriving depends upon the sea state, a hurricane may knock your house down, and a trip to the supermarket can take nine days and counting.

As to the food shortage at the marina we wonder if Jenny and her man have reached the stage of eyeing each other up yet. If they do, my money is on Jenny. She has the advantage of speed. And there are those Dalmation genes lurking somewhere.

David makes bread in the afternoon and we eat it hot from the oven. In the evening a contaminated tape mucks up the VCR. Unfortunately, the chemical needed to clean its heads gives off such a toxic vapour that you need to use it out in the cockpit, or risk expiring in your sleep. With the rain travelling horizontally at 30 knots out there we read instead.

The morning forecast for this area says the front is now stationary above us and that tomorrow will not be a good day to move on after all. We are not alone, however. When we listen to the Waterway Net, it seems that none of its members' boats - in the Caribbean, the Gulf of Mexico, Florida or the rest of The Bahamas - are on the move today. Everyone, it seems, is tucked in as tight as can be.

In the meantime the shackles on a nearby unoccupied yacht clank in a grey, wet, blustery day. But finally, after well over a week here, things seem to be settling and in the afternoon we go ashore and pay our outstanding fees. Jenny still looks well-fed and contented so we feel safe in letting her take us for one last walk along the lovely beach.

We are out at sea next morning when we spot a trawler yacht travelling towards us off our starboard beam. It is so low in the water, and given the course it is on, it is undoubtedly the couple from the Club heading back with supplies. They are so heavily laden, and there is such a swell from so many days of high winds and turbulent water, that they rise and fall alarmingly: lifted up in full view one moment; sinking so low the next that only the top of their flying bridge is visible.

37
Birthday Treat, Nassau

After so many days aboard, our first priority at Nassau is the supermarket. We find the town as friendly as last year and the harbour just as scruffy. The places that were slowly crumbling away then, still are. Apart from the BASRA dock which has fallen down completely. Now everyone uses the dinghy dock of a nearby bar to get ashore, but the owner doesn't seem to mind.

Our second priority is the Pond Wash Laundrette and our third is to get our empty propane bottle refilled. We leave the bottle at a marina for collection by the gas company, collect our mail from the post office, call Tony, check our emails and visit the new Straw Market. Since we were here last winter the old one burned down. It seems a local man, angry at being deserted by the love of his life, had set fire to it.

Late afternoon we return to the marina to collect our gas bottle. On our way back to *Voyager* with it the ex-New Zealand America's Cup contender passes on one side of us and a full-size replica of a Viking longboat on the other. It is a rather strange moment. Fifteen hundred years of nautical design, development and history - with our little aluminium dinghy in between.

Nassau is the cleanest commercial harbour we've ever been in, thanks to the fact that it is open at both ends and has a vigorous current running through it. This is perhaps as well given the detritus thrown into it. One nearby yachtsman lifts a huge truck battery with his anchor, with leads still attached, while another pulls up a rolled and bound carpet. And one afternoon we watch a large television float past.

Asked what I want to do for my birthday outing I plump for the Ardastra Gardens and Conservation Centre. I'm not a fan of zoos but having heard of its famous Marching Flamingos I *am* curious – while at the same time a little uneasy about how you persuade such flighty creatures as flamingos into something as regimented as marching.

I don't like to see animals and birds in cages either, but at the Ardastra Gardens not all of them are. For instance, the Meeter-and-Greeter at the entrance to the gardens is a Vietnamese pot-bellied pig. Although, to tell the truth, the day we visited she was asleep on the job, stretched out in the sunshine on a nice, springy bit of turf.

I need not have worried about the Marching Flamingos either. Mainly because it is more of a lurch than a march, with their human sergeant major expertly choreographing their natural inclination to surge off *en masse* in one direction, stop dead, and then surge off in another. Marching or not, it is humane as well as very entertaining.

Like ballet dancers, flamingos are graceful and absurd at the same time and require applause whenever they come to rest, blinking, beaks only inches from your camera lens. There is the odd bit of feather-plucking of their nearest neighbour, too. It is early mating season, apparently, and they are a bit skittish.

After their performance they hover outside the arena, or walk reflectively in large, shallow pools, relaxing, taking refreshment. Some rest on one leg, with their neck forming an S over their backs and their beaks half-buried in their wing feathers.

The gardens are lovely. The cages are a little on the small side, but everything is beautifully clean and cared for and there are at least two of nearly every species, so they do not live in solitary confinement. We see our first-ever sloth in the flesh – two-toed. It gazes at us sleepily. And there is a nice relaxed atmosphere without the usual Thou Shalt Not signs everywhere - except above the crocodile, which tells you that if you throw missiles at him you will be asked to leave.

If the Vietnamese pot-bellied pig works as the Meeter-and-Greeter at the entrance – some of the time anyway - a Moluccan cockatoo earns his living as the Thank-You-For-Coming at the exit. As we prepare to leave, his supervisor pops him onto my left shoulder and a scoop of bird seed into my right palm, ready for a photo-op.

I am not at all thrilled at having such a wicked-looking beak so close to my face. So I'm mortified when the man says, 'Give the lady a kiss, Toby,' and the bird dutifully lowers his head.

However, at the very moment my mind goes blank with panic I become aware of the most delightful sensation imaginable. Using only the smooth curve of his unexpectedly warm beak, and his warm round tongue, Toby is gently, seductively, caressing my left earlobe.

Afterwards, he resumes his quiet, upright pose on my shoulder. My relieved response is to burst out laughing. Moluccan cockatoos don't give much away facially and looking at the photograph later I cannot tell if he looks offended, or quietly pleased at the effect he has achieved. I'd like to think he was pleased. I know I was.

38
The Exumas

From Nassau we make our way south-east on an aquamarine sea under an azure sky. But as so often in these islands, the light changes and by 10am the sea is a breath-taking pale green, opaque one moment when a cloud floats by, translucent the next.

Around mid-day there comes a spectacular sort of brightness. The light has an extraordinary clarity, a radiance. I have been down in the galley getting lunch, come up into the cockpit and say, 'Good heavens!' and David says, 'Yes. Isn't it?' At times the sea is so still you can see the bottom clearly 23 feet/7 metres below.

We are heading for the Exumas, stopping briefly on the way at a couple of the islands visited last winter - like Normans Cay with its wonderful swimming - but mostly those we have not seen before.

Normans Cay
Unlike last year, we are anchored at the southern end of the island and it is here that you encounter evidence of a blot on the recent history of Normans Cay. And indeed on The Bahamas itself when, for a relatively brief period, both were involved in the narcotics trade.

In the late 1970s Carlos Lehder, co-founder of an infamous Colombian drug cartel, bought half the island. After buying up local properties, or scaring the residents away, he extended the small airfield's runway and turned Normans Cay into a base for importing cocaine into the United States. He is also reputed to have gathered a small army of people around him to run the business, provide protection and keep outsiders away. A number of unsolved homicides were linked to the cartel's activities, including that of an over-inquisitive yachtsman.

The drug lord's reign came to an end in the mid-80s when he was handed a prison sentence of life without parole plus – as seems to be a belt-and-braces sort of thing with US courts – an additional 135 years.

What now remains of the cocaine empire around the anchorage is a ruined dock, the wreck of a DC3 Dakota aircraft half-submerged in the bay and some abandoned buildings ashore. Although even now, the tiled and stainless steel kitchens and bars have an almost recent look to them, while the ransacked offices still contain a lot of filing cabinets and some impressively large desks.

We had read that a sense of evil permeates the place, but felt none. Perhaps because The Bahamas is doing its usual thing – what the hurricanes and tropical storms don't reduce to rubble, the undergrowth consumes. Although the airfield is now used by the local hotel.

We have a beer at MacDuff's, a small bar on the west side of the airstrip and, as we leave through its garden, watch a tiny hummingbird feed on nectar from a long red trumpet flower.

We go for a swim, off a beach resembling a cartoon desert island, with three little palm trees on it. The water is shallow and warm, the sand creamy and soft.

As we return to *Voyager* the sun is setting. Most of the sky is blue although you can't see the actual sun for a handful of small, pale grey clouds lying across it. The sun's deep orange rays pierce them, sending long shafts into the sea and rimming the clouds themselves with gold.

It's still my birthday. One day never seems enough for things like birthdays and anniversaries so we always spread them out over two or three. Same as a long weekend. We have dinner in a candle-lit cockpit and David gets to watch my favourite film. Again. He knows it so well by now he sometimes murmurs the dialogue along with the actors.

The velvety night sky is awash with stars. Our *Stars and Planets* book says that this is the last time until next year that the Winter Hexagon can be seen – six stars belonging to some of the most beautiful constellations: Capella, Pollux , Aldebaran, Procyon, Rigel and Sirius. But you don't need to worry too much about names. Just seeing is enough.

Big Majors Spot

Another of last year's locations is Big Majors Spot. There are some lovely beaches here – one of them with a very contented-looking black pig on it. Sometimes it forages above the waterline. Sometimes it paddles along the shore. We swim among coral and caves and on one return to *Voyager* I am convinced I have been eyeballed by a barracuda. David reckons it was more likely a harmless bonefish. But he didn't see it, did he?

We are swimming more than we have in years, sleep like the dead and wake blinking into another sun-filled day. Sun and moon set together at present providing glittering night skies fit to blow your mind. You lie on your back in the cockpit, with the stars reaching down to the horizon all around you, and feel as if you are being gathered up into the universe.

Little Farmers Cay

To get to Little Farmers means sailing down the coast of Great Guana Cay. Our chart for the area to the west of this long, skinny island is sketchy and the water worryingly shallow, so David decides to head out into the Atlantic on the island's eastern side.

To get there we have to navigate our way through Big Rock Cut, which is deeply troubling. It looks all wrong as you approach it. There are shoals, rocks and the turbulence of the water is disturbing. We know we have no option but to pass through it but are not at all happy about it until we clatter out the other side. Once into the Atlantic, however, we are in for another bumpy sail until finally we surf into Farmers Cay Cut and anchor on the west side of the island. All is now tranquil. We settle in glorious isolation off a small beach and dinghy to it late afternoon. A rocky road across the island takes us past neat wooden buildings in pinks, yellows and greens - a tiny store, grocery and post office.

On the far side of the island there is a small harbour with a tiny wooden dock called, rather grandly, Little Farmers Cay Yacht Club. Two local fishing boats are tied up to it and half a dozen men are busy. On the pontoon is a newly-stripped and bloody turtle shell. A second turtle, still intact but unmoving, lies on its back, one of its rear legs pathetically bent from its normal angle.

There is an official hunting season for two of the three most commonly-seen turtles in The Bahamas. It's just that we've only ever seen them swimming in the sea before today.

Rudder Cut Cay

Leaving for Rudder Cut Cay next day is not simply a matter of consulting the chart because, once again, it is not that helpful. For a start, there are no depths on it. And the sky is cloudy, denying you the option of colour-coded sailing in safety.

The notion of sailing by colour is something we first encountered in the Caribbean. The theory is that if the water is dark blue, it is deep. If it is turquoise, it is 15-20 feet/4-6m. But if it is bright green with brown in the middle you are heading for a reef. In the old days of sailing ships - before echo-sounders and with only a lead-line to determine depth - sailing by colour was an additional aid for mariners. But, to be effective, height was needed to be able to see any changes early enough to yell a warning to the helmsman; so a crewman was sent up the mast to the crow's nest to keep a look-out.

Two things militate against this technique being of any use to us. One is that cloud has a dramatic effect on colour, turning even the palest of shades to dark blue. The other is that *Voyager*'s only crewmember refuses to climb any higher up the mast than the coach house roof.

Unfortunately, in the absence of any depths, or warnings of underwater obstacles, all the chart provides in the form of a safe passage between the two islands is a red line with a sharp bend in it. Turning to the cruising guide, its advice is to find a channel of deep (that means dark) water. Looking for dark water under moving cloud is like seeking greener grass on the other side of the hill – when you get there, it appears to be somewhere else.

Before embarking on what we hoped equated to the red line on the chart, we had watched the progress of a yacht that had set out earlier and done our best to memorize its course. Sometime after leaving ourselves we are confused as to what we can see ahead of us. As we get closer it turns out to be the alternating stern and bow of a rusty fishing boat. It is turning constantly without going anywhere, while a crew member rushes around it in a dinghy. It struggles free just before we reach it, and begins travelling very slowly towards Little Farmers Cay, led very gingerly by the man in the dinghy. It is always disconcerting when even local fishermen go aground.

In the end we do our usual, me on the bow staring into the water ahead, and David watching the depth gauge while going slowly and hoping we are accurately following the chart's red line. At times we get close, but never quite touch bottom.

We could have avoided this route between reefs and sandbars by heading into deeper water on the ocean side of the Exuma chain. But having seen two yachts out there earlier, tossing and heaving about, we had decided against it. It is a nine hour passage and watching them it was obviously proving a very uncomfortable one. A detour via Rudder Cut Cay not only provides a more sheltered route - and a visit to another island – it also shortens a turbulent ocean passage by more than two hours.

We anchor at Rudder Cut Cay for the night opposite a creamy beach with a large cave at its northern end. At slack tide, around 5pm, we swim to the beach. The big domed cave is full of holes, and you have visions of historic winter tides and foaming water being forced up through its roof onto the land above.

In the evening a huge, molten gold sun sinks into the sea, dripping at its lower edge and spreading out across the horizon. As the enormous disk finally disappears into the sea its green flash - our second sighting now - leaves a green haze in the sky.

39
Great Exuma Island

Our passage to Great Exuma Island is nowhere near as turbulent as it would have been had we attempted it yesterday. This island gives its name to the chain known as The Exumas, and also contains one of the more famous settlements in The Bahamas. It is very popular with Americans. In fact, George Town is effectively small-town America afloat.

The approach to it is a four-mile dogleg through five sharp changes of direction between reefs, coral heads and sand bars, with the turns necessarily fast to get you safely between them. Sailing into the sun makes identification by colour impossible, and the cruising guide advises yachtsmen to ignore any navigation markers even if there are any - there are two but they make no sense at all - so we are grateful for the GPS co-ordinates that the guide provides.

By the time we anchor, around 4pm, the wind has died almost completely and it is very hot. The anchorage is shallow and crowded but passing dinghy-riders, with typical American friendliness, all give a cheerful greeting.

George Town
After the weather forecast next morning we go ashore to the landing stage owned by the supermarket known as Exuma Markets. To get to it you dinghy under a little road bridge into Lake Victoria, a sizable pond, and leave the dinghy at the supermarket's generous dock.

A walk over the little bridge takes us into town to check out the facilities: laundromat, tourist office, and so on; and visit the white, wooden Anglican Church on a small hill. It has blue shutters and stained glass in the top section of its windows. It is a light, cool, airy building and very peaceful.

Back at the busy supermarket we shop for essentials. With them loaded on board we head away from the crowded anchorage. The Twenty-Second Cruiser Regatta ended today. There have been 390 boats here this week.

Stocking Island, long and narrow and very tranquil, is only a mile across the channel from George Town and has an excellent anchorage. It is now very hot as there is almost no wind, but a cold front is supposed to be coming through tonight which should refresh the atmosphere.

Weather plays a persistent part in conversations in The Bahamas because of the tendency to have three or four quiet days interspersed with periods of very strong winds. As a result, yachtsmen become forecast junkies, listening to both the Nassau and Miami Met Offices and trying to work out which one is the right one on any particular day. The two rarely agree. But if a strong high pressure system or a cold front begins to move in, we all head for shelter. As long as you find a sheltered spot to anchor, it is still nice enough to swim and explore the islands.

The anticipated cold front passes through in the early hours of the morning accompanied by torrential rain and the most spectacular thunder and lightning - including one huge red explosion right over our heads. One meteorologist talks about this being 'a quasi cold front wandering up and down between the central and southern Bahamas.' We wonder what makes for a *quasi* cold front. And what the difference might be between that and a real one. A water spout is spotted near a neighbouring island.

After some days we return to George Town, our intention being to do some shopping, some laundry, check our emails and collect the post we know is waiting for us. When we arrive in the anchorage, one of the boats is flying signalling flags for some reason. Perhaps its skipper thinks they are bunting.

But each signal flag has a specific meaning and the information he is sending out to his fellow yachtsmen - despite his being at anchor - is: I am altering course to port; I am operating astern propulsion; I have a pilot on board; man overboard; I am disabled, communicate with me; and the nice little blue and white check one that declares an uncompromising 'No'. The final one is a Bahamian courtesy flag, so at least one of them is appropriate.

We give him as wide a berth as possible in the crowded anchorage in case his anchoring skills are as limited as his knowledge of flags.

Exuma Markets very kindly allows yachtsmen to have their mail sent there, and the Morning Net announces your name over the VHF when something has arrived for you, thereby saving wasted journeys.

With so many boaters colonizing George Town and its environs for the winter, they have created a vibrant social life for themselves. The Morning Net announces which events will be taking place on that particular day: aerobics, painting classes, AA meetings, Bible study, picnics, book clubs, coffee mornings and charity work.

Even sunset is a social event with boaters up on their bows blowing conch shells to celebrate it. Huge conch shells lie around on most beaches in The Bahamas, so finding one to blow into is the easy part. Some people manage long drawn out bellows, others strangulated peeps. One thing is certain, you always know the exact moment the sun is going down.

In fact, so completely has George Town been Americanized that the supermarket shelves cater almost exclusively to North American tastes. Or as one matron explains, still shocked at the memory: 'When we first started coming here they didn't even stock Doritos!'

Naturally the town makes much of its living during this winter visitation. For example, the supermarket has a small car park but a large dinghy dock. Many boaters stay here for a full six months, with their anchors slowly sinking deeper and deeper into the sandy bottom, which can be quite a problem apparently when it comes time to leave.

In fact, so dominant are US visitors that they have even named the beaches. Anchored not far from Volley Ball Beach David takes us ashore expectantly, given the scantily-clad Brazilian lovelies shown in TV coverage of The Olympics over the years. However, although there is a match in progress when we get there, the sight of the overweight and middle-aged in baggy shorts and shapeless T-shirts proves something of a disappointment. So we take a long walk instead and finish up with a beer at the Chat and Chill bar.

Another morning we go to Hamburger Beach which as might be expected has a barbecue on it, but more importantly some beautiful nature trails. Every now and again there are plaques describing the adjacent bush or tree and we eventually pluck up courage to try one of the edible fruits.

It is described as being especially popular with children and used like chewing gum. A white juice oozes from it which has quite a pleasant tangy taste. Unfortunately it also sticks our lips and fingers together and prevents any further experiments with wild fruit.

Islanders naturally know their stuff regarding shrubs and trees, some of which provide not only tasty treats and wild chewing gum, but a regular pharmacopeia of remedies for various ailments. However, I remember once lying on a beach under a most beautiful tree with some of its leaves and fruit lying in the sand around us and thought how utterly perfect it was to be able to stretch out on our beach towels under it, with the sea lapping gently at our feet, for as long as we wanted, safe in its shade from any threat of sunburn. It was only later, browsing through a book, that I noticed a photograph of the lovely tree. Whatever you do, warned the text, do not touch any part of this tree as it is poisonous to humans and animals and even mere contact with the skin can prove fatal.

Before leaving the Exumas we visit the marina to refuel. Diesel is $1.92 a US gallon and the small, indignant man with luxuriant moustaches ahead of us says a friend of his had recently returned from Venezuela where he had paid only eight cents a gallon. 'It just shows how much tax and profit there is on our fuel,' he shouts, roaring away, a life-size incarnation of Yosemite Sam. Goodness knows how he would react if he sailed in British waters and was charged the equivalent of six or seven dollars per US gallon.

With our enjoyment of tranquil places and quiet anchorages we had not expected to like George Town. Truth is, we only came here in the first place because it has the only supermarket in over a hundred miles and was somewhere we could have our mail delivered. But we have enjoyed it and stayed longer than expected. And despite a little over-crowding the atmosphere has never been less than pleasurable.

40
Islands In Between

We now head towards that other famous Bahamian cruising ground, the Abacos, but want to take in three other islands on the way.

Cat Island
Once offshore it is an eight-hour passage across Exuma Sound to Cat Island and a brisk sail under the genoa of 6-7 knots. The sea is the most

extraordinary blue. We see only one other boat all day, quite a few flying fish and a lot of sun, but not a single bird or mammal.

Our waypoint is the southwest corner of Cat Island, called Hawks Nest Point. From there it a two-hour journey across a huge bay to an area called The Bight. Only four other boats are anchored there. Quite a difference from George Town's three hundred and ninety.

Bahamian life has a strong religious element, most noticeable from the number of churches in these islands – and their large congregations - plus the many religious programmes broadcast on terrestrial TV. Some of the strongly Methodist islands even prohibit the sale of alcohol. But nowhere is a religious presence so uniquely expressed as on Cat Island.

The highest point in The Bahamas - all 206 feet of it - is here, rising up above our anchorage and the settlement of New Bight. Once called Como Hill, it was renamed Mount Alvernia by Englishman John Hawes (1876-1956) who then built a one-man monastery on the top of it.

Originally an Anglican minister, he designed and built churches in England and came to The Bahamas to re-build some of those destroyed by hurricanes. Just as his inspiration, St Francis of Assisi, had done before him in 12th century Italy - The Reverend Mr John Hawes subsequently adopted a nomadic life, becoming a labourer and railway worker in North America. During a visit to Rome he converted to Catholicism, was later ordained a Catholic priest and spent several decades in Australia as priest and builder of churches. In his fifties, after a heart attack, he returned to The Bahamas and began work on his hermitage on the hill that he renamed after the small cell at La Verna in the Tuscan mountains where St Francis is reputed to have received the stigmata, the wounds of the cross.

Despite modelling himself on Saint Francis, the hermitage that Monsignor John Hawes built for himself - with the help of local people, it should be said - could never be called 'a cell'. It is to all intents and purposes a complete monastery, albeit designed on a very small scale for the personal use of one man who as well as renaming the hill, also renamed himself - as Father Jerome.

To reach it we walk past the ruins of what was once a substantial plantation house, and its slave quarters - forbidding stone barracks being consumed by the undergrowth. Along the way we walk through what was once the plantation's garden, where an elderly local woman is picking tomatoes. And then we begin climbing the winding rocky track, aware of what an effort it must have been to haul building materials up here.

The hermitage at the top is head-crackingly small, with a chapel containing a one-man pew, a very small bell tower, tiny living quarters and a guest room only slightly larger than its bed. If not exactly driven to our knees, we are perpetually stooped for the sake of our skulls.

Despite its size, the hermitage is airy and light from apertures in all directions, while the only thing breaking the silence around it is birdsong. And the view is breath-taking - out over the harbour and a sparkling blue sea. At the same time that we admire it we also notice that all four of our neighbours are up-anchoring, and hope their leaving has nothing to do with us.

Monsignor Hawes/Father Jerome was in his 70s when he completed the work, died a few years later in Florida, and was buried here at his own request beneath his hermitage. Someone clearly still looks after it. It is clean and swept and the doors and window shutters have been opened to keep it aired in this fine weather. In fact it looks, even fifty years after he left it, as if the hermit who once lived here has only just popped out for a few minutes.

I have to confess to negative feelings about it. A man who is not a native imposes a new name on a country's highest peak and build's a monument to himself and his (changed) beliefs on the top of it. Also, the whole place seems so exclusive. But then, attitudes have changed in the half century since Father Jerome built it. Nowadays the tendency is towards inclusiveness and the wider community.

After lunch we wander round the town. Ruined slave houses and abandoned homes crumble between habited ones, some of them recently built. It gives a strange effect, like building in a graveyard, the living among the departed. A metaphor, perhaps, for the legacy of slavery which seems to hover over this place.

Late afternoon we go for a swim off the beautiful long beach. The water is warm and perfectly transparent, the sunset is glorious and there's not a single conch shell to be heard as we paddle back to *Voyager*.

Little San Salvador

The island of Little San Salvador lies between Cat Island and Eleuthera and has been re-named Half Moon Cay by the cruise ship company which now owns it. Our cruising guide says that although the company has declared anchoring in the island's gorgeous West Bay to be off-limits to yachtsmen they are turning a blind eye for the present.

It's a bit like fetching up in a leisure park. To reach the anchorage we pass behind two cruise ships, one of them built to resemble a five-masted sailing ship, whose passengers are taking advantage of a one-day stop-over and the water sports provided here. Above us a parascender under a gaily-coloured parachute waves nervously to her friends in the tow boat below, who are offering up their enthusiastic encouragement. A RIB passes, towing an inflated, undulating banana whose passengers bounce up and down on it shrieking happily.

Eleuthera

Just after dawn we set off around the southern tip of Eleuthera and up its west coast. By mid-day we are in the Davis Channel working our way through the sandbanks and by 2pm we are in Governors Harbour which is half-way to where we are going - and also the bustling metropolis of Eleuthera. You know this is so because it has the only traffic light on the island. It also has a deserved reputation for the worst holding in The Bahamas.

Another early start finds us continuing up the Eleutheran coast under a heavy sky. We can see squalls all round us and, at one point, a distant water spout. This is not something you want to experience up close - a funnel of water being sucked up into a massive overhead cloud. Water spouts are a serious danger to both yachts and small aircraft.

At the northern end of the island there is a long headland out to the west with shoals around it. These can be avoided by taking Current Cut which divides the headland and shortens the journey by two hours, but it is essential to arrive there at slack tide and hence the early start.

Our destination is Royal Island which, as we know from last year, is not only delightful but sheltered and with a big cold front forecast for the day-after-tomorrow our plan had been to sit out the bad weather there. Unfortunately, when we anchor in it, we have a boat on our starboard side with a man on deck talking loudly and endlessly about his business problems, and another on our port side with the noisiest portable generator we have ever heard.

The anchorage is very crowded and there is no other space big enough for us to move into. Like us, a lot of people have headed here for shelter from the coming cold front. But we could be stuck here for a week between the human foghorn and the portable generator. So we decide to make a run for the Abacos, and Marsh Harbour where we had sheltered during our last visit to The Bahamas.

41
The Abacos

The Abacos are the northernmost group of islands in The Bahamas and, like the Exumas, a very popular cruising ground.

We set off just before 6am into a calm morning. The Nassau forecast is West 10-15 knots. Miami reckons SE to SW 15-20. Any of them would do. All wrong, of course. The wind slowly increases to 27 knots and moves to the North West. On the nose.

Conditions become really nasty. And then the starboard engine cuts out. David bleeds it and it starts again, but it falters several times. David fears that we have picked up dirty fuel somewhere. We are getting low on diesel anyway and, combined with the turbulent conditions, any sediment that might have settled on the bottom of our fuel tank will have been driven up into our engine's fuel filters.

When we had set off in settled conditions this morning we had expected to reduce the journey with a short-cut through Little Harbour Bar. Unfortunately it is not something to attempt with a failing engine and we are not going to reach Marsh Harbour before nightfall given the time we have lost through a strong headwind and a faulty engine.

We have a choice. We can return to Royal Island Harbour and hope to find a place to anchor, or head for Cherokee Point on Great Abaco. We decide to try the latter but be prepared to make a night passage back to where we've come from. The trouble is our lack of information about Cherokee Point but it turns out to be an easy entry and a sheltered anchorage.

The winds drop overnight but in the morning, still very aware of the approaching cold front, we head off early for Marsh Harbour and have an easy entrance through North Bar Channel into the Sea of Abaco where we begin working our way around its sand bars.

After a while we have enough wind to raise a sail and are happily motor sailing when both engines cut out. David tries to bleed them but to no avail. Apart from anything else it means we shall have to anchor under sail, and Marsh Harbour's anchorage is invisible until you reach it. We make the necessary left-hand turn into it and are faced with a wall of anchored boats all gathered for shelter from the imminent cold front.

We turn into the wind behind them. David drops the anchor and I release the sheet to spill the wind from the sail. Happily we come to a stop just where we want to be, and the anchor holds.

Marsh Harbour

The good news is that we have done a perfect anchor under sail. The bad news is that we are slap bang in the middle of the big ship channel. We lower the dinghy and David goes off to fill our cans with fuel so that we can move as soon as possible. While a man called Steve, whom we've met before, emerges from the anchorage in his dinghy with a couple more cans of fuel for us.

When David returns he has to change the large fuel filter on the starboard engine as it is clogged with gunge. Then after some difficulty he manages to bleed the system through on both engines. In the meantime, a cargo boat, the Duke of Topsail, is preparing to leave its berth a short distance from the anchorage and get underway.

David gets both engines started just as Steve comes alongside and says he and his friend will tow us, with their dinghies, out of the path of the cargo boat. We thank them for their kind offer but are ready to go now. I call up the skipper of the Duke of Topsail to apologise for inconveniencing him, and he is very nice and says he will take it slowly while we haul up our anchor and get out of the way.

David looks weary. The heat doesn't help.

The promised cold front arrives next day. How can it be a cold front when it is still just as hot? And when we turn on the starboard engine to chill the fridge, to our horror it dies almost immediately. David soon discovers the problem. When he had worked on the engine yesterday he had turned the fuel off while he replaced the bleed screw, so we had run the system dry. He sets to and bleeds it yet again and is now convinced he has done a Master's Course in bleeding Yanmar 3-cylinder engines. A fairly specialised area of expertise admittedly.

With the bad weather finally gone and our fuel tank topped up we set off to see what the Abacos has to offer.

Hope Town

Only a couple of hours' sail away Hope Town, on Elbow Cay, has a long and very beautiful beach. This village has the feel of a real community about it, with its small Voluntary Fire and Rescue building, its tiny Burial Society and the big rusty tanker from the Dolphin Water Company trundling along the road. There is only the one road. The rest are wide footpaths with no traffic except the odd golf cart. The houses are wooden, painted in pastel shades and rather pretty.

There is one unpainted one that had been owned by Lily Bethel known locally as The Cat Lady. She died two months ago, a neighbour tells us, although people are still leaving fresh flowers at her door and trying to find homes for the stray cats she cared for. As we walk past the house, small faces gaze back at us from the undergrowth, bewildered by the disappearance of their friend.

Man-O-War Cay

We sail around the shoals to Man-O-War Cay and navigate the narrow entrance into a sheltered lagoon which is also the island's southern anchorage. It is very peaceful and pretty with lots of trees, a few houses and some attractive traditional boats. Most of the anchored boats are unoccupied which adds to the peace.

As well as being narrow, the lagoon's entrance also has a sandbar and during the afternoon a yacht runs aground on it. It soon becomes apparent that the couple aboard are stuck fast, so David lowers our dinghy and sets off to help.

When he gets there the yacht's skipper, Jim, is furiously winding away at his winch as he tries to use his kedge anchor to pull himself off. David suggests he takes over the winch while Jim uses his RIB to push the boat off the sandbar, since our aluminium dinghy isn't suitable. They are having trouble getting the kedge anchor to hold when a small sports fishing boat with two 175hp engines arrives and offers to tow them off. With that much power the yacht is soon afloat and joins us in the anchorage.

As Rhona and I chat later, she says wryly that she and Jim have been married 47 years but is not sure if they will make it to 48. Originally from Idaho, until they retired to Florida recently Jim had done all his cruising in magazines. This is their first real one and it has been a bit traumatic.

Man-O-War' village is very neat and tidy, and very prosperous. It is also one of the islands with a strong religious influence – in this case, Methodism – and it is illegal to sell liquor here. Although one of the shops does have Rum Cake for sale.

Treasure Cay

Our wanderings take us to extremes, from small traditional communities like Hope Town and Man-O-War, to commercial ventures like Treasure

Cay. We have heard a lot about the latter, not least its claim to have one of the world's top ten beaches. It also has a public telephone so we can ring Tony.

Treasure Cay isn't a cay at all but a bay in a large island. And I suppose when you are building a new resort, a cay sounds better in the brochure. But if it does have one of the world's top ten beaches, why is its most prominent feature a swimming pool? Perhaps it's just a bad day but the beach itself looks trampled, littered and a little seedy and we have seen much better ones all over The Bahamas let alone the world. Still, if you are selling a vacation resort, it's good PR.

Bakers Bay

Another, even more ambitious resort, is famous now only because it failed so spectacularly. Bakers Bay was purchased some years ago, renamed Treasure Island Resort, and intended as a one-day stop-over for cruise ship passengers. A multi-million dollar complex was built here but when the ships started to arrive it was discovered that the East Channel, by which they had to enter, becomes impassable when winds are over 15 knots from the east. Unfortunately for the resort, the prevailing winds are from the east and often brisk. The surrounding area is also very shallow and although a channel was dredged to get the ships in, it kept silting up again and the project was finally abandoned.

In the late afternoon we go ashore and walk through the ruins which are slowly being consumed by the undergrowth. Small fir trees are growing between the seats in the open air theatre and other flora is pushing its way up through bars and restaurants.

The decking between them remains surprisingly unmarked by time, forming high-quality timber passageways, winding their way between facilities and out onto the wonderful beach. Oddly it is this decking that fools part of your mind into thinking that this could all just be the latest craziness in theme parks and that in a minute or two you will turn a corner and find a liveried staff member welcoming you to Treasure Island Resort. It is the lack of any other people among this wealth of leisure facilities, for children as well as adults, which gives the place its eeriness until finally, with a slight chill between the shoulder blades, you follow the decking back out onto the wonderful beach.

It seems hardly credible that no-one checked the entry problems before committing to building this complex of extensive timber structures and expensive fittings. Especially since that, in readiness to get the big ships into it, the builders had dredged a channel to such an extent that a whole new island was created from the spoil, and which nature is currently claiming.

Nor was it only the structures that were abandoned. There was, apparently, a marine circus to entertain the cruise ship passengers and several of its dolphins, at liberty now, are still in the area.

After our walk through the ruins we enjoy a sunset swim off the beach. Shoals of fish eye us curiously and some accompany us. Back on board a small dark shark glides around our stern for some time, and we wonder if he accompanied us on our swim, too.

A shift in the wind, now from the south, and something unforeseen by the weathermen in either Nassau or Miami, provides ideal conditions to get to Green Turtle Cay. It is one of the Abaco's out islands – the chain of small cays, islets and large rocks that forms the outer rim of the Sea of Abaco - a long wide stretch of water that provides a barrier between the large island of Abaco and the Atlantic. These islands are quite literally the outer edge, with their backs to the Atlantic Ocean and very vulnerable to bad weather, especially hurricanes.

The wind is behind us all the way and it is a glorious sail. However, the route through the Sea of Abaco is littered with sand bars – or as our chart calls them 'sand bores'.

As we discovered on our first arrival in The Bahamas, charts in this part of the world can be a problem. That you can, in fact, turn a page of your chart book and find yourself in another century – and not even the last one - with charts using surveys from as early as 1836.

One clue to the age of our present chart is that in ten years of sailing and navigation we have never before encountered one that used the words 'sand bores' for sandbanks. Another clue is that all the depths are marked in fathoms whereas modern charts are either in metres, if European, or feet if American. And by the time we approach the area near Whale Cay our present chart shows depths as little as a quarter of a fathom – which means 18 inches/0.45m) of water. Not 18 inches below our keel, just 18 inches of water.

The difficulty with sandbanks is their tendency to shift. So you need to be wary, even when using a modern chart. And, since this one was drawn, its 'bores' have had a century and a half in which to move about. To avoid the worst of them we skirt around Whale Cay and out into the Atlantic, then back into the Sea of Abaco when depths increase.

Although shallow the Sea of Abaco is sheltered, at least for some of the way to Green Turtle Cay. However, there is quite a long break in the island chain where a vessel is exposed to the Atlantic, and winds from the east can make this route unthinkable. In fact, the local description for the sea state at such times is The Rage. Fortunately the present southerly wind continues to give us an excellent sail on a slight sea.

Green Turtle Cay

Our reason for coming to Green Turtle Cay is to visit the settlement of New Plymouth on the island's southern tip. It was settled around 1790 by Loyalists escaping from, or driven out by, the victors of the War of the Rebellion. It is a very pretty, neat and friendly little town. We walk the narrow streets and visit the Albert Lowe Museum which is a house on Parliament Street built in 1825.

It is essentially an affluent family home, light and airy with big windows and furnished in the style of the time with velvet sofas and high-backed chairs downstairs, while upstairs an attic bedroom with a sloping roof, has twin dark oak beds and roses on the wallpaper. Of particular interest are the house's artefacts and old framed photographs which provide an insight into the history of out-island life.

We find the old jail, an ominous-looking concrete blockhouse. And the library whose exterior is barely less intimidating. There is also a sculpture garden, created in the 1980s, whose centrepiece is life-size statues of two women - one black, one white – and dedicated to the community's Loyalist past. As well as busts of prominent residents it also includes a tribute from former students to inspired teachers at the local schools. It seems a very nice idea, and I like to think those dedicated teachers inspired their students to spend more time in the library and stay out of the gaol altogether.

Delia's Cay

Delia's Cay is a tiny islet off Great Guana. Like its neighbour, Green Turtle Cay, it also takes great pride in its Loyalist history. The days have become extremely hot and our dinghy's outboard is on the blink again. So, in the cool of a very pleasant morning, David rows us ashore and we follow an unmade road across the island into the settlement. It is a lovely little town with a pretty harbour (but bad holding) and the people are most friendly.

A very nice man invites us to walk around the new marina complex being built and offers to take our picture. And a very nice woman with two Jack Russell terriers gives us a lift back to our dinghy on the back seat of her golf cart. One dog rides in style up front, the other running resolutely alongside and taking only one detour – over somebody's front lawn to invite the impotent rage of two large dogs on the balcony above. The little dog's action is so swift and confident I get the feeling he does this daily.

The lady herself is sixth generation Bahamian, she tells us, her ancestors having come as Loyalists. 'We didn't mind paying the Tea Tax,' she says, as if all that unseemly fuss in Boston Harbour happened only yesterday. 'Now Americans still do, but we don't pay any taxes at all.'

And I get the feeling that, like her small terrier with the dogs on the balcony, she has wound up more than a few visiting Americans – whose descendants so unceremoniously uprooted her own - with this little tidbit.

Back on *Voyager*, in masks and snorkels, we each tie a paint scrapper to our right wrist and swim around her hull, removing any bits of wildlife living there in preparation for our next passage. The bilge pump stops working, the water maker is on the blink and we've been without the outboard engine for some days now. It's a sure sign we're planning a long voyage; things always start breaking down. It is a very hot afternoon. It is also the first night of a full moon, and stunning; rising like polished brass above the little town and illuminating us, and all the sea around us, all night long.

Getting Ready To Leave

Marsh Harbour is the only place for all the things we need and we anchor as close to town as we can to make rowing ashore easier until David can get the outboard engine fixed. The temperature on board is in the lower 90s at its peak, 120 out of doors. We have not seen rain since George Town, five weeks ago.

The following morning David rows to the head of the harbour and delivers the Evinrude to The Outboard Shop for repairs. On the way back he stops off at the bank for money, takes some film in for developing, buys some blackened hogfish for lunch and checks our emails. This is the first time in three weeks we have found anywhere to access our emails but apparently that's too long for Hotmail which has wiped our account. Everything, not only incoming messages, but the email addresses of every friend, relative and essential company have gone.

After lunch we get a radio call from The Outboard Shop and David rows off again. He returns delighted. The outboard runs better than it ever did. Not only that, it no longer gives him electric shocks. Jason, the repairman, said that while he was working on it he recorded one measuring 500 volts.

The days are windless and very hot with high humidity. You tend to stick to whatever you touch. The meteorological forecasts from Miami and Nassau at present are so far out, on both wind direction and strength, it is barely worth taking them down. The only thing they seem to agree on is the promise of isolated showers, which never arrive anyway. The Waterway Net says the US is having record high temperatures for this time of the year.

Today is the 2nd of May and the day of the Bahamian General Election. There has been plenty of political activity. Most cars have carried flags for one or other of the parties and all the telephone poles have posters on them. Some of the advertisements in the press even accuse named politicians of bullying and corruption. Before the previous election, the party in power had been in government for a long time and at the last election, we are told, Bahamians had voted for change.

The results of today's election are announced just after 10 pm and soon a procession of horn-blowing cars are parading along the waterfront. The previous government has returned to power with a landslide victory. It seems the electorate got tired of their experiment with change. 'At least,' a local man says darkly, 'there's been no funny business like last time'.

The following day we leave Marsh Harbour. The Sea of Abaco is a brilliant turquoise. It has been a long and lovely sojourn on this second visit to The Bahamas. We have spent time at some delightful little settlements and enjoyed the facilities provided by three of the largest. But mostly we have lingered among the kind of truly uninhabited, 'desert islands' that have a special place in so many a traveller's heart.

The Bahamas is not a soft touch for winter cruisers. Its very shallowness can make it dangerous. The Atlantic Ocean, rushing around a small island creates currents which can surprise with their speed. Some of its anchorages may be less than tranquil given the strength of the sea swell. Entry into harbours and bays can sometimes be a challenge. And the weather is changeable as cold fronts or Northers sweep down from the US bringing high winds and turbulent water.

Food can be expensive because, like the Caribbean, most of it is imported, and with so few inhabited islands it is often not the cost that is an issue but finding somewhere to restock. Nevertheless, it is surprising how inventive you can be with the canned and dry goods you already have on board.

And once you find your sheltered cove, and your anchor sinks into that pristine sand, you are in Paradise. The water has the colour and clarity of gemstones. The swimming is wonderful and the coral reefs are a snorkeler's delight.

Days begin and end in a blaze of colour in many places, but here even the moon rises the colour of polished brass and sinks blood red. And with most of the islands uninhabited – which means no pollution or street lighting - when the day is over, the night sky is mesmerizing.

42
Heading for Bermuda

Once out of the Sea of Abaco and into the Atlantic we set a course for Bermuda, 725 miles away. Mid-afternoon we have our last sight of the islands before they disappear below the horizon. By late afternoon there are just the flying fish and the seagulls.

You don't do much on a sea voyage beyond attending to the routine demands of sailing: the navigational checks, the log, the night watches and catching up on the broken sleep afterwards so that even if you are not actually sleeping, lying on your bunk resting is required. This routine serves a vital purpose. It keeps you relaxed and rested so that you are ready to respond to problems if and when they occur - like actors in the wings, calm but alert to what is going on around them until they receive their cue.

Repairs and provisioning for a voyage can be busy, hot and tiring, sometimes frustrating. But, by degrees, you slow down. You give yourself over to the sea and the sky – their colours and their moods. Everything becomes suspended, elemental, eternal.

Sunset and supper are at 7.30 tonight. At eight, David goes to bed and I begin the first watch of the night. By now Venus and a few of the brighter stars are visible. The sky is a soft azure blue and the horizon cinnamon.

Within an hour Venus is so bright she sends a shaft of gold, as vivid as moonlight, across the water to our port quarter. The lower the planet descends the brighter she becomes, until finally she sinks into the sea. Deprived of her light I turn on the radar because with scattered low cloud, no moon and Venus gone, the horizon is now invisible. Even the stars, a vast dome reaching down to the sea, hide more than they reveal and it is impossible to tell if a ship's light is among them.

A glance at the chart tells me that the Atlantic under our hull is over three miles deep here. I didn't really need to know that.

Our mid-day to midnight run is 69 miles which is good for the conditions but the wind is weakening and we doubt if we will be able to maintain this speed.

Apart from the wind getting flukier, requiring an increase in engine revs, it is an uneventful night. The moon is in its third quarter and rises a little after 2am. The morning starts to get light at around 5.30.

It is Saturday and our second day at sea. The Waterway Net reports that we are passing under a ridge of high pressure and once north of it we should get stronger south-westerlies - which would be perfect for us - but to expect a change later to the north, which won't be so good.

The Net also reports that a 32ft fishing boat is missing on a journey from Miami to Freeport in The Bahamas. BASRA, the islands' search and rescue organisation, had received a VHF call from it saying it was out of fuel but was unable to get a position. We also learn that a barge has been blocking the ICW at Barefoot Landing, South Carolina, for almost a week.

We remember the two tugs aground there when we passed through a few months ago, but at least the waterway was still passable then. People are becoming worried that, without more government funding for dredging, whole sections of their beloved Intracoastal Waterway will become unusable except by very small boats.

We have also begun picking up forecasts from Herb at last. Full name Herb Hilgenberg but known to anybody offshore simply as Herb, he lives in Canada and broadcasts every day except December 25th. He is prodigiously experienced at ship routing and weather forecasting, and his information during our Atlantic crossing from the Canaries to the Caribbean last year was invaluable.

Herb gives his information free to yachtsmen with SSB radio transmitter/receivers. We have an SSB receiver only, and David listens for boats which are closest to us which gives us a good idea of the weather for our immediate area.

Herb confirms that we should have light south-westerly winds tomorrow but to expect moderate north winds on Monday shifting to the north-east and easing. Unfortunately, north-east will be right on our nose.

Today is a slow day with the occasional freighter and little else. One advantage of the motor-sailing forced on us in these light conditions is that it produces enough juice for us to put the radar on during the nights, which are currently *very* dark.

Anyone who reads 19th century English novels such as Dickens or Jane Austen may have noticed that when evening events are being planned there is an occasional reference to the moon. I never thought anything of it until we became offshore sailors; but for guests to reach an evening ball or dinner party a carriage journey needed to be undertaken, and without moonlight – and no headlights or streetlights either - the poor coachman could end up driving the horses and the carriage into a ditch.

At sea, apart from weather forecasts, the log and sleep, the other major events of the day are meals, which may sound boring but it is always best if things stay boring. They rarely do. Tonight there comes a jerky rhythm to the sea and we need to hold onto something solid whenever we move about or else risk falling over.

It is far too violent to think of venturing beyond the cockpit, although even here, in its central, protected well, we bounce so much that only one of us moves about in it at any one time otherwise we get knocked into one another.

Yet just after dawn the morning is so tranquil we go out onto the foredeck to watch when dozens of common dolphins arrive to play in our bow wave.

Unfortunately, the Morning Net's weather report is obliterated by someone speaking over it very loudly in Spanish. But Herb gives us the bad news later: adverse winds for the next couple of days.

I see a turtle and think how handy it must be to simply dive down into the deep, still waters during bad weather and only return for those necessary quick gulps of air.

On one of my watches two very large freighters pass. From first sighting to disappearing takes all of ten minutes, which is why our small, portable kitchen timer is back on duty again, in the pocket of whichever one of us is on watch, with its ten-minute setting pinging us back out on deck to check the horizon.

Our fourth day out is David's birthday. Around 3am, the wind rises and, as predicted, shifts to the north-east and near the nose. We turn more towards the east to keep it in our sails and cut the engine. It is nice to have some pure sailing even if it's not exactly where we want to go. So we decide to tack, making a change in direction every two hours. Unfortunately, catamarans are not good at this type of sailing and after an hour's tacking we are no closer to our destination.

The forecast from the Morning Net says we will have at least two days of this. It also reports that the small fishing boat, out of fuel and missing for several days, has been spotted by a search plane near the Bahamian island of Andros and that a boat has been sent to rescue the two men aboard. But there is no further news of the grounded tug on the ICW.

The wind slowly begins to rise and gradually so does the sea until it is very bouncy, then deeply uncomfortable and ultimately rather nasty. I feel tired and queasy. As the day has progressed, the wind speed has not only increased but has crept even closer to the nose and although we cover 98 miles we get only 68 closer to Bermuda. David joins me in feeling tired and queasy and neither of us feels like celebrating his birthday.

Before setting out David had carefully researched the best time of year to make this journey with favourable winds. However, be it El Niño, climate change or our failure to make libations to the appropriate gods before shoving off, the desired conditions elude us.

With the wind still on the nose next morning – our fifth day at sea - conditions are still very unpleasant. We have trouble hearing the morning forecast but it sounds as if we can expect 22-knot winds or more from the north by Friday, in three days' time, which would be nice but not soon enough for us.

The problem is, we do not have enough fuel to motor all the way to Bermuda in strong head winds. We discuss the options and wait to hear what Herb has to say later in the day.

One possibility is to head out directly east into the Atlantic with our remaining fuel and then use the north-east winds to get to Bermuda. Unfortunately this would lengthen our journey and if the forecast winds do not arrive we could miss Bermuda altogether.

Another option would be to head for the US coast and either try again after rest and refuelling or request another 6-month stay there. Or we could return to The Abacos and await another attempt.

The USA seems the best option until Herb predicts light winds, some from the south-east and some from the south-west, until Sunday - which would mean we could sail directly to Bermuda. We decide to wait and see if his prediction holds good.

In the meantime we put all but one of our spare cans of fuel into the tank, make our calculations, stop tacking and turn directly towards Bermuda, running on one engine. David is disturbed by the fact that at 2500 revs we are only doing three knots and had expected more. We make 83 miles today but are only 35 closer to Bermuda.

By the early hours our speed has improved and the wind is slowly edging to the south and behind us where it is the most use. By dawn, although it is fluctuating, we are making 4 knots in the right direction and calculate we have enough fuel to motor-sail to Bermuda even if the winds do not get any stronger.

Dawn also ushers in one of those blissful days: of bright blue sky, small fluffy white clouds, a light sea swell, the awning up, warmth and bright sunshine. Just sitting in the cockpit with a chopping board on your knees, cutting up vegetables for a pasta sauce is heavenly. So different from recent days, with the waves slamming against the bridge deck so hard that you totter like small children who haven't yet learned to walk properly. The present, gentle sea around us is an incredibly deep blue.

It rains briefly around 3pm – the first rainwater *Voyager* has had on her since George Town six weeks ago, and an indicator of just how dry this region is at this time.

It has also been a day without much in the way of forecasts. The Morning Net suffers from interference and Herb's is totally distorted by atmospherics, or 'poor propagation' as radio experts call it.

We have been in deep water since just after we started, anything between two and three miles deep, so we pay little attention to the echo sounder. However, every so often it will register a 'last depth found' of just a few feet and you can't help wondering what just swam under you.

Two storm petrels arrive. Tiny birds that live on the wing, they delight in something different on their patch and fly towards and away from us numerous times. They also like to fly alongside boats, skimming the surface of the water so close beside us that we look down on their backs. At even a short distance away they are so near the water that even a slight swell hides them from view.

Late afternoon the light wind rises and falls. It also shifts backwards and forwards across our stern and we are only able to have the genoa out for short periods because the rest of the time it flaps listlessly. Then the sky clouds over providing enough rain to wash away the salt caked all over the boat. We seem to have passed through a front and by 9pm when we change watches we haul out the genoa again. Finally, it seems, the promised wind change has arrived.

With luck we may arrive in time on Friday. More likely we shall arrive just after dark and have to hang around offshore until dawn as Bermuda is not somewhere to approach for the first time in the dark.

We have a most beautiful sunrise but the wind is dying and drifting towards the bow again. By mid-day it strengthens and we are able to cut the motors for a few hours. In the afternoon the wind drops again and we go back to motor sailing. We check the fuel level every three hours and worry that we are using too much; but all we can do is just keep plodding on towards our destination.

At 7am on Friday, our eighth day at sea, we put our last container of fuel in the tank, giving us about 30 US gallons. By now we are fairly confident that we can make it to Bermuda in daylight. For most of the morning we see south-east 3-4 winds, but continue to motor sail to ensure we arrive before dark. But the wind weakens in the afternoon and we have to use both engines to maintain enough speed to beat nightfall

BERMUDA

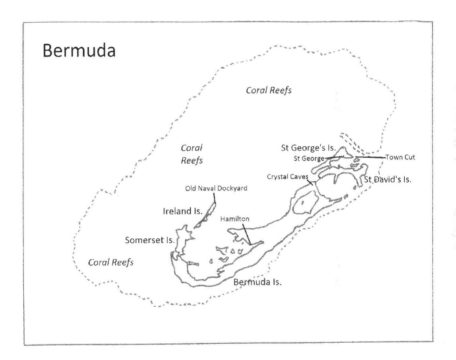

Dotted line indicates the outer edge of the reefs.

43
The Bermudan Archipelago

Bermuda is frequently referred to as 'an island' but is in fact a collection of islands surrounded by an enormous area of rocks and reefs. The two largest towns are: St George's, the original settlement dating from 1612; and Hamilton which subsequently became the country's capital. We intend to head for St George's as it is not only the closest but also the most popular for yachts in transit. To reach it you have to pass through Town Cut, which is surprisingly narrow. So it is no wonder that the Harbour Master's Office is manned around the clock seven days a week given the fact that massive cruise ships go in and out. Meeting one of them half way could be quite a problem.

As required, we contact the Harbour Master on the VHF. The man on duty is super, even asking if we have been before and do we need assistance to enter. We thank him, but our only difficulty is trying to spot the marker posts while staring into a very low, bright sun.

We arrive at the customs dock in St George's Harbour just as the sun begins to set over a spotless little town of pastel houses with white roofs. White not only deflects the sun, it seems, but provides a clean surface to channel rainwater into storage tanks. Water is at a premium here.

An elderly man helps us tie up and a tall, friendly young Customs Officer does our paperwork and offers advice. While David completes the forms, I sit on a bench and chat with the older man and watch the sun sink below the island. The tiny harbour has small houses right down to the waterfront. They look snug and welcoming in the early evening light.

The Customs Officer is *so* helpful – when you leave, he says, if you tell the last shop you spend money in that you are going they will give you your change in US dollars. His last words as he unties us from the dock are where to find a nice little spot in the anchorage and to enjoy our stay.

We are so happy to be settled before dark, crack open a bottle and have supper by candlelight in the cockpit. The town lights glow softly and there is just the sound of frogs. Some places are such a pleasure although other factors do apply, apart from scenery: things like your reception on arrival, how long you have been at sea, how relieved you are to be in, and how tired, hot and sticky you were before it all stopped. Soon after dinner we sink into dreamless sleep. Saturday morning we are delighted to wake up in Bermuda, go ashore early and take a walk around the town.

This little country was born out of a ship wreck. The *Sea Venture* had left Plymouth, on England's south coast, in June 1609 for Jamestown, the English settlement in Virginia. It had 150 passengers and crew and a dog, but never reached America's shores. It foundered off Bermuda a few weeks later in a storm – possibly a hurricane - as it had set sail into what we now know to be the North Atlantic Hurricane Season.

After three days fighting the storm, and with *Sea Venture* taking in water faster than crew and passengers could bail it out, her captain ran his ship aground rather than let her sink. This allowed all aboard – the dog included – to reach safety. William Shakespeare is believed to have drawn on the testimony of several of these survivors for *The Tempest,* his play about moral shipwreck and redemption.

Sea Venture's survivors built themselves another boat, which they called *Deliverance*, and subsequently reached Virginia and the Jamestown settlement for which they had originally set out. One of them was John Rolfe, later to found the tobacco industry and marry Pocahontas.

But a couple of years later, in 1612, another ship of emigrants sailed from England, expressly for Bermuda. And it was here, at St George's, that they established what is said to be the oldest, continuously-occupied settlement in the New World. The colony of Jamestown in Virginia, although established five years earlier, in 1607, and probably the most well-known, failed to thrive.

The archipelago's name comes from Juan de Bermudez, a Spanish explorer, who claimed the uninhabited islands for Spain around 1503 but never set foot on them. He apparently felt the risk posed by the surrounding reefs wasn't worth taking.

While the name on the chart may be Spanish, there is no escaping the country's antecedents as we visit St Peter's Anglican Church and lunch at Freddie's Pub on The Square, serving a mouth-watering steak and kidney pie in flaky pastry, real chips (not those anorexic little fries that need four to fill a fork) and a very good cider.

St Peter's, built in 1713, is light and airy thanks to its many windows, and currently filled with the fragrance of freshly-cut flowers. Parishioners are decorating it for tomorrow's Mothering Sunday service. It is a very pretty church with exposed beams and white-washed walls, box pews, and a lot of polished wood. It is also the oldest surviving Anglican Church in continuous use outside the British Isles.

Lunch on the balcony at Freddie's is a late celebration for David's birthday since neither of us had had the wherewithal to do much about it on the actual day. In fact, such was our antipathy to food for most of the passage that we arrived pounds lighter than when we set out.

St George's main square is most attractive, but there are some aspects of our shared history in one of its corners that are best left in the past rather than celebrated, such as the stocks and pillory. Then, as we wait for our order to arrive, a Town Crier in a blue frock coat, white hose and three-cornered hat strides onto the edge of the quay, reads an inaudible decree from a parchment scroll and then dunks some poor woman into the harbour on a ducking stool.

'It's a living,' she mutters as she sloshes past us on her way home. Personally, I'd have preferred to see the pompous, pot-bellied bloke in the blue coat, white stockings and three-cornered hat under water. But, there you go.

We also take in a tour of the American tall ship *Pride of Baltimore II*, a clipper topsail schooner we last saw in Annapolis harbour. But since she is now handily tied up to the quay here we accept an invitation to go aboard for a look around. After which, we embark on some general maintenance in preparation for our next voyage.

David begins on his list of mechanical checks, starting with the engines and EPIRB and has a go at the creak in the bathroom bulkhead. I set about repairing two damaged sections of the genoa outhaul – sitting on the side deck with a glass of red beside me and The Best of the Sixties on my Walkman, singing along with the groups. People who sing along like this are always something of a spectacle. Firstly, we can rarely remember all the words and just sing out the ones we know, leaving gaps while we wait for the recording to get to our next bit. Passing yachtsmen smile indulgently.

We also put a couple of small patches on the awning where a rope has worn through it. I spray the adhesive, David places the patch. We have done one, and while I wait for him to line up the other I finally get around to reading the tiny label on the back of the can.

'Have bottled oxygen available,' it says below the familiar icon of a skull and crossbones, 'and a physician on alert.'

In between maintenance work we continue to explore St George's. Its small parks are not so much mown as manicured, very neat and pretty. The houses are traditional and well-preserved with some dating back to the 18th century. The town has echoes of Devon and Cornwall, with neat, plastered houses fronting onto narrow, twisting streets.

It also looks quietly affluent. And on the subject of money, Bermudians pay no income tax but for the average earner this is probably offset somewhat by the higher cost of goods and services. Fuel, food and other commodities appear to be twice the price of those in the USA.

However, in terms of environment, the islands have a temperate climate - with the coldest month around 65°F and the warmest 85°F. And although the possibility of a hurricane cannot be entirely ruled out it is not considered a problem. Its streets are uncluttered since the law currently allows only one modest-sized car per household. And no hire cars are permitted at all, so neither traffic nor parking is a problem. Add all this to the good humour of the people and the general cleanliness and tidiness and you start to think that it would be a really nice place to settle.

Unfortunately a quick check shows that there are only a few houses available to non-Bermudians and the cheapest sells for several million dollars with an annual property tax starting well in excess of $100,000. True, a condo would be cheaper but still well out of our price range.

Bermuda, like the Azores to which we are headed, is a staging post for yachtsmen because both lie on one of the great sailing routes between America and Europe, and sooner or later a large number of yachtsmen pass through one or both of them.

Accordingly we meet up with a number of people we previously encountered as far away as Madeira, Massachusetts and the Caribbean, and spend many a lazy afternoon catching up.

We also go for picnics on glorious beaches such as Tobacco Bay and walk along the coast road. Bermuda has forts scattered all around it but as far as we are aware none has ever been used in anger. Like Canada's, they were mostly built just before or just after the War of 1812 but the US doesn't appear to have got around to invading.

On one afternoon ramble we encounter a man who asks us if we are enjoying our day and would we like to see the capture of a swarm of bees. He turns out to be Bermuda's Bee Man, with several hundred hives scattered around the island.

We follow him into a garden and there, in a small bush, is a swarm clamped around its main stem, one bee on top of another. He says their own hive has probably become overcrowded and this group has gone off in search of a new home. They look so vulnerable, embarking on a new life but only getting as far as this little shrub in somebody's garden.

He sprays them with a fine mist of water, to restrict their ability to fly, puts on protective clothing (which he says he probably won't need) and begins to scoop handfuls of them off the bush and lower them gently into a large bin. We stand there fascinated, with stray bees flying all around us. He says they are harmless in this state and will introduce them into one of his own hives.

St George's historic charm was saved for future generations by having the status of Capital removed from it in 1815 which meant the developers shifted their attention to Hamilton instead. This is not to say that Hamilton is not a very attractive place. We take the bus to have a look at it. And another to explore the Crystal Cave. The largest of Bermuda's subterranean caverns, it was discovered in 1905 by two twelve-year-old boys in search of a lost cricket ball.

On the way back to Voyager we stop off at the tourist office as it won't be open for the sale of tickets at the time we want to leave in the morning for a rather special trip.

Dolphin Day

We rise at 5.30 next morning to catch the 6.45 bus for the dockyard on Ireland Island at the nether reaches of the archipelago and some nineteen miles distant. The dockyard is the old Royal Navy base, which the British abandoned in 1951, and which houses Bermuda's excellent Maritime Museum.

The journey there takes us along the coast, past the southern beaches. It is a landscape of cliffs, rocky inlets, small harbours and beautiful little bays.

We had been at the bus stop with 20 minutes to spare, at the terminus with 30 minutes to spare, and at the dockyard 35 minutes before it opened – but that's in the nature of public transport. And we don't mind at all because today is the day of our guilty, but very special appointment.

In a corner of the Maritime Museum's enormous grounds we change into wet suits and floatation devices. We have masks but no snorkels because a snorkel could cause injury. Unfortunately, you are so used to having a snorkel attached to your mask that initially you keep forgetting, and breathe under water, which is disastrous.

As with zoos, neither of us enjoys performing marine mammals, yet both of us have longed to interact with dolphins. We've met people who've heard someone say they met somebody who achieved it in the wild. And we read an article once about someone who tried it but the dolphins kept pushing him back to shore because from his swimming technique - so different from their own - they'd assumed he was drowning. But for the two of us, on a solitary boat miles out at sea on a strong swell with wild, unsuspecting and possibly male dolphins, it was never going to happen.

Today there are only four of us humans in a very large pool – once part of a functioning naval dockyard - and supervised from ashore by a cheerful American called Gemma. She introduces three dolphins into the pool. I'm aware of them rushing past us underwater, very close, as though testing our responses. But it doesn't take long for them to get used to us so that we can stroke them, support them between us and hold their flippers as we swim alongside them. We share the pool with them for upwards of half an hour, then get out briefly for a chat (with a human) about conservation and the environment before returning to the water.

What we like about this place is that while the whole experience is hugely enjoyable for a visitor, it seems to be designed with the dolphins in mind. The first session allowed them to get to know us – minimizing the stress of having strangers introduced into their domain. In this second pool they come closer, enabling us to fondle them – holding their jaw in one hand and stroking their beak with the other, patting their melon, stroking their stomachs, and chests and tail fluke. In short, they glide through a gentle embrace, something they seem to enjoy very much. We are even invited to give 'em a kiss. Mine is a proxy one, to all the wild dolphins that have given me so much joy over the years.

The youngest is two years old and the oldest 28. They can live up to 40. The oldest one, a former Navy dolphin, is known affectionately as The Princess, mother of the two males. Utterly relaxed, she lies on her back before us with her eyes closed in an apparent state of bliss as Gemma explains her anatomy to us; the sheer tidiness of an enclosed marine mammal body.

In a third pool the young males perform for us. They weigh about 480lbs, Gemma says, and can reach speeds of around 30mph. The most awesome moment comes when one races off, banks round the far curve of the pool and roars directly at us. He stops dead a foot from us and then skyhops, vertical in the water, looking very pleased with himself and ready to be congratulated. Watching his speed and knowing his weight our applause is as much from relief as admiration.

The other male is sent off to retrieve two rings tossed by Gemma into the water at the far end of the pool with a, 'Let's see who he gives them to.' The young dolphin returns in moments with both of them on his nose and presents them to me. I am overcome.

The pools are visible from the public area of the museum and we wander across the cobbles afterwards to a bench, to digest our recent experience. A girl of around twelve, recognising us from the pools, glares at us. She comes over and proceeds to give us a lecture on dolphins being better left to lead natural lives in the wild while her mother, becoming increasingly embarrassed, tries to entice her away.

I look at the girl, with her flushed face and her small frame quivering with indignation. 'I agree with you,' I tell her. 'But I've just had one of the most fantastic experiences of my entire life.'

Bermuda has one last treat for us. Late afternoon the Gombeys arrive on the harbour front. The Gombeys are a Bermudan folk tradition, like England's Morris Men, in the sense that: nobody has a clue what it means; its roots are obscured by time; but it involves a bunch of men in daft clothes making a lot of noise and drinking beer.

Morris Men routinely wear knickerbockers, knee socks hung with bells, flowers in the brims of their hats and bang sticks together as they dance along the street. Then they all head off to the pub.

Today's Gombeys are wearing face masks, frilly, multi-coloured suits and matching, very tall hats topped with peacock feathers. They make their own distinctive noise with whistles and drums. When they have finished marching, whistling and drumming they wander around the quay companionably drinking bottled beer together, while their womenfolk hold their hats for them.

One thing I have to say as a female observer is that, like Morris Men, the Gombeys look to be having the most marvellous time. Their enjoyment is palpable. Although I suspect that it has more to do with male bonding and the beer talking than all that stuff about pre-Christian traditions, the Green Man and nature worship.

44
Weather Watching

We are now ready to set off for the Azores, but the weather has been slowly deteriorating. It now turns very blustery. Herb warns this could last a week and might get worse. It does. It is currently 30-40 knots gusting up to 45 and constantly changing direction. In fact, conditions become so bouncy that *Voyager* and every other boat in the anchorage begins rocking violently. One of them begins dragging towards the rocks and cannot start his engine. At the same time several boats abandon the marina, which is the opposite action to what one would normally expect but they had been moored Mediterranean style, have dragged up their kedge anchors and now have nothing to hold their bows off the concrete quay.

They begin milling about looking for a suitable place to anchor in an already crowded anchorage and one of them, with a total disregard for the poor man with a failed engine who is desperately trying to sail off the rocks, keeps getting in his way regardless of the man's distress; until someone in a RIB goes to his aid, towing him far enough around to get the wind into his sails and allow him to sail out of trouble.

The wind howls on into the night. We go to bed and try to sleep but fail. When we hear an Australian voice shouting we get up. For several days we had been anchored a respectable distance from his boat. But earlier today another yacht - without a name, a home port or an ensign to identify it – had inserted itself between us and the Australian, and is now dragging into his boat.

The Aussie is yelling at the three men inside to come out and shift their boat. 'I know yer in there,' he yells. 'I just saw ya put yer light out. It's no good hiding. Git out here, ya bahstards. That was nearly a hit.' But they stay put, in the dark, for a long time, before finally creeping out to address the problem.

Just after midnight there is a report from Bermuda Radio over the VHF. The Coast Guard has picked up a faint Mayday call but still has no position for the stricken vessel. It also repeats the gale warning. I feel heartily sorry for anyone out there tonight, but especially on a failing boat. I fall asleep on the sofa around half past two. David is still on watch when I wake up at daylight.

It is raining hard later in the morning when a cruise ship arrives. It must be very annoying to pay all that money for twenty-four hours in sunny Bermuda only to get Easter Monday in Blighty. We are wondering how much longer the conditions will prevent us from leaving. Sadly, in terms of weather, the ideal day for us to have left here turns out to have been the one after we arrived, but of course we had wanted to see something of Bermuda.

A lot of new boats have been anchored in the harbour for several days now. Cruising in company, they are heading back to Europe and this is their gathering point. The wind has lessened slightly, but has now shifted to the north-east, so it is a surprise when we see most of them milling about with every sign of leaving.

The skipper of one of them, who had anchored rather too close to us, has started to get his anchor up without warning, taking it for granted that we will rush out in the pouring rain to fend off his boat. We ask him, not a little irritably in the circumstances, where they are all going and he says the Azores. They must be mad. The conditions, and the forecast, are terrible. Heavy rain and a headwind. A few stay behind but the rest lurch out like lemmings. We hear later that they are having a terrible time with 30-knot headwinds, 20-foot seas and torrential rain.

After three days the first of the casualties returns to the anchorage. Its roller reefing has broken. Others begin to trickle in. One of them is a catamaran with a state-of-the–art rotating wing mast. The design is said to be more efficient than traditional sails and easier to use short-handed. Unfortunately its roller reefing has broken, too, and there is a crack in its boom.

Herb is worried by the strange weather patterns we are getting and the fact that the three international computer models - which forecasters use - keep getting their predictions wrong. However, two days from now seems a distinct possibility. It would mean having to beat into moderate winds and being pushed to the north but south-westerlies *are* expected by the end of the week which would allow us to return to lower latitudes.

We meet the couple from the catamaran. They have just received a quotation for $25,000 to ship their boat back home and are in a state of shock. David suggests they could motor to the US and just ship the boom back for repair. While this was being done they could still use their boat as a motor boat and cruise the USA. He gives them our copy of Skipper Bob's Marina Guide and information on the boatyards we have used.

Herb suggests that waiting another day or two before leaving would be best. Bermuda Harbour Radio puts out a forecast for 25 knots tomorrow and 30 to 35 the day after, all from the south-east and which is too much for us to beat into.

Next day the couple from the catamaran stop by in their dinghy to say they have been able to talk to the manufacturer of their revolutionary wing mast. His advice with regard to the crack in the boom is, 'Slap a patch on it.' They are much happier. They can get their roller reefing fixed here and expect to be ready to travel in a matter of days.

Herb's advice is not to leave before Friday and so the wait goes on. He says the weather patterns for the lows coming off the US East Coast are defying all three computer weather modelling programmes. They are all giving different predictions and the only thing they have in common is that they are all getting it wrong.

Friday will see the end of our legal stay in Bermuda and we shall need to get an extension to our documentation. It will also be the last day before the official start of the hurricane season – Bermuda lies within the hurricane belt - and our insurance company will not cover any resulting damage. So we need to remove ourselves from the hurricane zone as soon as possible. The wind begins to shift to the south and Friday looks as if it could well be a good day to leave. Although we shall initially get pushed slightly north, within a day we should be back on a direct route.

And so it is that on Friday morning, on the last day of May, we go ashore early to clear out with Immigration and call Tony to let him know we are setting off for the Azores. Back on board we stow away the outboard, tie the dinghy upside down on the foredeck, fasten the washboards over the bow windows and lay the safety line along the side deck.

David has done his best to find the optimum time for us to set sail. At present he has forecasts from three sources. One says gales to the north, another says gales to the south and the third says gales to the west. All indicate reasonable conditions to the east, where we want to go. David will also be tuning in to Herb's broadcast each evening from around 7pm.

At 3pm we raise the anchor, call Harbour Radio for permission to leave, wave our goodbyes to fellow-yachtsmen in the anchorage and motor out of the harbour. Beyond the heads it is quite bumpy but we get the genoa and the main up and enjoy a sail. The local forecast is not much different to Herb's, south 15-20 knots, going south-west by morning. So the bumpy conditions should lessen during the night.

45
To The Azores

It is not a good night. In fact, it is so turbulent that neither of us sleeps off-watch and we both have dodgy stomachs. I just about manage to hang on to my supper but David loses his overboard. We make good progress with more than six knots until shortly before dawn when the wind drops.

The bad night is followed by a bleak, overcast day with a lumpy sea; our only sighting a couple of shearwaters grazing in our wake. Herb says winds should be OK for the next two days but could then be from the east or north-east by the third. We also learn that a number of other boats set out shortly after we did, and others have done so today.

Sunday is overcast, squally and nasty outside; damp and muggy indoors. And very uncomfortable. At around 2.30pm a huge wave hits our starboard hull, rises into the air and breaks over the doghouse roof - and us. It turns out to be the first of many. With the wind rising we start to reef the genoa, but the reefing line jams. The only answer is to go forward and free it.

David buckles himself into a harness and clips it onto the safety line running down the length of the boat. Then he makes his way down a rolling side deck on hands and knees – the only way to avoid being knocked over by breaking waves and the roll of the boat. Once at the bow, he discovers the exit line of the roller reefing has doubled back into the entry section, putting three thicknesses of rope where only one should be. He releases it but it will need careful handling in future.

Herb says we are running through a trough but that when we get to the other side of it, the wind will be coming from the south, which will give us a broad reach. The down side is that we could have similar conditions to those at present for three more days. Winds are gusting at near gale force. We still have motion sickness and are eating little.

Our fourth day out is overcast with strong winds, heavy rain and a nasty sea but just after dawn the wind eases and we let out a reef on the genoa. Soon after, David turns on the starboard engine to top up the batteries and hears a strange whistling noise. He can't find the source in the engine bay but out on deck finds half a dozen False Killer Whales - who seem attracted by the groans from our self-steering gear - swimming as tight as they can get to our stern where the noise is at its greatest.

Slender-bodied, with an elongated head and snub nose, the false killer whale is not a whale at all but a large dolphin. However, like its partial namesake, the killer whale, it does kill and eat other marine mammals. Perhaps this group had mistaken our self-steering's protests for some ailing creature and easy prey. Or maybe they were simply curious. But as soon as they spot David gazing down at them from the stern they vanish.

The wind begins gusting to near gale force again. We need to put a reef back in the genoa or we shall have too much canvas up. But despite taking care, the same thing happens as yesterday. The furling mechanism gets stuck.

The easiest thing to do would be to take the genoa down. But we can't because it already has a reef in it making it impossible to lower. With the wind rising rapidly David puts on his harness and clips himself onto the safety line again. His journey forward is even more violent than yesterday and it is one of the few times I have been really afraid for him.

When he gets to the furling mechanism he finds that as before the rope has folded back on itself inside the reefing drum, but this time it is jammed solid. While he works on it, it is not possible to keep any tension on the genoa and when the self-steering falters the sail begins to flog. Within moments it has caught around the radar reflector which it tears from its mounting and hurls into the sea. But not before the reflector has caused a gash in the genoa. The wind catches it and in no time the gash has become a long tear between the sacrificial strip and the sail itself.

David, meanwhile, is crouched right on the edge of the bow struggling with the furling gear, in gale-force winds and with big greenies crashing over him. Each time the bow plunges, he disappears below my line of vision and I hold my breath in case he isn't there when the bow rears up again. All I can do is sit at the helm and steer, desperate to keep *Voyager* on a course which prevents the sail from thrashing from one side to the other and sending David flying, or else pounding the mast and causing even more damage. I am horrified that I might allow the boat to drift. It takes over an hour to free the rope and finally furl the genoa.

Unfortunately, as with most British catamarans, the genoa is our major sail. We try to make progress under the much smaller mainsail and even put up the tiny staysail – which is really only a storm sail - to help it along but they are an unbalanced pair and the self-steering gear becomes ineffective. We keep lurching off course and have visions of hand-steering for the next two weeks. We eventually solve the problem by running an engine - at just 1500 revs for economy but enough to hold the bow on course. We now have torrential rain.

Herb says the current conditions will remain for the next two days at least. And some of the boats which left Bermuda just after we did have begun turning back.

Voyager is crashing into the waves and groaning terribly. The dinghy breaks loose on the foredeck and David makes his way forward again to re-tie it. It has a dent in its side where the breaking waves have pushed it, in its loosened state, into the staysail furling gear. The self-steering gear is making the most awful noises while at the same time the wind generator, howling in all this wind, is vibrating so much that it seems about to dismantle the section of gantry it shares with our GPS aerial.

We have already lost our radar reflector overboard, making us less visible to the radar scanners of other vessels. The last thing we need now is to lose the use of our GPS.

Approaching a wind generator in a gale-force wind is like walking into the propeller of a small aeroplane. Unlike a plane's, however, the spinning blades of a wind generator do not remain facing in one direction. The nose cone holding the blades rotates 360 degrees so that it can find wind from any direction in order to produce electricity for you. That also makes it infinitely more dangerous and harder to catch. At the same time we don't want to damage its blades as we shall need them to produce power for our batteries as soon as we are fully under sail again.

Behind its circle of blades the generator has a wind vane which turns the blades directly into the wind. Our plan is to insert the boat hook into the small hole in this vane, turn it so that the blades face away from the wind until they stop spinning, and then tie the thing down.

Our task is made more difficult because we are teetering on the edge of a wildly plunging stern as well as working with our arms at full stretch above our heads because, apart from needing a wind generator up high to catch any available wind, you can't install one where it is likely to spin its vicious little blades into your face.

Our first few attempts fail as the boat hook is simply thrown violently back by the swinging vane, but finally David snares it, turns the blades away from the wind, and when they slow sufficiently I throw a rope over them and tie the thing fast to the gantry.

As we stand there for a few moments, panting at the effort and congratulating ourselves that we both still have all our fingers, I think how bizarre we must have looked – David with his 'spear' and me with the 'net' – like a gladiatorial team in some Roman arena ducking and diving to contain a dangerous beast. With the wind generator under control David resumes his search for the source of the complaints coming from the self-steering, but finds nothing.

It has not been a day we would ever want to repeat: waves constantly crashing over us, torrential rain, leaks everywhere and noises we cannot identify. We are also worried about how much fuel we shall use if we have to continue using an engine to keep *Voyager* on course. We are both very tired but still only four days into a seventeen-day passage.

The time has come when we must decide whether to go on or turn back. *Voyager* is at last clear of the trough of low pressure which had produced the gale, but we still have a violent sea. And without our genoa we are beating into near gale-force winds with an underpowered rig and making slow progress.

On the other hand, the forecast promises a south-westerly wind which would provide ideal sailing conditions. To return to Bermuda would also take us back through the slow-moving gale we are only just now leaving behind. And even if it does blow itself out, to be replaced by the promised south-westerly, we should then have to beat into a south-west wind all the way back to Bermuda. We decide to carry on.

There is, of course, the problem that we are being pushed steadily north. Herb has warned that winds are even stronger up there. But we have made our decision and all we can do is try to limit the amount we are being pushed northwards while we wait for the promised favourable wind.

An Unexpected Visitor

The only thing spotted yesterday was an aluminium beer keg. Sightings for today are one freighter and a loose fishing buoy until late afternoon when, after circling *Voyager* for some time, a Brown Noddy lands on the lid of the stern locker. A medium-sized sea bird of the Tern family, he is not happy once he gets there as his webbed feet and long claws keep slipping on its surface. Not to mention our looming presence.

He takes off again and perches on the doghouse roof instead, but is severely buffeted up there and shortly before dark flutters down onto the cockpit sole. His eyes are only half open, like a hung-over drunk. With barely the strength to right himself, he staggers with every roll of the boat. He looks ill and almost past the point of caring. And now that I get to see him properly it is apparent that he is a juvenile. For a species which thrives in colonies of thousands of other birds, he is not only alone and in ferocious weather, but is not even fully grown.

I coil a short piece of rope into a small mat and shoo him onto it. At least he stops staggering, but he keeps shaking his head and looks cold so I roll up a bath towel lengthways, tie it up with string to stop it unrolling and flapping in the wind, and curl it into a barrier around him. He sinks down into this rope and terry towelling nest, lowers his head and does not move again. We do not expect him to survive the night, but avoid shining a torch near him on our watches anyway, just in case. If anything is likely to save him, it is sleep.

Herb says we will get high winds for the next two days but they should then moderate and veer to the south and south-west. He repeats his warning about not going north but unfortunately we are unable to prevent our track northwards.

He says all the various countries' computer models are at variance with one another in their predictions and he can only use his own experience - which is, of course, what so many of us rely on. To add to his dilemma the weather patterns are, he says, unlike anything he has known for this time of year.

The only yacht left of those that set out from Bermuda at a similar time as us, and which is in contact with Herb, is called *Machismo*. Like us, its skipper has problems. He has a broken chain plate and cannot use his sails on this tack so is motoring. But he also has engine trouble. Herb has advised that he return to Bermuda.

His response: 'I never turn back!' is fortunate for us because his is the only vessel giving us access to Herb's predictions in our particular sea area.

Like the bird out in our cockpit, sleep is what David and I need most. Because of the violent conditions we have not slept properly since leaving Bermuda. Normally, even in the roughest of night watches, one of us has gone to lie down, if not to sleep then at least to get some physical rest, to be fit for purpose on our next watch. But there is no physical rest to be had and sleep is out of the question.

A Dark Night of the Soul

Our fifth night at sea is the worst we have ever experienced. We are both braced against a bulkhead in the saloon, our bodies juddering with every wave that slams against the hull. The wind is howling like a banshee and the creaks and groans coming from *Voyager* are unlike anything we have ever heard her make before.

At around 3am, when body and mind are at their lowest ebb anyway, I begin to think the unthinkable. It becomes manifest when I realize that, while clinging to the chart table for physical support, David is also quietly gathering together a few essentials – passports, ship's papers, credit cards, and so on - things we should need to take with us were we to abandon ship.

It is the response of a moment, the result of the exhaustion that comes from too long without sleep and the stress of a constantly heaving environment. It passes and we stagger on, taking data from the instruments hourly, filling in the log and lurching out into the cockpit every ten minutes to keep a lookout for other vessels.

In the early hours I notice our guest's back feathers fluttering in the cold wind. Obviously I can't lay a cover over him. If he is still alive it will panic him, but in case he is, I slide his draft excluder a little closer round him so that at least the rest of him will be warm. Which, when I think about it later, was pretty stupid, even if my mental processes weren't up to much at the time. After all, this is not a small child or a puppy but a creature which lives its life out in the elements. Even though the current ones may have proved too much for him.

Nevertheless, at daybreak his wings emerge, one at a time, and his head goes through the most amazing contortions as he sets about his grooming routine. His long, vicious-looking beak slips delicately along every flight feather and, after each long glean, he dabs his beak decorously on the towel, first one side then the other, like a barber wiping his razor. Then he plumps up his back feathers and addresses his undercarriage. This will go on in spasms for three hours, plus a fair bit of stretching in between, and all done still inside his draft excluder on his non-slip mat. And at least he is able to complete his ablutions without falling over because, since reaching a peak during the night, conditions have become less violent. There is less roll now and the wind has almost dropped away.

Meanwhile, David notices that our mainsail has started to come down and is sagging at the bottom. We need to restore some tension. It isn't causing a performance problem but we shall be unable to reef it should that become necessary. We have already lost the use of our genoa. We cannot afford to lose the main as well.

I climb up onto the doghouse roof and crouch against the mast, supporting the mainsail with my left hand and with my right feeding its luff into the slot in the mast, while David works the winch to haul it aloft. And naturally, whenever you begin to do anything with the sails, the wind begins to rise. It is soon up to 20 knots. Our first attempt fails. Despite managing to raise the sail back up, we are unable to tie it off in time before it sinks again. David releases the tension on the winch and we get ready to try again.

Our Guest Leaves

With his grooming and exercises complete, our guest decides this is the moment to leave. He tries to fly up out of the cockpit but his wings are too long and his runway too short. A Brown Noddy is not designed to do a vertical take-off out of what to him is effectively a deep pit. I don't want him to be exhausted before he starts his journey, so I ask David to hang on a minute and climb down.

At the bird's next attempt I put my hands underneath him and scoop him up the last few inches to get him onto the stern locker. He is so unexpectedly light and his rich brown feathers so very soft. There is a bit of an unseemly scrabble out onto the afterdeck, because of the 20-knot wind, as he makes an awkward, slipping, web-footed beeline for the stern toe rail. What he wants is a clear take-off with no obstructions and this is the place for him to do it. But just as he lifts off, the wind gusts and blows him against the lower part of the stern handrail. It catches him under his head and sends him back onto the deck. But he gets it right the second time and sails off. In his element. Flying strongly into the distance.

I scramble back up onto my perch on the doghouse roof to continue the struggle with the main, but within a few minutes am surprised to see a small, dark shape out of the corner of my eye. The Brown Noddy is back.

I have no idea why, and at the time do not have the leisure to think about it. All my energy is going into forcing the mainsail up into its groove in the mast while trying not to fall off the doghouse roof. But later I can only think it was curiosity. In terms of his survival he had done everything right and in the proper order: slept through the night and recovered his strength; prepared his feathers next morning; then tested himself in flight. Only after all that had he come back to take a look at the strange creatures who had sheltered him.

He flies around the boat three times, observing us carefully, before setting off strongly to the west. He has a long way to go – 565 miles to Bermuda - and all on an empty stomach. I had tried tempting him with tinned sardine after his morning ablutions but one touch with his beak had made his eyes water. The bits of raw meat and wholemeal bread left for him overnight still lie untouched. At least he misses the squall which comes through at mid-day.

Wild creatures leave such a hole when they go. Especially this one. His small, vulnerable presence had brought relief to the horrors of the previous night. Concern for another's predicament stops you fixating quite so much on your own.

After the squall has passed through, the weather brightens and even the sun peeps out. We take advantage of it to string the cockpit with our clothing, some of which has been wet so long it has begun to smell.

The wind gets less and we begin eating again. We are also handling the sea roll a little better. Although to watch one another crossing the saloon is like observing the under-twos tottering across a room, rushing headlong for the furniture and occasionally reeling backwards. Best of all, we are able to get some sleep.

On Wednesday, Herb explains the reduction in our wind speed. We (that is to say *Machismo* and ourselves) have wandered into a narrow, weak high-pressure ridge about 120 miles wide between two systems. If we can stay within it we should get our longed-for wind shift from the south-west.

There are still gales or near-gales to the north and the south, which would account for why we are getting such a lumpy sea in moderate to light winds.

We also keep finding current against us. There are lots of circular eddies between Bermuda and the Azores. Some are warm and others cold. Both create currents. The warm ones move in a clockwise direction, the cold ones anti-clockwise. Depending on whether you are at top or the bottom of one of these circles, you either have current with you or against you. We cannot know if the eddy we are in at present is warm or cold, but it is definitely against us.

By Thursday we do at least, finally, get a warm day and a clear sky. Our only sightings in twenty-four hours are another aluminium beer keg and a freighter.

Our first warm day is followed by our first starry night. But with the arrival of darkness we discover that our masthead tri-colour is no longer working. These are not the conditions to contemplate climbing to the top of the mast, so we shall have to use our anchor light instead. Apart from being illegal, it will also look rather odd to any passing ships – the sea being over a mile deep here – but at least they will be aware of our presence.

Improvising

Before we set off from England we bought a new mainsail for *Voyager*, her old one being a little baggy and not as efficient as it might have been. Gazing up at its replacement flying in the wind today reminds me that we still have the old one on board and I ask David if we couldn't try hoisting it in place of the damaged genoa. It is nothing like the shape and size of the genoa but it *is* a sail, and will hold *some* wind. By evening the sea is more settled and if it is the same in the morning we will try it.

Herb advises *Machismo* to keep going due east and the longed-for south-westerly will arrive in a couple of days. Unfortunately we are being slowly pushed to the north-east and can do little about it. Herb also puts out an alert for a white 64ft schooner which left the Caribbean on April 21 and has not been seen in the six weeks since.

At around three o'clock on Friday morning the moon emerging through cloud makes me jump. For an instant it looks like a masthead light too close for comfort. A pair of jeans, still not dry days after being soaked in sea water, hang malodorously beside the steering wheel.

Dawn sees conditions still good for the sail change and we plan it like a military campaign, complete with check list. It goes well. Despite wind and a rolling deck we get the genoa down and bag it without too much trouble. Then the old main is hauled up. The luff is much shorter than the genoa's, so when we get it up the mast its foot is about six feet higher than it should be. It looks very odd. And because we are close hauled at the moment, the shape is all wrong and the leech flutters madly. But, with a bit of juggling, it works - and we are able to turn the engine off.

While conditions are such we take the opportunity to do a few other jobs: retie the dinghy on the foredeck; move the gash bags from the stern locker (near our noses) to the chain locker (at the bow); empty three cans of diesel into the fuel tank and, lastly, set the wind generator loose again.

Doing anything while compensating for the constant roll of the boat uses up a lot of energy. But although tired at the end of it we are very happy with the result. Fortunately, the skies stay more or less clear, the wind mostly under 15 knots and even the sea gets a little calmer. We are back to three meals a day and have established that running the engine at 1500 rpm uses only about 1 litre per hour, so worry less about the amount of time we can afford to motor when we need to.

Herb reports tonight that the expected south-westerly has been delayed yet again - until Monday now, which is three days away. He also suggests boats stay below 34°North. Unfortunately we have been pushed close to 35°North but conditions seem no different to those which the boats below 34°N are reporting. We are still sailing without engines and happy about that.

On my early Saturday morning watch, a shooting star curves across the sky like a huge firework. It is bright green.

Wind strength and direction become erratic and we are constantly adjusting our course to stay as close-hauled as we can, given the limitations of our sails. Herb says we could get a south-westerly wind tomorrow, and that most of the boats which were behind us, but turned back, have left Bermuda again.

The wind at last starts to veer further south and gradually we are able to alter our course more and more in an attempt to get below Herb's 34°N. During the night there is a lot of phosphorous in our wake. Its silvery glitter in the darkness is always a little eerie. Today we average 3.9 knots and cover 94 miles without an engine, which is better than expected and makes us optimistic.

Sunday. At last, eight days late, the wind begins to move towards the west and we start to pick up speed. It slowly increases during the day and we cover 110 miles. But by evening it rains and conditions are again choppy and uncomfortable. Indoors it is muggy and everything feels damp to the touch. Herb warns of a gale system to our north and we hope we are well enough south to avoid it, although the wind *is* getting stronger. We are still above 35°N and alter course again to try and get below 34.

It is a wild bumpy, lurching ride trying to get further south and below the predicted gale. And *Voyager* is finding a whole new range of noises with which to torment us. By mid-morning Monday, however, we are below 35°N but have yet to achieve the magic figure of 34. We alter to a more easterly course anyway. It is a great relief because the new course quietens everything down so that the only one stressed is the self-steering gear which continues making terrible groans.

We are still 1,000 miles from the Azores, but at least past the half-way mark. We have also had another engineless day and so preserved our precious fuel supply. Because the winds are constantly above 20 knots our day's run has been 129 miles.

Our optimism ends when Herb says there are low pressure cells all along 35°N and we just hope we are far enough south of them. Listening to Herb has become an ordeal. Not only do we get high-pitched atmospheric whines and screams, but someone keeps turning on his microphone and whistling. Worse still, foreign voices hold long conversations on his frequency with several speaking at the same time. It's like being tuned into the Tower of Babel and, unfortunately, to be sure he gets every bit of information available David can be listening for up to two hours. He emerges from the earphones with his eyes glazed and his brain scrambled.

The weather meanwhile has been almost constantly overcast with rain again today. We are tired and sleep as much as we can in between watches.

In the early hours of Tuesday morning, our anchor light stops working. Now we have no masthead lights at all and have to use our steaming lights instead. They are at deck level and therefore not so visible in a plunging sea and our wild, bumpy ride has resumed with a vengeance. In fact, clinging to the helm in the darkness I am convinced on one occasion that we even become airborne briefly before crashing back into the water.

By 7am, (we are still on Bermuda time), the makeshift 'genoa' is shaking and flapping so much we begin to fear for the mast. Unable to furl it from the cockpit David clips himself onto the safety line again and goes forward onto a heaving foredeck in breaking seas. Once there, he tries to furl the sail but cannot. The problem this time is not the self-furling gear. It is the fact that when we had raised the old mainsail in place of the damaged genoa, we had not hoisted it right to the top of the rigging, because it was so much shorter than the sail it was replacing. Unfortunately, the result is that it has jammed at the top of the forestay.

So David tries to take the sail down instead, but is unable to do that either. Finally, after a long struggle, he manages to furl it. The wind is now Gale Force 8.

Just as David looks like disappearing over the bow in a huge wave, the wind generator works itself up to such a pitch that it begins to prise itself off the gantry. Over the years, one way or another, the wind generator has distressed me greatly. Now I simply gaze at it impassively like an old but despised enemy on the brink of well-deserved doom and wait for it to fall into the sea. To hell with the consequences. But, like some vindictive being having its bluff called, it remains on its perch.

Deprived of our foresail, and with only our main, we are now being pushed off course at a quite alarming rate. But with David back in the cockpit we let out the staysail and turn on an engine at 1500 rpm to keep *Voyager*'s nose pointed in the direction we want to go.

The wind is still at gale force. And waves are still breaking over the doghouse roof. To add to the amount of water we are taking on, it begins to rain. There is a worrying groaning noise coming from the steering gear and the port rudder is clunking. Apart from one brief respite we have been at the mercy of these conditions for eleven days.

In the evening, Herb says there is yet another front ahead of us which will affect our next 24 hours. But by Friday - three days from now - we should be able to turn towards the island of Faial.

Our original plan had been to head for Flores which is the most westerly island in the Azores archipelago and for a time the nearest. However, we are now so far south that Faial is closer and its capital, Horta, has all the facilities for the repair work we shall need to do.

Tradition says, 'South-west winds to the Doldrums and then put out your spinnaker for the *drift* into Horta.'

'Drift,' my *eye*!

By 10pm the wind is roaring behind our stern. The sea is hitting the bridge deck with a monstrous booming sound then sucking and sluicing up the drain holes under the companionway grille. It is pitch dark and there is an overwhelming heaviness to the air that feels not simply damp but oppressive.

Wednesday finds us wringing out the towels under the bow windows every hour because the weather boards meant to be protecting them have had their rubber strips dislodged by the sheer force of the waves hitting them and are no longer providing any kind of seal. Seawater is also seeping into the galley from under the small fridge, having forced its way in through the gas exhaust vent. It is also finding its way in through the boat's other vents although fortunately that is going directly into the bilges. We pump the bilges two or three times a day and just plod on.

We are under heavy cloud, and it rains constantly, yet in the far distance - tantalising, but never reached - is a patch of clear blue sky. A small part of our substitute genoa's leech has unfurled and flutters persistently. When David had hauled it in on the foredeck, the sheets were not at the right angle and it didn't wrap evenly, but it was the best he could do at the time.

By mid-day we are well into Herb's latest safety zone, alter course and things become more comfortable – although the sea state does not abate, sending Voyager surfing down waves at 8 knots.

David finds a small puddle of diesel under the starboard engine and sets about tracing the leak. Otherwise it is yet another job for our To Do list at Horta.

We finally work out how to furl the 'genoa' correctly using a block on our centre cleat to get the sheet angle right. At last it is completely furled and quiet. By evening the gale is subsiding and our speed is falling. We contemplate putting it out again but are very tired and decide to leave things as they are and get some rest.

Herb reports that a front will go through in the night followed by north-west winds which will go to the south-west and we should be able to turn towards Horta. During the night the wind keeps easing and going directly behind us and we cannot keep it in the staysail so we furl it and continue under main alone.

But, as forecast, in the early hours the wind does shift to the north-west and for the first time since we left Bermuda we are not taking waves on our starboard side. So far the doghouse roof and decks have been almost constantly awash. Perhaps now we can begin to dry out a little.

Just after midnight I spot a ship not far off our starboard quarter and call it up to make sure its captain is aware of our presence since we have no masthead lights anymore and no radar reflector. VHF reception is poor and the man's English is limited but he understands me perfectly and confirms that he knows we are here. Even from the security and comfort of a commercial ship's bridge he is obviously aware of what the present conditions must be like for a small boat because he surprises me as we part by saying a halting, but heartfelt, 'I am very sorry for you.' I think that very kind.

Just after dawn on Thursday we let out the staysail and turn towards Horta. And we have sunshine - with clouds admittedly, but nevertheless, *sunshine*. It must be our warmest day since Bermuda. The winds are light now but we have a current with us which helps. It is setting us more to the east than we should like but we *are* heading towards Horta and we are happy.

Until evening, that is, when Herb reports that there is a chain of four separate gale systems between the Azores and Bermuda and more low pressure cells keep spawning. He adds that another gale will come out of Horta on Saturday and boats in our area shouldn't go further north. We groan and alter course again. Tonight we have a bright first quarter moon and Venus shines like old gold in a starry sky.

The kitchen timer is a tyrant which gives no peace. You are tired, you want to sit comfortably in a warm, dry saloon but no sooner you are, it seems, then off it goes again, and you have to get up and take a 360° survey out in the cockpit to make sure *Voyager* is safe. Not to mention *wake up*, since you are supposed to be on watch after all.

Just before dawn on Friday morning a Tern tries to land on our portside lifebuoy. It wobbles and then flies away again. It is a shock to realise how long it is since we saw a bird, apart from a very tired Brown Noddy blown seriously off course.

It is another sunny day, with some cloud, but nice. We put the staysail out but the wind fluctuates between 12 and 17 knots. At 17 the wind is south-west and the staysail works, at 12 it is west-south-west so that the main stops the wind getting to the staysail and it flaps aimlessly.

This apart Friday is a restful day and we enjoy it. The wind very slowly increases and our speed gets to a consistent 5 knots. Then Herb reports that tomorrow's front will be 25 knots gusting higher and boats should go *south*. Once it has passed, we can turn towards Horta once more - if we *can*, because the wind *may* come from the north-east instead. Reluctantly we head south-east again. At this rate we are going to miss the Azores altogether.

In the early hours of Saturday a strong squall goes over us with lashing rain and gale-force winds. Presumably we can expect more of both before the front goes through. Afterwards the wind falls to 11 knots but slowly builds again. We are now accompanied by shearwaters much of the time.

The wind keeps fluctuating between the west and south-west. By mid-afternoon the expected front has still not arrived. It's a bit like a loaded gun being waved around – you don't know if or when it will go off and whether it will hit you or not. Alternatively, was that squall the front? Or is the front still to come? We decide to turn back towards Horta and if it does arrive we will head east to get through it quickly, we hope.

Herb comes on at his usual time and describes a very complex weather system. There is a weak high at 37N 40W, a front stretching from 40N 20W to 34N 30W to 33N 40W and also a warm front somewhere else which David is unable to record. Because of this Herb then gives a very different forecast for each of the boats on his list, so we are not much wiser because we aren't near to any of them; *Machismo*, with his large engines having pulled well clear of us. Although at least we now know that the front has not yet gone through. David is perplexed and decides to go south-east. Two hours later, and unable to sleep because he keeps mulling over the problem, he changes his mind and turns us towards the north-east and Horta again.

Our zig zag course continues. Horta is still 350 miles away. It has been another rainy, overcast day. There is another squall in the small hours of Sunday morning. After that has done its worst, the wind goes to the north and then north-north-east which means we are unable to maintain our course.

In the afternoon the wind drops, the current comes against us and our speed falls to 2 knots. On the plus side the sun pierces the clouds in places. By evening the wind had risen somewhat and we get up to 4 knots. It has not been so bad a day and I bake bread. At least we are more rested and are definitely eating well. We even get a relatively quiet night.

A Kind Dutchman

Today, Monday the 17th of June, was originally our estimated time of arrival, yet seventeen and a half days out from Bermuda it now looks like being another two before we reach the Azores. Herb has mentioned another front due out from Horta during that time so we also have more fun to look forward to. Although for the present the wind has become very light, dropping down to as little as two or three knots, and the only progress we make comes from the engine. We have upped the revs to 2000, still on just one engine, and plod very slowly on. David's calculations suggest we might be all right to run the engine faster but we could end up with no reserve. We decide not to risk it.

Along with the lack of wind, the sky becomes overcast and ominously dark. David listens to Herb, although he cannot expect much help as none of Herb's boats are in this area and we are the only one with light winds. In the meantime I have spotted a sail behind us and when Herb's broadcast has ended I call the boat up for a chat.

It is called *Dutch Concrete*, appropriately enough since her owner, Jack is Dutch and the boat is made of concrete. He and his crew are having to steer by hand as their autopilot is not working and they have water in the engine. Asked how we are getting on I tell him: down a sail, low on fuel, but plodding on. He has an engine to deal with and I sign off. But he calls back a short time later and offers us fuel.

We are startled. It had not occurred to us that anyone would have any to spare after such a journey as this. Nor is it a manoeuvre we have ever done before. Jack, however, is a pro and says he will tie two containers together with a length of rope between and then tie a float to them with another length of rope on that. He will then pass in front of us and throw them over the side so that we can pick them up over our starboard beam. It is pitch dark and raining and we hope we don't miss them and have to turn round for a second attempt.

We slow down, they steer close to us, Jack heaves the containers into the water and we can see them clearly, yellow, in the glow of our deck lights. David lunges with the boat hook but can't reach them, he lunges again and misses. It is my fault. I am steering but have become so anxious about getting *Voyager* close enough to the cans but not so close that I go over them and their ropes connect with our propellers that I have forgotten to turn off the autopilot. So no matter how I steer I am having no effect.

Realizing just in time, and with the sea lurching and the wind driving us away from the cans, this is our last chance and David just manages to get the boathook around the rope of the pickup buoy. By now he is at full stretch, with the cans a considerable weight in the heaving water. I leave the helm and rush to help get them on board, surprising myself with my own strength. Desperate needs produce desperate measures and I am desperate for this journey to end.

We radio up our thanks to *Dutch Concrete* and say we will see them in Horta. Then we put the fuel in our tanks, turn on both engines at 2250 revs and our speed reaches six knots. Our arrival time immediately becomes tomorrow and we should be in before the gale. It is a black, wet, nasty, turbulent night but we feel good. And very, very grateful to a very generous Dutchman in a concrete boat.

The wind slowly builds next morning and settles between 17 and 21 knots. In normal circumstances we would turn off the engines and just sail but that would mean not arriving until the small hours of the morning and we want to be tied up before the forecast gale blasts through.

It is a wet, nasty day with poor visibility but made beautiful by the fact that our journey is almost over. We know we are getting close to land when we are joined by large numbers of common dolphins in the late afternoon. The rain, however, is unremitting and the sea violently choppy. The gale is getting close.

THE AZORES

46
Faial

We edge into Horta Harbour and the night watchman waves us into a space on the dock with his torch. We tie up with relief and turn off the engines at twenty minutes after midnight local time. Then we walk along the quay to *Dutch Concrete*, moored two boats away, say a heartfelt thank you, return to *Voyager* and crawl into bed.

Oh, how we sleep.

Our journey has been 2,047 miles – it wouldn't have been quite that far but for our zigzag course – and ended up taking 18 days, 9 hours and 20 minutes at an average speed of 4.6 knots. Not bad for a boat without its most important sail and so many adverse winds.

For very many people who have made this voyage in the past it will be remembered as a pleasant, leisurely sail. But ever since the last *El Niño*, which turned out to be the strongest on record, weather patterns have been changing globally in all sorts of ways. This has been one of them.

Later in the morning we complete the entry formalities, fill our fuel tank and cans plus those belonging to *Dutch Concrete*, return Jack's to him with our sincere thanks and arrange for the four of us to meet up in town the following day to say thank you properly.

We then move onto a berth inside the marina between an Italian couple and a Canadian with an English wife. From the boat we look out across the Straights at the island of Pico, less than five miles away, looking magnificent with a line of cloud lying just below the volcano's peak.

Settled in with our new neighbours we go off to find a bank, call Tony to say we have arrived safely, and order lunch at the legendary Café Sport. This bar, with its charts, foreign ensigns, pennants and sailing bric-a-brac, is a yachting institution, and part of the island's history of welcoming tired, hungry and thirsty seafarers between and betwixt the Americas, the Caribbean and Europe.

The first Portuguese ships reached the Azores in 1427 and the nine major islands that make up the archipelago were settled gradually over the following two centuries, giving each a distinctive character. Still part of Portugal, the islands now have the status of an autonomous region with their own assembly and government. All are volcanic in origin, although some have experienced no activity since they were settled.

The harbours at Portugal's Atlantic islands are the only places we have ever been where graffiti is not discouraged. At Horta it is an institution. Many yachtsmen paint a picture of their boats, cartoons of the crew, or simply leave a yacht name and date to record their passing. They cover the street, the sea walls, even bollards - anywhere with a flat surface. Mostly they are simply an exuberant testimony to having completed the journey here. A few are superb.

Those around the commercial dock, where yachts used to tie up before the marina was built, date back to the 1970s. Their survival is surprising, given the attrition of Atlantic gales – like the one currently battering Faial's shoreline, even though it is June.

This journey has left us feeling unusually tired and our enthusiasm for some much-needed maintenance is muted. However, our priority is arranging for a sailmaker to visit. A nice man, his quote for repairing our big genoa and replacing its sacrificial strip, as well as our staysail's, is less than Annapolis quoted for just a new strip on the little staysail.

Given the force of the north-easterly winds at the moment, some yachts moored on the outside of the marina wall have sought shelter inside. There are now four boats rafted up directly behind us and our neighbours so, if any of us wants to leave, three of them will have to cast off to let us out.

Nobody is planning to go anywhere for now, however. Although everybody seems to be using the time constructively. The whole marina echoes to the sound of boats being patched up and repaired.

With our energy returning David goes into town to get our empty propane gas bottle refilled. I glue the rubber seals back onto the washboards for the bow windows, do a great deal of laundry and provide hearty meals. David deals with various leaks – engine oil and seawater – we repair the roller reefing, address the problem of our masthead lights and replace our lost radar reflector.

In between we visit the town. Although Faial is a small island - 67 square miles - Horta is a substantial town and an attractive one. Its historic buildings follow a Portuguese tradition of using black basalt to highlight white stucco walls which is very pleasing to the eye. And there are the same mosaic pavements and cobbled streets to be found throughout Portugal.

Gradually, some of the people we left in Bermuda – or who set out after us and turned back - begin to arrive. One of them says it wasn't too bad until 50 miles off the island of Flores where they ran into 50-knot winds. 'We were doing 12 knots down the waves,' he tells us, 'under bare poles.' They had to put out a drogue and hand steer for eleven hours.

Another lost his steering three days before getting here and, after his emergency rudder arm broke, ended up steering with a large pair of pliers clamped onto the rudder stock. A woman is still shocked, days after arriving, at the size of the waves that had been breaking over her boat.

We decide we have earned a break, so when one of the mornings finally dawns dry and bright, we hire a car, because just beyond the busy town of Horta and its crowded marina is the most beautiful, unspoiled countryside imaginable.

Two things strike you immediately. One is that there are no walls or privet hedges dividing the fields or separating them from the roads. Instead, there are hydrangea bushes. Miles upon miles of blue hydrangeas. The other thing you notice are the flowers. There are flowers everywhere; in the cottage gardens, the roadside verges and the hedges of the coast road. Roses, blue agapanthus, hibiscus, lilies, red-orange nasturtiums, sunflowers, white agapanthus, dahlias and sweet peas.

Faial is lush and green and filled with colour. The only barren place on the island is the area surrounding Capelinhos, which is a uniform grey and devoid of any foliage beyond a little grass struggling to establish itself on the margins. The volcanic eruption here began in September 1957 and lasted for thirteen months. The tower of the lighthouse remains – half-filled with volcanic dust - although its light has gone from the top. And there is a fireplace with an oven in one corner of the building at its base; an eerie reminder of the domestic life once lived by the keepers of the vanished light. No-one perished in the eruption thanks to someone noticing a patch of heaving seawater half a mile offshore. But the loss of homes, farms and livelihoods in such a long eruption was devastating and led to substantial migration abroad.

On one of the shores there are thermal baths and small bathing pools among the lava boulders, connected by small pathways ending in a large natural pool formed by the sea rocks.

At a handicrafts workshop we discover with surprise that the delicate white flowers on sale are made from fish scales. Only the day before, while prising one off what I'd thought was a well-scrubbed chopping board, I had grumbled that surely there must be some use for fish scales after the fish had finished with them as they appear to be indestructible.

And here in the Azores they have found one. Delicate flowers in small glass frames. Beautiful and unique. A delight to the eye created out of something that other people throw away.

We follow a sign for a forest reserve and find plantings of native species carefully labelled. They don't seem to be surviving too well, while in the island's gardens and hedgerows the foreign interlopers thrive. Geraniums, Aunt Elizas, carnations, fuchsia, white clover and foxglove, with dragonflies the size of small birds.

There are steep paths into the forest – one of which we take, and find lots of elderly people playing cards on picnic tables around a barbecue area. Even the wood has been provided for the barbecues, cut to size and neatly stacked, and we wonder about the wisdom of encouraging people to light fires in a forest but there is no evidence of bush fires anywhere on the island.

The volcano Cabeço Gordo (Fat Mountain) is Faial's highest and the tiny, ground-hugging flora at the top is reminiscent of moorland. Many I've never seen before: bright yellow with four round petals; white bells, or deep red, like upturned snowdrops. And wild strawberries. We stand on the crater's rim and look down into its centre – quite flat with a cone in the middle.

A third volcano, Monte da Guia, is the one we can see from the marina and which sometimes looks purple, depending on the light. Standing on it now, it is a green semi-circle, the seaward side of the cone having eroded to form a small curved bay called Caldeira do Inferno. Behind it is the simple but pretty little church also visible from the boat.

Our sails are returned to us. The genoa repair looks good but we won't know for sure until we put it up and we need a little less wind for that.

We visit the town's small museum. It has two extraordinary handicraft collections. The first is tissue paper which has been folded and cut into patterns so intricate that at first sight the items appear to be made of fine lace.

The second is a collection of model ships and street scenes crafted from bamboo core. Like islanders everywhere, the people of the Azores have traditionally used whatever is to hand.

There is also a photographic exhibition of some of the best visiting yachtsmen's wall paintings from the harbour. It is good to see that they are being recorded before the Atlantic gales, and later arrivals' zeal, can damage them.

The big catamaran with the revolutionary rig arrives and its skipper stops by. His forestay had broken and he and his wife did most of the journey under main alone. He also says they'd passed an Italian yacht which had lost its engine and was dependent on sail. Its crew had already been 21 days at sea, since leaving St Martin in the Caribbean, and given the present headwinds looked like spending a lot more time out there yet. They'd declared themselves quite OK, however - plenty of booze and cigarettes left.

He also tells us that around thirty yachts left Bermuda after he did and that most should be here in the next few days. Very few are leaving Horta at present owing to a renewal of gale-force, north-east winds so it is going to get pretty crowded. The harbour master, meanwhile, is doing a superb job fitting everybody in.

With the wind from the wrong direction, and too strong to set off, we find ourselves gazing as always at the island across the water from us. Ever since we arrived here, and wherever we are - on deck, in the galley, the saloon or our cabin - we have looked out upon Mount Pico, with the white cloud wreathing its volcanic peak.

There are only three spaces left on the Pico ferry's wooden bench. As we settle into two of them, the third is taken by The Tourist from Hell. Floral shorts. Massive thighs widely spread, his left one taking up half my space as well as his own.

Unable to be still for a moment, he turns the small act of stowing two hiking poles underneath the bench into an epic performance, almost taking my eyes out with the pointed ends in the process. After that he brings out an aerosol sunscreen and vigorously coats himself and me with its contents. It has a strong perfume that starts David sneezing - the first time the allergies have kicked in for a long time.

Then the elbows come into play as he energetically inspects his picture gallery on his camera while intermittently scratching at his arms and legs where the skin is peeling off. Happily it is only a short ferry ride to the pretty town of Madalena.

47
Pico

We hire a car for the day, rattle over a narrow, cobbled street between pollarded trees and disappear into the island. It folds itself around you. There is no other traffic about.

The vineyards begin immediately. Large, light-green, floppy leaves against black walls. The roadsides run wild with blue hydrangeas ten-foot high, the brambles squeezing in between are heavy with white flowers.

As with the other islands, Pico emerged from the sea through volcanic eruption but at 7,713 feet/2,351m Mount Pico provides Portugal with its highest point. The early settlers used its black lava rocks like the sheep owners of northern England's Peak District used their grey granite – to build walls. Walls inside walls, until here they sometimes enclose an area as small as six feet square, protecting Pico's grape vines from Atlantic winds and retaining the day's warmth overnight.

In both countries the walls served a dual purpose. You can't use land for viticulture, or grazing, until you've done something about all the rocks – be they basalt or granite – that are cluttering it up.

We get lost once, down an unmarked road, trying to find the village made of lava. We ask a man carrying the biggest cabbage we have ever seen. Everything grows in this volcanic soil and much of it bigger than most other places. It is incredibly fertile here – grape vines, figs, corn, bamboo, banana trees – and everywhere, *everywhere* flowers.

Adegas is the name of the village where all the houses are built out of basalt, or black lava. A few have touches of white paint, but mostly they are uniformly black, as is the road, the soil, the lacy walls of smooth round rocks encircling the fields, the boulders along the coastline, and the beach. Add to that the brooding presence of Mount Pico and its cloud towering over it, and I wonder if living thus might produce a negative effect upon the spirits. I am not sorry to move on, yet an elderly resident sitting on a bench in the sunshine seems happy enough.

We stop at Santo Amaro, where they still build wooden boats in the same traditional way they once built open whaling boats. And drink in the flowers: hydrangeas of every shade from white through pale blue and pink to some deep combination of the two; rambling roses from pale pink to deep red, daisies of every kind – big white dog daisies, tiny pink and white moon daisies and everything in between – including some that even flourish on the saltwater margins of the sea. Big, rich blue agapanthus with deep green foliage. Satin-white lilies. In-your-face gladioli (no wonder Dame Edna Everage chose gladdies for her personal statement), marigolds and hollyhocks.

We gain altitude. The temperature begins to drop. The hydrangeas up here are still in tight, white bud and the trees have disappeared. A black and white cow, coming down the road towards us, drifts gracefully to the verge, her small white calf protected on her inside flank. She waits for us to pass, then continues on her way.

A kestrel hovers overhead. Finches and bananaquits dart. From the fields affable white cattle gaze back at you with polite interest. In the valleys below, the green landscape is broken by small lakes. And, in the smoky distance, lies the island of São Jorge shaped like a knife with a long, pointed blade.

We make the 5.45pm ferry from Madalena just in time, which saves a three-hour wait. The Tourist from Hell boards, clutching his hiking poles, but all the seats around us are taken.

The wind begins to lessen. The sea becomes less turbulent. We begin our preparations for moving on. When the wind becomes slight enough, we set about putting up our repaired sails. The little stay is no problem at all. And even the huge genoa goes up with far less effort than expected. It looks good.

With the weather's improvement continuing, we visit the supermarket and stock up on fresh foods. Tomorrow is Sunday and weather-wise a good day to set off.

48
Terceira

Initially there is little wind and we have to motor but after we round the north-west corner of Pico the wind picks up enough to try out our newly-repaired genoa. It not only looks good, it beats well. In fact, it seems to get closer to the wind than it used to.

After six hours we approach the anchorage of Caheta on the island of São Jorge – the one shaped like a knife with a long blade that we had gazed out on from Pico – and where we plan to spend the night. Unfortunately, there is a large dredger filling the only part of the anchorage that has reasonable depths while its tug, on a buoy close by, is rolling badly. It does not look very inviting so we decide to press on to Terceira. This means an overnight passage but is a better option. And around midnight we are treated to a grandstand view of Terceira's firework display, the culmination of the island's fiesta.

Monday is a grey overcast morning on which we know from the clock that the sun has risen but as yet have no evidence to prove it. It is also quite cold and we are well wrapped up. As we approach the harbour we can see that the sea wall has been badly damaged - the result, we find out later, of a huge storm last winter.

We anchor, then launch the dinghy and paddle into Praia da Vitoria and a small, newly-built marina. We have all our documents with us as yachtsmen are required to book into, and out of, each island they visit. Everyone is very helpful and invites us to tie up in their new marina which they say is free this month because it has not been officially opened yet. They even offer the use of their brand new washing machines – that great lure to cruisers everywhere. We take them up on their very generous offer then take a walk around town.

In the afternoon, a policeman ambles along the pontoon for a chat. A friendly man, he had once spent eighteen months in the English town of Colchester. He tells us about the storm last winter which demolished part of the sea wall and washed away one of the small lighthouses which had stood on the northern side of the harbour entrance.

He also clears up something which has been puzzling us. As we have travelled round the islands we have seen lots of single room buildings, quite small but too large to be shrines. They are where the religious artefacts of a street or small neighbourhood are stored, he tells us. Responsibility for their care is shared among the community, and each week one member will take the statues and relics into their home and provide a meal for the neighbours.

We get up early and are able to use the marina's super new washing machines and dryers before the workmen turn the water off again. We put the dinghy on to the foredeck and tie it down. Lastly, we top up our water tanks and are ready to go. We say our goodbyes to the people at the marina who have been so kind, and head out to sea. We clear the harbour by noon but can still see the island at nightfall.

When the new day dawns and I begin to fill in the log I hesitate at the space where we put in the date. Only a year ago today we had stood on New York's FDR Freeway, and watched Macy's Fourth of July fireworks display, without an inkling of how much would have changed in the world and for so many people.

49
Out at Sea

We head off - on a course which, should we continue on it, would eventually put us in Iceland – in search of the wind Herb has forecast above 40° North. When we find it, happily it is coming from the west and we set a direct course for Falmouth.

Tuning in to Herb is not much help to us at present because his nearest boat is at least two days ahead of us and as yet we have no one following. Fortunately there's not much happening, except acoustically. In the galley, preparing a meal, I can hear sounds like a distant brass band – not a discernible tune, but definitely brass.

The sounds you hear at sea, and the way the brain responds to them, never fail to fascinate. Your brain won't leave a sound unidentified so it attaches to it whatever is known, even if in practical terms what it comes up with is absurd. On the journey from Bermuda David heard a Russian choir and on one occasion, when he was off-watch, was so convinced I was calling him that he was half-way out of bed en route for the helm before he realized it wasn't me and fell back again.

When we had the previous outboard motor, sitting in the bow of the dinghy I regularly heard opera echoing up the mast hole – usually tenors. Our present outboard produces heavy metal. And, of course, there was that party in fully swing, a friend told of hearing, hundreds of miles out from the Azores and with no other boat in the vicinity.

On our third day out, and getting close to sunset, David spots whales. About twenty of them, off our port side. They are Fin Whales, between fifty and seventy feet in length and easily identifiable by the distinctive way they surface and dive. The head rises first. There is a slight pause followed by a very tall plume of water from the blow hole, and then a long sleek back curves out of the water for what seems like ages. The head disappears. A small dorsal fin rises, and then a long tail which follows the rest of the body below the water without exposing its flukes.

They probably pass us at 25mph, but the rhythm is leisurely as one member of the pod after another powers to the surface and then dives again. It is hypnotic: head, plume, back, fin, tail, descent; head, plume, back, fin, tail, descent. One after the other: up, along and down again. The sheer power of them is awesome. While we have been watching them, we can be sure they are observing us too, with those alert eyes on the sides of their sleek heads. We stand there for ages after they've gone, wanting more.

Despite being July, and technically summer, it is cold and grey with occasional poor visibility and the odd shower of rain. With fronts ahead of us we keep the 'genoa' reefed as we go into the nights. Herb has become extremely difficult to hear and we shall be glad when we can pick up forecasts from closer sources like the BBC.

Although overcast and grey, it is now getting light at around 4.30am so we have shorter nights to keep watch in. Turning on an engine to top up the batteries one morning brings a sudden eruption to starboard and a startled dolphin hurtles away.

Sometimes the wind dies and *Voyager* languishes. Then a period of wind-shifts leave a confused and lumpy sea with waves high enough for her to surf down them at 8 knots. Every day we have been accompanied by a pair of shearwaters and sometimes a solitary petrel.

By the seventh day we are identifying a lot of squalls on the radar, but manage to avoid most of them. There are a lot of wind shifts, however, and fluctuations in strength. Despite the sky being so overcast these days, we are getting really spectacular sunrises through the breaks in the heavy cloud. And though we don't see the sun rise, it gilds the edges of the clouds and hurls great shafts of gold down into the sea.

Herb is now inaudible, we are still unable to tune into the BBC shipping forecast and atmospherics make it impossible to decipher the French broadcasts. So, when we suddenly hear an English voice on the VHF, obviously very close, we call him up and ask him if he has a weather forecast.

He turns out to be an RAF pilot in the clouds just above our heads, who sighs and asks irritably if anybody on board has a shipping forecast. Then he asks someone in his cockpit plaintively, 'Can we go to a working channel?'

Pretty sniffy treatment, I thought, towards a civilian who helped train so many Royal Air Force pilots in low level flying – providing them, as I unwittingly did, with moving targets as I walked our poor dogs across the top of the hills above our house. Not to mention loosening our roof tiles with their swoops down into the valley.

But soon afterwards a container ship, *Royal Klipper*, passing a few hundred yards off our starboard side, responds positively to our request. We frequently have strong currents against us which slow our progress.

Over the Grand Bank next day we begin dodging Spanish fishing boats. This huge area of comparatively shallow water - stretching all the way around Ireland, the British Isles, and mainland Europe from France to Denmark and the Baltic Sea – is a popular fishing ground for commercial boats.

We see a submarine on the surface but decide against asking the Royal Navy for a weather forecast given our reception by the RAF yesterday. During the night, however, we are at last able to tune into the BBC shipping forecast and feel much happier. It seems they have changed their broadcast times while we have been away.

It has been an uneventful passage apart from a few squalls and, compared to the one between Bermuda and the Azores, almost idyllic - until shortly before midnight on our last full day at sea. During a lull in the wind we have been running the starboard engine and it suddenly dies. We have run into a large section of abandoned, heavy duty, blue nylon fishing net.

A traditional fisherman's Welcome Home.

Irrevocably caught around the starboard prop, David quickly hauls in its long trailing ends with the boat hook and ties them to our hand rail – keeping them away from the port propeller which fortunately has remained free. And, instead of heading for Falmouth we alter course for the much closer Hugh Town, on St Mary's in the Scilly Isles.

We can see Bishop Rock Lighthouse for most of the night. It is the most south-westerly point of the British Isles and protects mariners from the notorious rocks of the Isles of Scilly. We are also dodging fishing boats for much of the time, but fortunately acquire no more nets.

GREAT BRITAIN

50
The Isles of Scilly

St Mary's

Shortly after 7am we make our approach to Hugh Town on St Mary's and call up the harbour master on the VHF. We explain our problem with the net and he tells us we can dry out on Porth Mellon beach. We turn off the engine at half past eight on Saturday morning, three and a half hours short of ten days at sea.

The tide falls very quickly and *Voyager* settles nicely onto a firm sandy beach. Within a couple of hours we have the netting off the starboard prop and in a refuse trailer, and our decks ship-shape.

We open our bottle of celebratory fizz and have a cheese and wine party in the cockpit, the sun warm, the wind slight and lots of youngsters learning to sail on the water's edge. Not to mention a few adolescent girls who have clearly fallen in lust with their young male instructors.

Ashore, it is *very* pretty. Whitewashed cottages or stone-built. And flowers blooming everywhere, deep blue agapanthus and bright-eyed daisies. The coastline is relatively treeless, but incredibly green and neat, with its castle and stone fortifications. And the people are extremely nice.

It is a lovely day. Sunny and warm. We go to The Mermaid and have an all-day breakfast for lunch - our first English sausage and bacon in quite some time. It seems strange to be in a Cornish pub on English soil again. In one sense you feel almost like a foreign visitor and in another it's as if you have never been away.

A phone call to Tony, a trip to the Co-op. And though we really don't want to, after a brief sojourn in the cockpit to let our lunch fully digest we make the effort to take our diesel cans to a service station. With tomorrow being Sunday, it won't be open and if we have our fuel on board we can set off whenever wind and tide allow. We cart the full cans back on our small folding trolley and empty them into the tank.

Even when you are tired you can con yourself gently into things you don't want to do. We'll just stroll up and *get* the diesel, we'd told ourselves. We don't have to put it in today, just so long as we've got it. And then, rather than stow it away, and knowing you'll have to spend time, and energy you haven't got to spare, clearing up the small but inevitable poisonous spillage afterwards, you still talk yourself into putting it into the tank now and having done with it.

In fact, we've done rather well, really. A passage itself is tiring, always adjusting your balance and with rarely more than three hours continuous sleep. So, after ten days at sea, to have beached *Voyager*, removed a fishing net, unhitched the dinghy from the foredeck and lugged it onto the davits, tidied up, lunched, phoned home, shopped and topped up the fuel tanks is not bad. And, of course, we want to have a look around this lovely island.

When the tide returns and *Voyager* floats off the beach we put her onto a mooring buoy. It is the first mooring buoy I have lifted in a while and the chain on it weighs *a ton*. I think my strength must be failing until I discover that the EU has recently imposed new laws on member countries increasing the link size that harbour masters must now use. The increased weight is apparently raising fears, in many a sedate south coast marina, that elderly yachtsmen will be dropping like flies.

We sleep for eight hours, during which time I don't think either of us moves.

51
The Mainland

We need to get *Voyager* lifted out and know just where to go for the things we need – Emsworth, in Chichester, West Sussex - but decide to visit a few places on the way, before settling down to some weeks of serious work.

We have a delightful sail from Hugh Town, St Mary's in bright sunshine and light breezes. Early afternoon we pass Wolf Rock Lighthouse which got its name from the howling sound it produces in gale-force winds, caused by fissures in the rock on which it is built. The lighthouse is 18 nautical miles from St Mary's and 8 nautical miles from Land's End on the Cornish mainland, and given the notoriously treacherous weather here it must have been a remote, not to say eerie place to keep the light burning before automation in 1988.

We round The Lizard, the British mainland's most southerly point, at about 6pm and are tied up in Falmouth Harbour a couple of hours later. It is so nice to be in Falmouth again. We have such happy memories of it. Not least the lovely old Chain Locker pub on the quay.

Saint Just in Roseland is not somewhere we have been before, but years ago a Cornish friend had suggested that if we ever got near there to take time to pay a visit, as we wouldn't regret it. We anchor off overnight and early in the morning dinghy ashore onto a pebble beach. The village is hilly but well worth the climb. Below it, the lovely little 13th century Church of St Just in Roseland overlooks a tranquil creek and must have one of the prettiest churchyards we have ever seen - a semi-tropical garden, thanks to the Gulf Stream which warms the shores along this part of the English coast.

We also anchor up the River Fowey (pronounced Foy), off the small picturesque town that was already here when the Norman invaders made their survey of their recently-acquired English property – better known as the Domesday Book - in the late 11th century. The waterside is dominated by the Priory built shortly afterwards. Beside it, the crenulated Place House is almost as old, and well protected from prying eyes by high walls. Fowey was once home to Daphne du Maurier, author of classic novels such as *Rebecca*, *My Cousin Rachel* and *Jamaica Inn* which held my young mind spellbound but offered no happy endings.

We sojourn at Barn Pool in Plymouth Sound and re-acquaint ourselves with the British Sunday newspaper, the saloon awash with supplements, sections, magazines and advertising material. As we browse peacefully we can hear, though dimly, the International Power Boat Race taking place on the far side of the Sound.

Between Plymouth Sound and Portland Harbour we see a puzzling sight in the water. There is something dark and triangular ahead of us with what appears to be another, smaller triangle, moving steadily from side to side behind it. We continue carefully, overtake it, and discover a Basking Shark.

What we could see from behind had been its dorsal fin (the large triangle), with its smaller triangle of a tail moving it placidly along, while its enormous mouth takes in great quantities of seawater from which it filters out its food. Although large (up to 26 feet or 8 metres), and aggressive-looking with its great mouth, it poses no threat to anything much apart from plankton.

Our computer, which has endured much in the course of four years at sea, goes down. David tries all he knows but gives up for fear of losing all its data for ever. I add a computer expert to the items on our already lengthy To Do list. We are deeply depressed. However, Christchurch, a little further along the coast, soon cheers us up.

We make an early start to get the best from the tide and sail out on a clear morning, keeping well away from the overfalls off St Alban's Head where strong currents meet a submerged ridge and create rough water.

It is windy and bitterly cold. At about 9am, when I finally stop moving around and sit down to read, I feel so cold I keep getting up for more clothing. In the end I am wearing a shirt and trousers, sweat shirt, snug, body warmer, thermal scarf, baseball cap, and when the back of my head still remains too cold for comfort, a towel over the baseball cap. This, I remind myself, is an English July. How would I cope with a winter? In fact, the wind offshore is so brisk that at one stage it whips the top off David's coffee. Later, ashore, the weather is balmy.

Christchurch was a settlement when the Romans were here, its glorious cathedral is 900 years old and the Old Town is a joy. By the time we reach it we are also in dire need of a laundrette. Christchurch's turns out to be a one-off. It is run by a man very like Fletcher in the TV classic *Porridge*.

'You on holiday?' he says with wry, Fletcher-like sarcasm, eyeing our five bags of washing.

A gregarious, generous man, he is fascinated by the idea of our sea crossings and ensures we get the best service he can provide at minimum cost. This includes putting two of our loads into his big washer, but with so much soap powder *Voyager* reeks of it for days afterwards. Although everything *is* very clean. And he very generously identifies the hottest dryers to save us money.

He has an unusual interpretation of British coinage, identifying every specie resting on our outstretched palms as a Thatcher or a Healy or whoever was Premier at the time of its issue. And despite his own in-house signs as to how much money should be put into which machines, what he takes from us is always less than the sign above a machine says.

An informal social club, people drop in - a retired bus driver, a local farmer – and while the dryers do their work they bring us up to date about developments in our homeland while we've been away. One of our questions is the reason for the news media's constant reference to a TV programme called *Big Brother*, as yet unseen by us. Fletch's expression is reminiscent of someone watching life as we know it slowly but irrevocably slipping away.

'Give it a miss,' is his considered advice. The farmer nods.

We are anchored in a creek near the town. It is a rural idyll. Horses graze the banks, cows stand up to their knees in the water. There are families of young mallards learning to dive down to the weed. Some turn bottom-up with ease, others put their heads under water but then flap about, unable to control their own buoyancy. An angler is tormented by a large fish, leaping spectacularly out of the water only feet away from him, but not willing to take his bait. And there are swans everywhere, often by the dozen, travelling in pairs, six pairs in a line.

We have one of those blissful, restful nights and rise into a misty dawn to find swans asleep all around us, floating on the still water, heads tucked under their wings.

52
Full Circle

Four years to the day, after first setting out on our voyage, we are back in Chichester Harbour. We hadn't planned it this way. It just happens.

We settle onto our old mud berth at Emsworth with its shallow water and wading birds, and the dyke between the harbour and the water meadows lush with marsh grass and summer wild flowers. Before planning a major overhaul and anti-fouling for *Voyager*, and mulling over the next stage of our cruising life, we have some visits to make, family and friends to see.

Since leaving here, on that August afternoon four years ago, we have covered 23,137 nautical miles (26,657 land miles) and visited 19 countries. Other yachtsmen have done far more, for a much longer period and to far more exotic places. But we never intended any sort of competition. The only thing we have ever competed against is the weather, and if asked how my time at sea has changed me I should have to include my relationship with the elements.

In an environment defined by a house, an office and a car the only real inconvenience we suffered from weather was being snowed in once. Whereas living on a small vessel, either out on the ocean or at anchor on its margins, is to understand for the first time the sheer power of weather and the sea conditions it produces. For it not only determines when and where you go, but whether you should even go at all. On the choices you make, may depend your survival.

One of the many things I discovered from living largely out-of-doors is the way you become attuned to the natural world. You notice even the smallest changes – to sky, wind, waves, even the colours of the sea – and so protect yourself instinctively.

Initially a reluctant sailor, I fell in love with the cruising life. I began to revel in the prospect of waking up each morning in a different place - but still with my own bed, bathroom and kitchen. Also the satisfaction of a life pared down to the essentials, yet all you really need. And understanding what is most important in your life. What actually makes you *happy*.

We have visited so many beautiful places – coastal towns, fishing villages, even major cities – each made more enjoyable still by being able to sail into their harbours and simply wander on foot into the heart of them. And the lovely unspoilt islands, of course, many of which, without our own boat, we should not have reached. Nor can I express sufficiently our gratitude for the very many people, in all the countries through which we have passed, who are so extraordinarily kind, helpful and courteous to passing strangers.

One of the revelations the sea has to offer is marine life. Not just the thrill of a visiting family of dolphins putting on a show, or a curious pod of whales, but the way that wild creatures become a mirror image of human existence. Their various types, emotions and responses seeming no different from our own.

The easy-going, forgiving nature of the pelican; the nervy, suspicious cormorant always tensed to flee; a young tern blown off course and so tired it allows itself to be put to bed. An adolescent whale honing its skills under our hulls. Or a small group of big fish, preying on a large group of very little fish, until the former have satisfied all their wants and left the latter devastated and decimated. And whoever said it takes a village to raise a child would have rejoiced to see a whole family of dolphins teaching two tiny calves to swim safely between our bows. In short, they seem not unlike the rest of us in their curiosity, love of novelty, devotion, patience, cruelty, intelligence and vulnerability.

We have also been brought face to face with the damage which we, as human beings, are doing to them. As our populations and our demand for material goods increase, the resulting detritus - in terms of effluent, oil spillages and especially plastics - is turning the world's beautiful but fragile seas into toxic dustbins. At the same time, our own over-fishing is depleting the main source of food on which marine animals and birds have to live, while entanglement in discarded fishing nets causes millions of them to starve or drown every year.

Our last whale sighting – the Fin whales - was the most spectacular of all. Each one of the twenty-odd mammals was greater than *Voyager*'s length and maybe six times her weight. They were also travelling around five times our speed, yet they were never going to be a threat to us. Sadly, by our increasing demands on the environment, we are a constant and growing threat to them and to all living things for which the ocean is home.

As well as beautiful places and landscapes we have witnessed some extraordinary things on the night-time sea. Blazing debris returning from Space, although a bit too close for comfort from where we were sitting at the time. An electrical storm of a kind we never knew existed and never want to be in the middle of ever again. The Milky Way on a clear, moonless night, stretching out to infinity is truly awe-inspiring while a meteor storm above your head is magical. And there is no more joyous way to begin or end the day than with the rising or setting of a vast, luminous sun.

To everyone who has travelled with us through my books, I sincerely hope the journey has proved worthwhile.

Epilogue

I have saved my final word for David. A modest man, he has always objected to my including a dedication at the front of the *Voyager* books, despite his enormous contribution to them - not least their technical accuracy and getting them into print - and his unstinting support generally. So I can't end this series without expressing my admiration and gratitude.

He came late to sailing, a daydream long deferred for all sorts of reasons. There was no boyhood dinghy sailing, which is how many yachtsmen start, and his skills were largely learned from books, plus a handful of practical courses.

The first of these came with an obnoxious instructor whose idea of training was to teach his hapless crew of six nothing, while constantly yelling at them to 'get it right' or 'do it faster'. Setting off home after a demoralizing week at sea with him they had decided to either abandon sailing altogether or consider a small motor boat instead, as obviously they were too old, too stupid or the wrong class to become yachtsmen.

The thing about David is that he rarely gives up and, in the process, provided me with some of the most fulfilling experiences of my life; not only at a time when I thought my best years were behind me, but of a kind I should never have considered for myself. For I hope I have not given the impression in these or any other pages that I am skipper material, because I'm not. I am essentially crew, and could never in my wildest imagination have enjoyed any of this but for him.

Glossary for Non-Sailors

Antifouling – paint put on the hull below the water line to deter marine growth and shellfish which reduces the speed of the boat.

Autopilot – device to hold the boat on a set course automatically.

Barrier Island - a long, broad sandy island lying parallel to a shore, which has built up through the action of sea and wind and which protects the shoreline from erosion.

Beam – the widest part of the hull.

Bitter end – one end of the anchor chain is shackled to the anchor, the other end to the chain locker. When you have played out the chain to its bitter end, there is no more chain left. Like so many other sailing terms, it has passed into common usage.

Blue water cruising – long-distance ocean sailing.

Boom – a hinged pole attached to the mast which holds the bottom of the main sail and allows it to be set in various positions to catch the wind.

Burgee – a triangular pennant flown from the rigging and carrying a sailing club's colours.

Clear in – like all foreign visitors, yachtsmen have to clear in with Customs and Immigration on arrival and clear out when they leave.

Close hauled – sailing yachts will not travel directly into the wind but when the wind moves a little off the bow, if the sail is tightly winched, progress can be made.

Davits – two small hoists to lift and hold a dinghy, usually at a boat's stern.

Doghouse roof – a fixed cover over the helm for weather protection.

Dory – typically a small, shallow-draft, flat-bottomed boat.

EPIRB – acronym for Emergency Position Indicating Radio Beacon. It will transmit a signal requesting the Coast Guard to either send a rescue vessel or divert a commercial vessel to come to your assistance.

Gale Force 8 – on the Beaufort Wind Force Scale, Gale 8 ranges between 34 and 40 knots (39-46mph); Strong Gale 9 is 41-47 knots (47-54mph).

Gash bag – all refuse (gash) on board is bagged and taken ashore for appropriate disposal.

Gelcoat – the hard shiny outer layer covering the fibreglass from which our boat is built.

Genoa – the large sail in front of our mast.

Hard or hard standing – the ground on which a boat rests when it is lifted out of the water to allow work to be done on its hull.

Holding tank – retains foul water from bath and toilet for proper disposal to avoid polluting beaches and harbours.

In-mast furling – this allows the mainsail to be rolled into the mast, either to reduce the amount of sail (reefing) or to roll it in completely when not in use.

Knot – one knot equals a nautical mile covered in one hour and is roughly equivalent to 1.15mph.

Lead line - a lead weight on the end of a length of thin rope with depths marked on it.

Leech – the outer edge of a sail.

Lines – ropes. See also Mooring line.

Luff – the straight edge of the sail alongside the mast.

Monohull – a conventional yacht has a single (mono) hull. A catamaran like *Voyager* has two, a trimaran has three, and are termed multihulls.

Mooring line – a rope used to tie a boat to the shore.

Oilies – slang for wet weather clothing from the days when the cloth or canvas, from which it was made, had to be oiled to make it waterproof.

Painter – a rope attached to a dinghy's bow to tie it up.

Port – left-hand side of a vessel looking forward.

Pulpit – a hand rail round the deck at the bow.

Pushpit – a hand rail round the deck at the stern.

Quarter – either side of a vessel aft of (i.e. behind) the beam.

Red ensign – the official flag flown by British Merchant Navy ships and British leisure boats. It has a red ground with the Union Flag in the top left-hand corner.

Reefing – reducing the amount of sail exposed to the wind, to reduce the yacht's speed or stress on its rigging.

Sacrificial strip – in traditional rigging, the sails are taken down, folded and put in a bag when not in use. With self-furling, or roller reefing gear, such as our genoa and stay sail, the sail is rolled in situ, with only the leech remaining exposed. Because this gets damaged by the sun, it is normal for a strip of fabric (often blue) to be sewn down the leech, which protects the sail and can be replaced when damaged.

Self-furling – the ability to roll a sail away by pulling on a rope from the cockpit instead of going forward along the deck to drop it into a bag or tie it down.

Scope – the amount of chain or rope needed to keep the anchor safely dug in and the vessel fixed in position.

Scurvy – a nutritional deficiency, once common among sailors, resulting in suppurating wounds, jaundice, fever, depression, spongy gums, loss of teeth and ultimately death.

Skeg – a fixed beam below the hull to which the rudder is attached.

Sound – a long, broad stretch of seawater, usually parallel with the coast and forming an inlet from the ocean.

Spring Tide – the highest tide in each fourteen-day period, as compared to the Neap Tide, which is the lowest in every two weeks.

Squall – sudden increase in wind-speed, often accompanied by brief but heavy precipitation.

Starboard – right-hand side of a vessel looking forward.

Topsides – the sides of the hull above the waterline.

Printed in Great Britain
by Amazon